Austria, Prussia and Germany, 1806–1871

SEMINAR STUDIES   IN HISTORY

Austria, Prussia and Germany, 1806–1871

JOHN BREUILLY

An imprint of Pearson Education

London · New York · Toronto · Sydney · Tokyo · Singapore · Hong Kong · Cape Town
New Delhi · Madrid · Paris · Amsterdam · Munich · Milan · Stockholm

Pearson Education Limited
Edinburgh Gate
Harlow
Essex CM20 2JE,
England

and Associated Companies throughout the world

Visit us on the World Wide Web at:
www.pearsoned.co.uk

First published in Great Britain in 2002

© Pearson Education Limited 2002

The right of Linda Benson to be identified as author
of this work has been asserted by her in accordance
with the Copyright, Designs and Patents Act 1988.

ISBN 978-0-582-43739-5

British Library Cataloguing in Publication Data
A CIP catalogue record for this book can be obtained from the British Library

Library of Congress Cataloging in Publication Data
A CIP catalog record for this book can be obtained from the Library of Congress

12 11 10 9 8 7
13 12 11 10

Typeset by 7 in 10/12 Sabon Roman
Printed and bound in Malaysia, KHL

The Publishers' policy is to use paper manufactured from sustainable forests.

CONTENTS

INTRODUCTION TO THE SERIES

Such is the pace of historical enquiry in the modern world that there is an ever-widening gap between the specialist article or monograph, incorporating the results of current research, and general surveys, which inevitably become out of date. *Seminar Studies in History* is designed to bridge this gap. The series was founded by Patrick Richardson in 1966 and his aim was to cover major themes in British, European and World history. Between 1980 and 1996 Roger Lockyer continued his work, before handing the editorship over to Clive Emsley and Gordon Martel. Clive Emsley is Professor of History at the Open University, while Gordon Martel is Professor of International History at the University of Northern British Columbia, Canada, and Senior Research Fellow at De Montfort University.

All the books are written by experts in their field who are not only familiar with the latest research but have often contributed to it. They are frequently revised, in order to take account of new information and interpretations. They provide a selection of documents to illustrate major themes and provoke discussion, and also a guide to further reading. The aim of *Seminar Studies in History* is to clarify complex issues without over-simplifying them, and to stimulate readers into deepening their knowledge and understanding of major themes and topics.

NOTE ON REFERENCING SYSTEM

Readers should note that numbers in square brackets [5] refer them to the corresponding entry in the Bibliography at the end of the book (specific page numbers are given in italics). A number in square brackets preceded by *Doc.* [*Doc. 5*] refers readers to the corresponding item in the Documents section which follows the main text.

ACKNOWLEDGEMENTS

My thanks to Clive Emsley, one of the series editors, for his comment on a draft of the book. Arden Bucholz provided me with some very helpful information and ideas concerning Moltke and the Prussian army. Librarians at the Wissenschaftskolleg zu Berlin helped me obtain many books during the last phase of writing. In particular, my thanks to Marianne Buck for help in tracking down the painting of the *Fürstentag* used for the front cover of the book.

We are grateful to the following for permission to reproduce copyright material:

Maps 1, 2, 3, 4 and 5 from *The Formation of the First German Nation-State, 1800–1871*, published by Macmillan, reproduced with permission of Palgrave (Breuilly, J. 1996).

In some instances we have been unable to trace the owners of copyright material, and we would appreciate any information that would enable us to do so.

CHRONOLOGY

1803	Territorial reshaping of the German lands with France gaining the left bank of the Rhine and a few German states receiving compensation on the right bank through the destruction of many small secular and ecclesiastical states which had belonged to the Holy Roman Empire.
1804	Francis II, Holy Roman Emperor, assumes the title of Francis I, Emperor of Austria.
1805	Newly enlarged states of Bavaria and Württemberg become kingdoms. The third war of coalition (Austria, Britain, Russia) against France. French victories over Russia and Austria. French naval defeat at Trafalgar. Peace of Pressburg: Austrian territorial losses.
1806	Francis formally ends the Holy Roman Empire. Confederation of the Rhine is founded. The fourth war of coalition (Prussia, Russia, Britain) against France. French victories over Prussia. Napoleon initiates the continental blockade of Britain
1807	Peace of Tilsit between France and Russia reduces Prussia to a rump state. Stein is appointed first minister in Prussia and begins making reforms.
1809	The fifth war of coalition (Austria, Britain) against France. Austrian defeat; Treaty of Schönbrunn.
1810	Napoleon marries Maria, daughter of Emperor Francis.
1811	Prussia joins military alliance with France.
1812	Napoleon invades Russia. Retreat begins in October. Prussian General Yorck signs Convention of Tauroggen with Russia in December.
1813	March: Prussia declares war on France. August: Austria declares war on France. September: Bavaria changes sides. October: Napoleon is defeated at Leipzig.
1814	Allies enter Paris. May: first Peace of Paris. Congress of Vienna meets.
1815	Napoleon escapes and is defeated at Waterloo. Final Act of the Congress of Vienna. German Confederation is established. Otto von Bismarck is born.
1817	German Student Association (*Burschenschaften*) organises nationalist festival at Wartburg.

1818	Constitutions are granted in Baden and Bavaria; Prussia abolishes all internal tariff barriers.
1819	Carlsbad decrees introduce political repression throughout Germany.
1820	Vienna 'Final Act' completes confederal constitution.
1823	Provincial Diets are established in Prussia.
1828	Customs union agreement between Prussia and Hesse-Darmstadt.
1830–31	Revolts in Hesse, Brunswick, Hannover and Saxony.
1831	Customs agreement between Prussia and Kurhesse.
1832	Nationalist festival in Hambach.
1834	*Zollverein* is established; a new set of repressive measures is imposed throughout Germany.
1837	The new King of Hannover abrogates the constitution and expels the university academics (the 'Göttingen Seven') who protest.
1840	Frederick William IV becomes King of Prussia; crisis with France.
1847	Meeting of the Prussian United Diet in Berlin.
1848	March: revolution in Germany, the Habsburg Empire and elsewhere. May: German National Assembly convenes. Prussia is at war with Denmark until armistice of September. October: insurrection is crushed in Vienna. December: Prussia imposes constitution; Franz Joseph becomes Emperor of Austria.
1849	April: Frederick William IV rejects the offer of hereditary emperorship of Germany from the German National Assembly. Spring: second revolutions are crushed in Germany; the Habsburgs restore control throughout the Empire.
1850	March: Frederick William IV summons a German parliament to Erfurt. July: peace is agreed between Prussia and Denmark. November: Prussia abandons its 'union' policy at Olmütz.
1851	The German Confederation is formally restored and coordinates counter-revolutionary repression throughout Germany; Bismarck is appointed first Prussian ambassador to the Confederation Diet. Customs union agreement between Hannover and Prussia.
1853	*Zollverein* is renewed for further twelve years; inclusion of Hannover but without the inclusion of Austria which instead concludes a commercial treaty with *Zollverein*.
1854–56	Crimean War.
1858	Agreement between France and Piedmont to act against Austria. William is appointed Regent in Prussia as Frederick William IV is mentally incapable. William appoints liberal ministers with the onset of a 'New Era'.
1859	France and Piedmont defeat Austria. Austria cedes Lombardy to France (which passes it on to Piedmont); Piedmont cedes Savoy and Nice to France. *Nationalverein* is established. Bismarck is appointed Prussian ambassador to Russia.

1860	Prussian Minister of War, Albert von Roon, introduces military reforms into the Prussian parliament. Austria returns to constitutional rule under the new Prime Minister, Schmerling.
1861	Death of Frederick William IV; William becomes King of Prussia. Constitutional crisis starts in Prussia.
1862	September: Bismarck is recalled from his recent appointment as Prussian ambassador to France and is appointed Minister-President. Free trade treaty is agreed between Prussia and France.
1863	Austria convenes a meeting of German princes to enact confederal reform; Denmark incorporates Schleswig; German Diet votes for action against Denmark; Hannoverian and Saxon troops enter Holstein.
1864	War of Austria and Prussia against Denmark. October: Treaty of Vienna; Denmark surrenders Schleswig and Holstein.
1865	August: Convention of Gastein: Austria and Prussia occupy and administer Holstein and Schleswig respectively. *Zollverein* adopts the Franco-Prussian trade treaty of 1862.
1866	January: renewal of *Zollverein* with the continued exclusion of Austria-Hungary. 8 April: three-month alliance of Italy and Prussia against Austria. June: Seven Weeks' War. August: Treaty of Prague excludes Austria from Germany. October: Treaty of Vienna, Austria cedes Venetia to Italy. Prussia annexes Schleswig-Holstein, Hannover, Hesse-Cassel and Frankfurt. The North German Confederation is established. Secret military agreement between Prussia and the south German states.
1867	Constitution is agreed for the North German Confederation. 'Dualist' constitution of Austria-Hungary is agreed.
1868	Establishment of a Customs Parliament with elections in the south German states.
1870–71	War of Prussia and other German states against France.
1871	January: German Second Empire is proclaimed at Versailles.
1879	Alliance between Germany and Austria-Hungary which lasts until 1918.

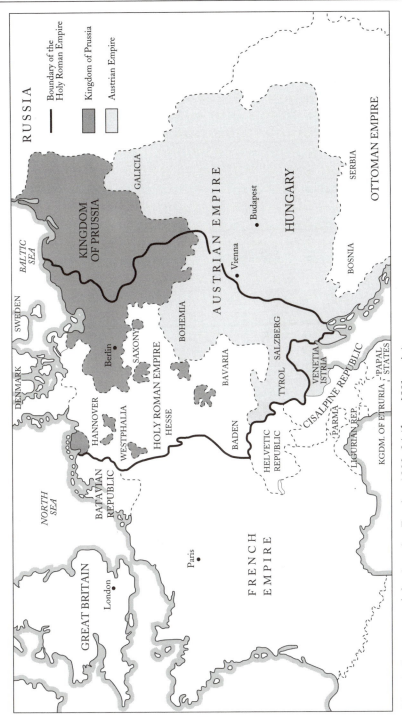

Map 1 Germany and the Austrian Empire, 1802–04 (from [50], p. ix)

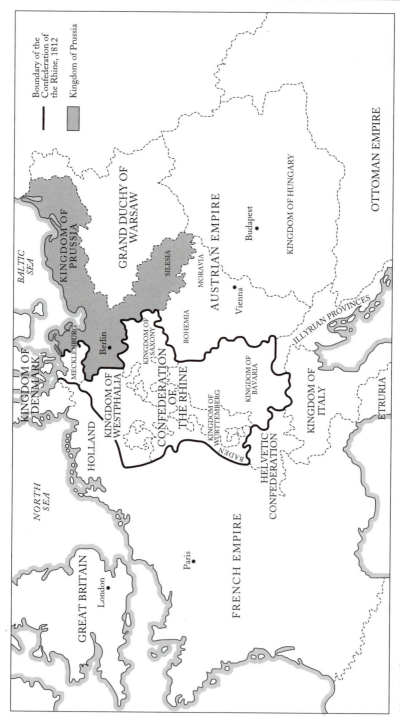

Map 2 The Austrian Empire, Prussia and the Confederation of the Rhine in 1812 (from [50], p. x)

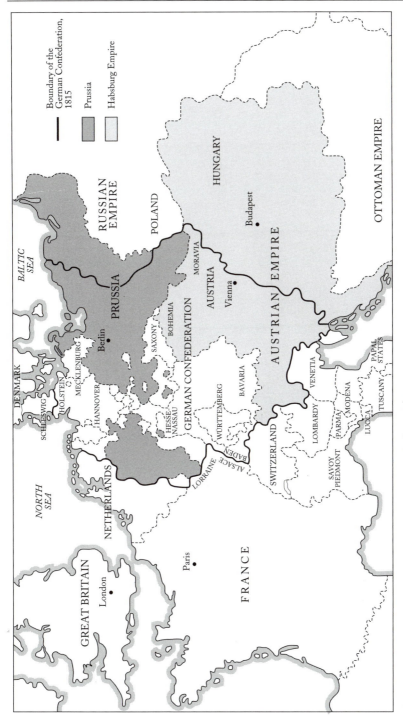

Map 3 Germany and the Austrian Empire in 1815 (from [50], p. xi)

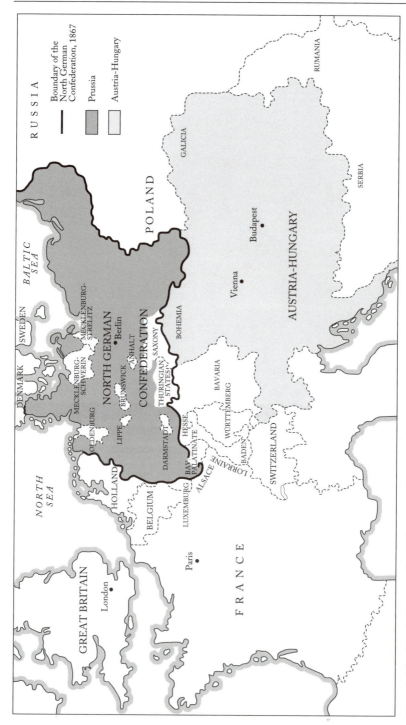

Map 4 The North German Confederation, the south German states and Austria–Hungary in 1867 (from [50], p. xii)

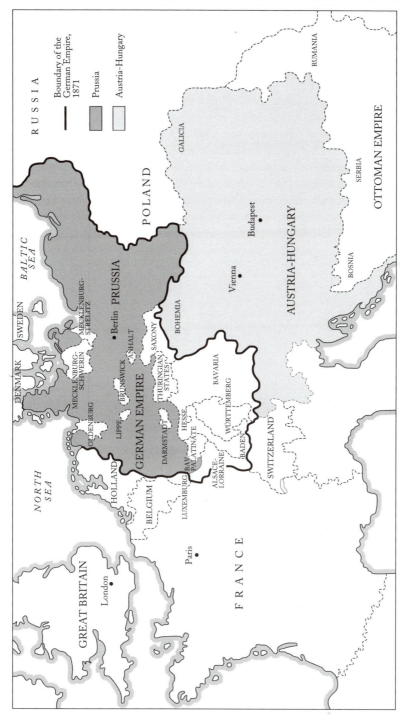

Map 5 The German Second Empire and Austria–Hungary (from [50], p. xiii)

CHAPTER ONE

THE SETTING

INTRODUCTION

In December 1805 Austria suffered defeat at the hands of France, resulting in the surrender of the Tyrol and her territories in Italy, Dalmatia and southern Germany. (See Chronology for the sequence of events and the maps for the territorial changes.) In June 1806 Napoleon presided over the territorial transformation of the German lands which had been under negotiation for some years. Most German states joined the Confederation of the Rhine (*Rheinbund*) with Napoleon as its Protector and Francis renounced the imperial crown [*Doc. 1 a–c*]. In October 1806 Prussian armies were defeated by Napoleon. Prussia continued the war in its eastern territories in alliance with Russia until July 1807 when Tsar Alexander I and Napoleon concluded the Peace of Tilsit. Prussia lost her possessions west of the Elbe as well as Polish territories, was placed under military occupation, saddled with a huge indemnity and had to join Napoleon's 'Continental System' which was designed to cut off trade with Britain [*Doc. 2*]. In 1809 Austria once more went to war with France, was defeated and compelled to cede Trieste and Illyria to France, Galicia to Saxony and Russia, some hereditary Austrian territory to Bavaria and to join the Continental System [*Doc. 4*].

The struggle for supremacy in Germany had apparently been settled and the winner was – *France*! This book considers how Austria and Prussia recovered great power status from the nadir of 1807–9, wrestling supremacy in Germany away from France and reorganising the German lands in 1814–15. Thereafter the focus is upon how cooperative domination of Germany by Austria and Prussia alternated with phases of competition or loss of control and ended with a war for supremacy. In this introduction I sketch the pre-1806 relationships between Austria, Prussia and Germany, outline various approaches towards the subject and explain how the book is arranged.

THE BACKGROUND

From 1792 until 1795 Austria and Prussia were allies against revolutionary France. Prussia then made a separate peace which lasted until 1806. Austria continued at war with France until October 1797 when it made a peace which, amongst other things, ceded control of the Netherlands. It resumed war against France in March 1799 in alliance with Russia and Britain. Further defeats led to another treaty with France in February 1801, by which France gained the left bank of the Rhine and effectively ended the Holy Roman Empire. From a position of neutrality Prussia exploited the situation to occupy Hannover in April 1801, although it was replaced by France in 1803. In 1804 Francis created an hereditary imperial title for his Austrian territories in imitation of Napoleon's own declaration as Emperor of the French. Austria joined the Third Coalition against France in August 1805. Prussia once again occupied Hannover.

This bare narrative shows that between 1792 and 1809 Austria and Prussia were distrustful allies for just the first three years of war with France. (Prussia effectively ceased war against France in 1794.) Prussia profited from Austrian setbacks, extending territory and influence in northern Germany. Both states exploited the destruction and territorial reorganisation of the Holy Roman Empire between 1797 and 1803, although these gains were undone between 1805 and 1809. There was no common cause against France; no commitment to the defence of 'Germany'. Austria had fought in four wars against France for some ten years (1792–97, 1799–1801, 1805, 1809); Prussia in two wars for about four years (1792–95, 1806–7). These two states were not natural allies in defence of either Germany or their own interests against the French threat [125 *chaps 2 and 3*].

That is hardly surprising when one considers the period between 1740 and 1792. For most of that time international relations were dominated by two conflicts – an 'inner' conflict between Austria and Prussia and an 'outer' conflict between Britain and France. Following Frederick II's seizure of Silesia from Austria in 1740, there followed two major wars from 1740–48 and 1756–63. In the first Prussia allied with France and Austria with Britain; in the second Prussia allied with Britain and Austria with France as well as Russia. An uneasy peace left Prussia in occupation of Silesia after 1763 and Austro-Prussian relations were marked by hostility and conflict up to the French revolution. Austria and France remained allies from 1763 to 1787 [41 *chap. 1*].

However, conflict between Austria and Prussia did not signal a 'struggle for supremacy in Germany'. Both states broadly accepted the institutions of the Holy Roman Empire, of which they were the two most important members, and sought influence in the rest of Germany by means of coalitions and the manipulation of imperial institutions. Apart from the contentious issue of Silesia, both states mainly sought gains outside Germany: Austria in Italy and south-eastern Europe; Prussia in Dutch and Swedish territories. Both had interests in Poland and, with Russia, effected the three partitions which by 1797 had wholly destroyed that state. Those partitions turned Prussia into a dual nationality dynasty with a quarter of its subjects having Polish as their first language. Austria had long been a multi-national empire; acquiring Galicia through the partitions of Poland simply added to that polyethnic makeup of Hungarian, Italian, German, Rumanian and various Slav language groups. 'Germany' was simply one zone amongst others in which Prussia and Austria acted in pursuit of their interests.

The combined impact of Polish partition and French revolution weakened France and strengthened Russia, which expanded into central Europe and had now come to share extensive frontiers with Austria and Prussia. They had to worry as much, if not more, about their Russian neighbour as about France or each other. Britain was the fifth, more distant, power, with German interests through the Hannoverian connection and concerns about Baltic trade but, more importantly, with a general concern to prevent any one power challenging its overseas interests or dominating Europe. This meant an anti-French orientation until well beyond 1815 as well as a growing concern about Russia. [41 provides the best overall treatment of international relations to 1848.]

The German lands apart from Austria and Prussia, organised in the Holy Roman Empire, constituted an 'intermediate zone', that is a region which separated the major powers from one another. The reduction of such zones to the direct control of one power could be destabilising because it brought major powers directly up against one another, as the Polish partitions had done with Austria, Prussia and Russia. Sometimes, in order to avoid such direct contact, a major power might prefer to exercise indirect influence rather than take over territory. Sometimes an intermediate zone was preserved as an area of neutrality or contest between two or more major powers. Switzerland is a good example. Sometimes such a zone was actually created as a neutral area. This was the case with the Netherlands after 1815 and continued with Belgium when it was recognised following an uprising against Dutch rule in 1830.

Clearly, the Holy Roman Empire, divided into hundreds of political units, was not a state. It did have provisions for making diplomacy and war but these were of minor importance. More importantly, it was what has been described as a legal or peace order, a channel for handling disputes between its members and between individual rulers and subjects. In these ways it was associated, at elite level, with a certain kind of German 'patriotism' which in turn Austria and Prussia claimed to represent when in conflict with one another and seeking support from elsewhere within the Empire. [For studies of the Holy Roman Empire, see 54; 62; 140.]

The formal destruction of the Holy Roman Empire in 1806 had several consequences. First, a number of medium-sized states were created which pursued more ambitious policies than their smaller and more numerous predecessors. Of these the most important which survived into the post-1815 period were the newly created kingdoms of Bavaria and Württemberg as well as the established kingdom of Saxony, the Grand Duchy of Baden and the Landgravate of Hesse-Darmstadt. Second, the *Rheinbund*, which replaced the Empire, was a Napoleonic creation designed for the extraction of money and soldiers.

Admirers of what had been achieved have tended to emphasise the first of these consequences, arguing that this created the basis for a more modern and progressive Germany preferable to Prussian, Austrian or external domination. They point to the many reforms made internally in these states during the Napoleonic period and also how constitutional advance and liberal movements developed most strongly in these parts of Germany after 1815. By contrast, critics have stressed the second consequence, contending that the new states were Napoleonic lackeys and that their preservation after 1815 allowed the selfish 'particularism' of this 'third Germany' to work as an obstacle to greater national unity and independence. (No one before 1815 and few for some time after 1815 seriously contemplated a single state but there were many calls for greater co-ordination by a federal authority in military, tariff and foreign policy spheres.) [On the Napoleonic impact on a European scale, see 28; 29; 45. Specifically for Germany, see 57a *chap. 1*; 59 *pp. 253–74*. The negative view was strongly argued by the 'Prussian school' of historians from the later nineteenth century: see 94 and 110.]

Whatever view one takes, it is difficult to deny that initially the *Rheinbund* was the brutal creation of power imposed from above, made with little reference to dynastic, ethnic or confessional traditions. The new states remained subject to arbitrary will, embodied in the restless, amoral and ruthless figure of Napoleon. However, what was at stake was not simply who held power, but also the principles on which states should be organised and relate to one another. In other words, we cannot simply look at the German states in terms of their geographical and population size or even their relative power.

The terms 'Germany', 'Austria' and 'Prussia' are elusive. They refer to political entities which underwent constant territorial and institutional change and shifts in relationships both amongst themselves and with the rest of Europe. In order to understand how 'Austria' and 'Prussia' regained great power status and how this in turn could lead to a struggle between them for supremacy in 'Germany', we need to clarify some of these terms and consider different approaches taken by historians.

APPROACHES

In 1866 Austria and Prussia fought a war for supremacy in Germany which Prussia won decisively. Triumph over France in 1870–71 led to the formation of the German Second Empire, in many ways the basis of present-day Germany. 1871 also marked the moment when the Habsburg government accepted the impossibility of reversing the outcome of 1866. Knowledge of Prussian success conditions the way historians look at previous chapters of the story. There is the danger of reading the ending back into those earlier stages. Indeed, the use of such words as 'chapters' or 'stages' can imply as much. Already by the 1850s and with increased influence after 1871, the 'Prussian school of history' presented Prussia as destined to play the role of maker of the German state [94; 110].

Yet to an observer in 1809 such an ending would have appeared most unlikely, not only because France was so dominant but also because Prussia was in an even more desperate state than Austria. If ever there was an improbable story-line, it is of the transformation of Prussia literally within one lifetime from the pliant rump state of 1807 to the triumphant creator of modern Germany in 1871. Prince William was ten years old when the Peace of Tilsit was signed; in 1871 he had seventeen years still to reign as King of Prussia and German Emperor.

Yet it would equally be a mistake to see the story as a series of accidents, a race in which the best or luckiest driver stays on the track while others, perhaps with better cars, crash, spin off, run out of fuel or suffer mechanical breakdown. For some historians the conflict between Prussia and Austria remained open to different outcomes right up to the 'accident' of 1866. For other historians this unfortunate accident actually in some sense derailed the ideal or normal course of events by subordinating the German nation to the power of the Prussian state. Clearly, Prussia needed luck and good drivers, but we must also consider the nature of the competition and the strengths and weaknesses of the various competitors if we are to be able to come to intelligent evaluations of these different views. In order to do this, however, we have to decide what kind of a competition was involved.

In focusing on the relationship between the two major German powers, broadly there are three levels at which analysis can be pitched: Europe, Germany, the two states of Austria and Prussia. That analysis in turn needs to take into account military, diplomatic, political, economic, cultural, intellectual and social history.

For a long time the emphasis in historical writing was on diplomacy and war, partly because these were strong interests amongst late nineteenth- and early twentieth-century historians but also because it appeared obvious that these were the crucial ingredients in the unification of Germany. From

1806 to 1815 the main concern was with war, above all the disastrous failure of Napoleon's invasion of Russia in 1812, the construction of a grand alliance against France in 1813 and the capacity of Austria and Prussia to put large and effective armies into the war effort, so ensuring a prominent place for themselves at the peace settlement. There was no war between major European states between 1815 and 1854, so attention shifted to diplomacy and the changing relationships between Austria, Prussia and Germany. Following the Crimean War in 1854, there was war in 1859 between France (with Piedmont) and Austria and then the three wars known retrospectively as the wars of German unification. The approach now mixed diplomatic and military history. At its 'purest' such an approach considers Austria and Prussia as two major states seeking to maintain or increase their power against one another, and Germany as the specific zone within which this happened. The approach can even take on a personal form, stressing the superiority of Bismarck over his diplomatic counterparts in Vienna, Paris and elsewhere, or of Moltke over those in charge of Austrian and French military strategy. [The classic study which coined the term 'struggle for supremacy' is 77.]

Historians of political ideas and culture object that this is too narrow a view. States are not mechanical objects which seek 'power' by whatever method seems appropriate. Individuals, no matter how great, have to achieve key positions and control the right resources to succeed. These individuals and the states within which they operate need to be understood as arising out of conflicts between groups of people who have assumptions and passions about what they want to achieve. In particular we must examine such assumptions and passions in relation to the role of German nationalism in the events leading to 1871.

Napoleonic domination evoked nationalist resistance. From 1815 onwards nationalist sentiment influenced, or even directly shaped, policy making. By 1860 nationalism in Germany and elsewhere was sufficiently strong to make the pursuit of any overtly anti-national policy difficult, if not impossible. Prussia was better placed than Austria to hitch itself to the national wagon because it had no important non-German territories or interests. However, this same nationalism turned Prussian success from territorial aggrandisement of the kind pursued by Frederick the Great into *national unification*, providing the popular legitimacy needed but lacking in German states since the Napoleonic period. Bismarck may have thought he was manipulating nationalism, but without it, at the very least, his achievement cannot be understood. [For general studies of German nationalism, see 49; 50; 55.]

But why did nationalism develop? Why was Prussia able to forge links with nationalism and to organise its diplomacy and war-making so as to effect national unification rather than Prussian expansion? 'Nationalism' is as problematic a driving force as is 'Prussia' or 'Bismarck'. [For some idea of the debates, see the books cited in the section of the bibliography on nationalism.]

Some historians have insisted that we must turn our attention to changes taking place within the German economy and society. The trend towards an urban and industrial society with much greater social and geographical mobility provided the basis for the growth of national consciousness and made political fragmentation appear obsolete [30]. Some argue that Prussia's leading role in such modernisation provided it with both the inclination and capacity to lead the way to national unification. For others, such a view goes back to the Prussian-centred approach with its air of inevitability, only now based on social and economic rather than diplomatic and military history. (For example, the famous expression of John Maynard Keynes that Germany was unified not by 'blood and iron' but by 'coal and iron'.) Instead, within this socio-economic framework, some historians argue that there were other possibilities of bringing closer links between German states, whether through Austria or the medium-sized states or the emergence of a powerful national movement led by modernising middle-class elites within state officialdom, the professions and, above all, the economy. Furthermore, one might argue that such links did not necessarily have to take the form of a single state under the domination of Prussia or Austria but could have been within a strongly federalist framework (as in Switzerland or the USA) or even a larger central European setting in which the German lands took a leading role.

These different approaches reflect shifts of interest within historical study, from diplomatic and military, to intellectual and political, to social, cultural and economic history. They also are related to changes over time, for example with a very positive 'Prussian' view from 1870 to 1914, with the development of more critical views after 1918, which became extremely negative after 1945, and since 1990 with a concern about federalist arrangements both at national and European levels. Finally, differences in part relate to the political or national viewpoint of the historian. Without conceding to the view that all history is a matter of opinion, one must recognise that all the historical writing on this subject is conditioned by such influences.

PLAN OF THE BOOK

I will try to do justice to these various approaches. This book is not a general history of the formation of the first German nation-state (which I have already written [50]) but focuses on the Austro-Prussian relationship and its impact on Germany. Given that focus, I argue that the overall pattern was neither one of inevitable Prussian success nor a matter of chance and inspired leadership.

In each of the narrative Chapters (2–7) I give separate attention to European developments, changes within Germany and how these shaped relations between Austria and Prussia. (The exception is Chapter 4. I explain why at the beginning of that chapter.) 1806–15 (Chapter 2) witnessed the consolidation and then the destruction of French domination of the German lands. This coincided with Austrian and Prussian defeat, followed by recovery. This chapter finishes with the formation of a new organisation for Germany, the German Confederation or *Deutsche Bund* (henceforth I will use the term *Bund*) at the Congress of Vienna.

From 1815 until 1848 (Chapter 3) Prussia largely accepted Austrian leadership in what amounted to a joint hegemony over the rest of Germany operated through the *Bund*. However, the emergence of oppositional political movements as well as the formation of a Customs Union (henceforth *Zollverein*) under Prussian leadership provided new ideological, economic and institutional orientations for those envisaging or seeking to bring about a more unified Germany.

During the revolutions of 1848–49 (Chapter 4) the old Austrian and Prussian regimes temporarily lost control. Initiative towards a national state shifted to a popularly elected German parliament. However, by the middle of 1849 the revolution had largely been suppressed and with it any possibility of this non-state guided path to unity.

Chapter 5 opens with a brief period of open conflict between Austria and Prussia in 1849–50, after which both states retreated from a forward policy in Germany. The *Bund* was formally restored in 1851. For the next seven or eight years the two German powers once again reverted to a policy of conservative and cooperative domination of the rest of Germany. However, this policy was pursued in a more unstable context than between 1815 and 1848. Competition for economic supremacy in Germany intensified with large-scale industrialisation taking place on an international scale. This was, above all, expressed in the attempts by Austria to join the *Zollverein* and Prussia to prevent this happening. The Crimean War was the first between major European powers since 1815 and had a major impact on Austria with implications for Austro-Prussian relations in Germany.

Chapter 6 begins with Austrian difficulties turning into crisis with military defeat at the hands of France in northern Italy in 1859. Domestic politics throughout Germany escaped from the counter-revolutionary grip in which it had been contained since 1850. Relations between Austria and Prussia veered unstably between intense cooperation, as in the war against Denmark in 1864, and open competition. I take the story to its dramatic conclusion in 1866 when that competition turned into war, unavoidably overlapping with one book in the series as well as finishing where another one starts [21; 26]. Finally, it is necessary to add a short postscript on the period 1866–71 (Chapter 7) because only with the formation of the Second

Empire was it clear to most contemporaries that the struggle for supremacy in Germany had been won by Prussia and had taken the form of national unification.

Thus I divide the story into six periods. The documents are chronologically organised and are selected especially to cast light on Austrian and Prussian policies towards one another and how others regarded those policies. There is a final chapter which departs from this narrative approach. In Chapter 8 I seek to analyse, with the aid of some statistics, the relative power of Austria and Prussia, how this changed over time, and how this helps us understand the triumph of Prussia and the defeat of Austria.

The maps, chronology, glossary and who's who are designed to help readers understand territorial changes, the sequence of events and key terms and people. The bibliography indicates some of the sources and secondary literature I have used in writing this book as well as providing readers with opportunities to follow up on various aspects of the subject.

PART TWO   THE NARRATIVE

CHAPTER TWO

FROM DEFEAT TO TRIUMPH, 1806–15

EUROPE

The principal actor to whom others had to respond in this period was Napoleon and his imperial system. In 1809–10 he was at the height of his powers. Admittedly the Spanish insurrection rumbled on, aided by British money and arms, and Britain continued at war, but it did not seem likely that this could threaten Napoleon's empire in the foreseeable future.

The German states were treated as instruments in Napoleon's imperial system. The *Rheinbund* states had to furnish Napoleon with men and money just like other of his satellites. Many of the troops serving in Spain were from Italy, Germany and Poland. *Rheinbund* soldiers fought against Prussia and Russia in 1806–7, against Austria and Tyrolean insurgents in 1809, and formed part of the *Grande Armée* that invaded Russia. [See Metternich's protest to Napoleon, *Doc. 11 and 25*.] The *Rheinbund* states, as well as Austria, Prussia and Russia, were compelled to break off all trade with Britain as part of Napoleon's 'Continental System' [*Docs 1a, 2 and 4*]. Prussia became a military ally and Austria a political ally shortly before Napoleon invaded Russia in 1812. Although Napoleon recognised the need to offer benefits to those who worked with him outside France, and sometimes conceived of himself as a European ruler – whether a Charlemagne, an enlightened despot or the man who brought order out of revolutionary chaos – generally his policies served French national interests rather than broader imperial purposes [28; 29; 45]. The sovereignty of Napoleon's *Rheinbund* and other allies was further compromised by extensive land grants designed to lay the foundation of an imperial nobility. The Continental System was undermined by making exceptions to the blockade of British trade which favoured French economic interests. French tariff policy damaged allies outside this tariff zone [45 *chap. 4*].

By the end of 1811 Napoleon's Continental System was clearly failing. Smuggling had become a major branch of economic activity. Russia was refusing to support the policy, for example in relation to trade with Britain. Whether this was the principal motive for Napoleon's invasion of Russia is a much debated question. Whatever the reasons, huge financial, economic and manpower burdens were laid upon the German lands in the preparation of this campaign.

The campaign failed disastrously [71]. As Napoleon retreated from Moscow his allies confronted a difficult problem – if, how and when to abandon him. Prussia made the first move, beginning with an unauthorised, local neutrality agreement between Prussian and Russian troops in December 1812 [*Doc. 6*], followed by a secret alliance in February 1813, made public in March [*Doc. 10*]. Austria moved more slowly, only declaring war on France in August and concluding a formal alliance with Prussia in September. Most *Rheinbund* states abandoned Napoleon shortly before the great Battle at Leipzig in October, joining the growing alliance system, especially on the basis of agreements with Austria such as that of Teplitz, concluded between Austria and Bavaria. A key point of these agreements was that Austria guaranteed the continued existence of the possessions of these princes, thereby prejudging aspects of a postwar settlement. [See 82 for Metternich's German policy.]

With allied victory at Leipzig the end of French hegemony had become a matter of time, although precisely how it would take place remained unclear. By early 1814 Napoleon was forced to abdicate; Louis XVIII was placed on the French throne and a peace congress convened. Its deliberations were disrupted by Napoleon's escape from Elba. The general terms of the peace settlement were already determined but the Hundred Days (the period of Napoleon's return brought to an end by the Battle of Waterloo) meant that a harsher peace was imposed on France and a harsher restoration policy pursued by the Bourbons than had appeared likely at an earlier stage of peacemaking. The victors each had their own interests to consider but also a common concern to make arrangements designed to prevent revolution and war in the future. How the 'German question' was handled has to be placed within the general framework of a European, even global, peace settlement. [Generally on international relations, see 41.]

GERMANY

What policies did the German states pursue during the Napoleonic period?

The *Rheinbund* states could not act independently of France until the autumn of 1813. They were, in effect, military satellites [99]. Although this might create bitterness and resentment, the German princes knew they could not openly resist. Some indeed prided themselves on performing with military distinction. The little we know of 'ordinary people' suggests they resented and even resisted French burdens, but on economic and possibly religious rather than national grounds. Rulers and their ministers sought discreetly to reduce Napoleon's interference as much as possible and concentrated upon internal consolidation. The last years of 1811–13, with the preparation for the invasion of Russia and then the Russian campaign itself, made this increasingly difficult. It probably also contributed to a growing anti-French feeling, though that is not the same thing as German nationalism.

The *Rheinbund* rulers, deprived of any independence of action in the foreign policy and military fields, concentrated upon consolidating rule over their new territories, often by stratagems such as issuing constitutions and creating a better-trained, more highly paid bureaucracy. Some princes adopted French principles, removing legal distinctions between town and countryside, decreeing peasant emancipation, guild abolition, Jewish emancipation and the adoption of the new French civil code. However, much of this was pragmatic and constantly threatened by Napoleon's intervention and exploitation [*59 pp. 253–74*].

However, the 'German' reaction to Napoleon goes beyond the policies of the German princes. For some historians, the most important feature of the period of French domination was that it laid the foundations of modern German nationalism. For example, the lectures given by the philosopher Fichte in Berlin in 1808, 'Addresses to the German Nation', express full-blooded nationalism. The French are rejected not just as conquerors but as aliens. Only the cultivation of national virtue can save Germany. The justification for authority is not dynastic, Christian, liberal or democratic, but rooted in nationality understood as collective cultural identity.

Ideas of 'Germandom' were expressed through the gymnastic movement established under the leadership of 'Father' Jahn, which aimed to rekindle the manly qualities associated with the original German people. The call for military action against Napoleon led to the formation of volunteer units pledged to the German cause. Radical patriots such as Baron Stein, Prime Minister of Prussia in 1807–8, who had taken service with the Tsar and who headed the commission charged with organising the occupation of postwar Germany, asserted that their commitment was to Germany, not to particular German states [*Doc. 5*]. Stein's secretary, Arndt, wrote a number of popular pamphlets and songs which expressed strongly German nationalist and anti-French sentiments [*Doc. 7*].

However, one must not exaggerate the importance of these ideas and actions. The late nineteenth-century age of mass nationalism made a myth of the war of the fourth coalition (1813–15) which is known in Germany as the 'war of liberation' (*Befreiungskrieg*). Still later, in the mid-twentieth century, after extreme nationalism in Germany had been discredited and defeated, the myth persisted, whether regarded as 'good' nationalism or forming the roots of 'bad' nationalism. Indeed, for some writers it was the German reaction against Napoleon which laid the foundations for modern nationalism generally [*33 chap. 1*].

Yet Fichte spoke to a tiny audience. The French censor allowed the lectures to be given, partly on the grounds that they did not advocate insurrection or guerrilla warfare but argued abstractly for long-term educational reform. Fichte's notions of a closed state, collectivised economy, 'total' education and the extinction of any individuality outside the national community were fantasies which only began to have influence in the twentieth century when it was possible to conceive of a nation-state actually accumulating such power. Fichte had little in common with Baron Stein, for whom Germany was not a cultural nation based on language but the hierarchical, multi-state and mixed nationality world of the old empire. Stein was politically more significant than Fichte but he was quickly marginalised. The authority of his occupation commission was undermined by the agreements Metternich made with *Rheinbund* princes to preserve them against attempts to break up their states, whether by returning to old imperial arrangements, punishing them as allies of Napoleon or providing territory for states such as Prussia – all policies Stein advocated in 1813–14.

The gymnastic movement had limited popularity and after 1815 backed away from politics. The volunteer units were militarily unimportant compared to conscription into regular units officered by royalists. Mass mobilisation probably owed more to anti-French feeling, based on material oppression, Christian appeals and obedience to monarchical authority than to German nationalism. [55; 59 *chaps 5 and 6*]

Yet there *were* constant appeals, even by the princes, to ideas of the people and Germany [*Docs 8, 9, 10*]. This was a significant change from the rhetoric of pre-1789 wars which tended to focus on dynastic and confessional matters, although Britain and France had started appealing to a national or public opinion and Frederick the Great moved a little in this direction towards the end of his reign. The change reflected the awareness of the princes that they had to respond positively to new ideas about their ruling being justified in relation to their subjects. However, the appeal was more often to the people (*Volk*) than to the more politically-loaded *Nation*. Furthermore, this as often meant the subjects of a particular ruler as it did 'Germans'. In the case of the Prussian *Volk* [*Doc. 9*], the king explicitly addresses: 'Brandenburgers, Prussians, Silesians, Pomeranians, Lithuanians!'. King Frederick William III of Prussia, Tsar Alexander of Russia and Emperor Francis of Austria all understood their *Volk* to be politically passive and loyal to the monarchy. At the same time, promises of constitutions [*Doc. 13*] implied some recognition of the need to give subjects opportunities for political participation. Therefore, although it had little practical significance at the time, the introduction of such appeals into the public rhetoric of governments was important. If political opposition to the princes, which sought popular support, developed, especially if such opposition also tried to make connections across individual states, then appeals to the nation could take on a very different significance. At that point it became possible to envisage a 'German nation' independent of, even opposed to, the German princes.

AUSTRIA AND PRUSSIA

Austria and Prussia cleaved to alliance with Napoleon until early 1813. Having been excluded from Germany and Italy, Austria focused active foreign policy towards the Balkans, leading to tensions with Russia. Austria had no expectation of alliance with Britain. Metternich, who had assumed responsibility for Austrian policy following defeat in the 1809 war, was happy to see Emperor Francis's daughter marry Napoleon. The appeal to the people, especially the German subjects of the empire, had been a feature of the propaganda of the 1809 war and was something Metternich had no wish to repeat. Austria sought to fulfil obligations such as indemnity payments and cutting off trade with Britain. Metternich thought the only way to restrain Napoleon was as a subordinate ally [59 *pp. 274–91*; 41; 136].

Frederick William III of Prussia shared this view, dismissing ministers Napoleon considered 'refractory', such as his Prime Minister Stein (who was accused by informers to Napoleon of supporting Austrian preparations for war in 1809), refusing to follow the advice of radical patriots and taking a cautious line on domestic reforms which might incur French disapproval. When the radical soldier Gneisenau submitted a memorandum which advocated universal conscription and a rallying of the Prussian people to resistance, the king wrote 'Poesie' (poetic dreaming) in the margin [59 *pp. 291–310*].

This was understandable given the harsh constraints to which Prussia was subjected. Prussia had to keep its army limited to 40,000 men and to pay a large indemnity. Frederick's decision to enter a military alliance with France – committing 20,000 troops to the *Grande Armée* against his recent ally, Russia – caused radical patriots like Gneisenau and the soldier and military theorist Clausewitz to leave his service for that of Russia, the only continental power which remained independent of Napoleon. There they joined Stein and his secretary, the rabidly anti-French publicist and poet Arndt.

For many historians the important difference between Prussia and Austria in the years before 1813 is to be located not in the field of foreign policy and diplomacy but in domestic politics. Prussia embarked upon major reforms in response to the defeat of 1807. By contrast Austria slowed down or reversed earlier reforms, especially those associated with the rule of Joseph II (1780–90). This had begun in the early 1790s but there had been new reforms (particularly in military matters) in preparation for the war of 1809. Defeat in this war led to the removal of reformers from office. In Austria, reforms in 1808–9 were *preparation* for war; defeat discredited them. In Prussia after 1807 reforms were a *reaction* against defeat which had discredited conservatives. For some Prussian reformers the goal was to recover a measure of independence; for others to deal with financial and economic collapse or as worthwhile ends in themselves. [*Doc. 3* is an example of such thinking from the man who was Prussia's first minister from 1810 until 1822.] In contrast to Hardenberg, Metternich noted how earlier reforms in Austria had precipitated internal conflicts and weakened the state [59 *chap. 5*].

It is difficult to estimate the contribution of reforms to the defeat of Napoleon. Reforms undertaken by the *Rheinbund* states had no military significance. Some Prussian reforms did help state finances. Self-administration measures like the urban law of 1808 reduced state commitment. The abolition of the guilds cleared the way for a tax on all artisans. Quasi-constitutional assemblies provided security for loans and support for taxes. These reforms were supposed to make the economy and government work more efficiently and to build up a spirit of patriotism, but some historians have considered their fiscal aspect as more important in the short term. In economic terms there was not time by 1815 for reforms such as peasant emancipation or the abolition of guilds to produce more productive agriculture and manufacturing. As for stimulating patriotism by offering people economic and political freedom, some reforms, such as the introduction of a constitution, never got beyond the status of a promise from the king [*Doc. 13*]; some, such as peasant emancipation, were restricted by later measures in favour of the privileged; yet others, like urban self-administration, were regarded by townspeople as a burden rather than an opportunity.

Yet the reforms signalled the purge of old officials and the coming to power of an energetic minority of reformers. They reduced the financial impact of defeat and territorial loss. They established more streamlined administration. All this helped the military reforms. Whether the motive for fighting was nationalist, monarchist, hatred of the French, or fear of the Russians, such motives had to be channelled effectively. New ideas about military organisation and methods of fighting meant that once the troops were raised they were used to good effect, as Napoleon himself ruefully observed. (Nevertheless, mobilisation in 1813 revived pre-1806 practices, for example on punishments, previously condemned by military reformers, and required the wholesale recall of officers dismissed in 1807.) More importantly, the greater scope of reform in Prussia compared to Austria arguably laid a long-term basis for modernisation after 1815 and also made Prussia, despite its authoritarian monarchy, more attractive than Austria to Germans looking to one of the major powers to take the lead in national and liberal reforms. [For the reform process in Prussia and the *Rheinbund* states, see 59 *chap. 5*; specifically on Austria, see 58 *chap. 3*.]

However, in 1812–13 the overwhelming short-term priority was how to respond to the failure of Napoleon's Russian campaign. As Napoleon retreated westwards, a Prussian military contingent concluded a pact with Russia in December 1813 [*Doc. 6*]. Soon regional assemblies in eastern Prussian provinces started to raise troops and declare against Napoleon. This went against the official policy of the king in Berlin, still occupied by French troops. When Frederick William did feel able to change sides, the emphasis was on alliance as a subordinate power to Russia [*Doc. 10*]. By June 1813 Russia and Prussia had reached agreement with Britain, thereby ensuring generous supplies of money and material for the war effort.

Metternich was more cautious. He neither envisaged nor wanted an early and complete defeat for Napoleon. A strong France was needed to prevent Austria and much of Germany lurching from the grip of one protector to that of another, Russia. Napoleon's limited military successes in early 1813, along with his reputation as a military genius, meant turning against him was seen as a huge risk. However, his refusal to engage in serious negotiations which would force France back to its national territory compelled Austria to join the general alliance against him [*Doc. 11*]. Metternich's next concern was to bring the *Rheinbund* states into this alliance which meant promising those states that the defeat of France would not lead to their own destruction. Already some of the contours of Metternich's policy at the Congress of Vienna and beyond were becoming clear [82 *chaps 6–8*; 41 *chap. 10*].

From the autumn of 1813 to the spring of 1814 the main concern of the Austrian and Prussian governments was with the effective prosecution of war [71]. Napoleon, despite huge losses in the Russian campaign, was raising large numbers of soldiers again, mainly by increasing the burden upon the French people. The Russians had an inexhaustible supply of men and, with British backing, could equip their armies once the decision to invade western Europe was made.

If German states were to retain independence or have any say in the future course of events and the decisions to be taken after Napoleon's defeat, Austria and Prussia had to play an important part in this war. That meant mobilising large armies. The Austrians still had a large population from which to draw and actually put the largest number of soldiers of all the allies into the field. The most impressive mobilisation, however, was that of Prussia, which finally adopted the radical 'French' principle of universal conscription, long urged by the reformers but resisted by the king [*Doc. 8*]. The *Rheinbund* states did little positive, with the notable exception of Saxony which remained a French ally at the Battle of Leipzig.

The sheer number of soldiers involved at this stage of the war was higher than at any previous time in European history [*Doc. 12*]. Adding garrisons as well as the British, Spanish and Napoleonic armies operating in the Iberian peninsula, it would appear that the best part of two million men were under arms. Austria and Prussia each mobilised over 250,000 combat troops, comparable to the Russian army. For Austria this was well under 10 per cent of her adult male population; in the reduced post-1807 Prussia the proportion was more like 15 per cent. Prussia could, therefore, appear as powerful as Austria but it required a much greater effort and was probably only sustainable for a short period, and under certain conditions, such as British financial and material aid. Frederick the Great had described Prussia as an 'artificial power' in comparison with Britain, France, Russia and Austria. By this he meant that those four powers possessed some combination of territory, material resources and population to an extent which automatically placed them in a leading position, irrespective of state organisation or policy, whereas Prussia could only obtain such a position through superior harnessing of more modest resources. This point still applied in 1815. (See Chapter 8 for how it no longer applied by 1866.)

THE SETTLEMENT OF 1815

Europe

By outdoing Napoleon in mass military mobilisation and preparedness to fight pitched battles the allies successfully concluded the war. Austria and Prussia had ensured their return to the ranks of the major powers. In territorial terms the settlement made at the Congress of Vienna confirmed rather than undid much of Napoleon's achievement. (Compare maps 2 and 3.) His reduction of the states of Germany and Italy from hundreds to tens was preserved. Russia advanced further into Poland. Prussia took compensation for Polish losses in Germany. Austria secured territory in northern Italy and south-eastern Europe. Britain had little interest in European territory (an exception was the restoration of Hannover, in personal union with the British monarchy) and more in security achieved through balancing continental powers against each other. Her major gain was the destruction of the French global challenge. Britain and Austria resisted an over-harsh treatment of France because they did not wish to shift from an unbalanced Europe in which France was too powerful to an equally unbalanced Europe in which she was too weak [41 *chaps 11 and 12*].

Germany

Arrangements also had to be made for the German lands. The agreements made with the *Rheinbund* states by Metternich, along with the restoration of Hannover, blocked either the restoration of many tiny political units (including ecclesiastical states which had been so important in the Holy

Roman Empire) or extensive territorial acquisitions by Austria and Prussia. The French creations of Berg and Westphalia were destroyed and territories returned to Prussia and Hannover. Prussia also acquired additional territory on the left and right banks of the Rhine from which she formed two western provinces of Rhineland and Westphalia. Prussia also sought to acquire all of Saxony with initial Russian support but was blocked by the other powers (including France) and only gained the northern part. Austria made no territorial gains in Germany. The south German states which had grown so much under Napoleon – Baden, Bavaria and Württemberg – were largely confirmed in their territories, with Bavaria receiving the Rhenish Palatinate in compensation for the return of the Tyrol to Austria. As with Prussia, this meant Bavaria's Rhenish possessions were physically divided from the rest of the state [83 *passim*; 41 *chap. 12*; 125 *pp. 105–10*].

It was deemed essential to bind these German states together to forestall radical change from within and interference from outside. This was the purpose of the *Bund*, drawing on the models of the Holy Roman Empire and the *Rheinbund* but different from these in important ways. [For the constitution of the *Bund*, see *Docs 14 and 15*.] As with the old empire, there was to be a regionally organised army based on contributions according to the size of the state. There was a special concern with a strong military presence in fortresses on the French border. Member states were forbidden to enter into agreements with non-member states which could be deemed a threat to the *Bund* or any of its members. There was to be an Austrian presidency, a pale shadow of the imperial title held by the Habsburgs until 1806. However, unlike the old Empire, there was to be no Confederal court or legal system or any executive authority. There was no question of a national representative institution; instead, the composition of the *Bundestag* was made up of state envoys with a weighted voting system which prevented any simple Austro-Prussian majority (again as in the Holy Roman Empire). The absence of judicial or executive institutions made it appear that sovereignty was vested in the individual states, unlike the Holy Roman Empire. However, this idea of state sovereignty jarred with certain provisions in the *Bund* constitution. There was a (very brief and unclear) stipulation that all states should grant constitutions based on the various social estates [*Doc. 14*, article 13]. There was provision for the *Bund* to enforce settlements of disputes between member states. Quite how the tension between state sovereignty and Confederal authority would be handled was unclear. This problem was compounded with the 1820 completion of the *Bund* constitution [*Doc. 15*] which shifted the balance of authority away from the states to the *Bund*.

There was also the question of how 'national' was the *Bund*. As a product of an international peace settlement it was 'guaranteed' by eight powers (the five major ones plus Sweden, Spain and Portugal) which implied rights of intervention. Prussia and Austria were divided into 'German' and 'non-German' areas (again, as they had been in the Holy Roman Empire and indeed involving much the same territory). This also enabled Austria and Prussia to act as *Bund* members or non-members as it suited them. Some parts of the *Bund* were ruled in personal union by princes whose major territories lay outside the *Bund*, for example, the King of Denmark in Holstein, the King of Holland in the Grand Duchy of Luxemburg, the British King in the Kingdom of Hannover. (This ceased in 1837 when Victoria became Queen because Hannoverian law did not permit a female monarch.)

Austria and Prussia

The *Bund* was not pre-destined to take the form that it did. Some of its features have to be understood in terms of the Austro-Prussian relationship.

First, in the initial stages of negotiation both Metternich and the chief Prussian negotiators (Hardenberg and Wilhelm von Humboldt) had envisaged a more centralised *Bund* with clear provision for Austria and Prussia together to exercise control over the other German states [83; 138 *pp. 181–219*]. This did not elicit any great disagreement from the other major powers. Understandably, the other German states, especially the 'medium' states (by which I mean the four other kingdoms – Bavaria, Hannover, Saxony, Württemberg – and the larger grand duchies or duchies of Baden, Hesse-Cassel, Hesse-Darmstadt and Nassau) objected to such an arrangement, having become used to internal autonomy within the *Rheinbund*. However, it is difficult to see how these states could have resisted Austro-Prussian agreement. (See Chapter 8, Table I.1 which makes clear the demographic domination of Austria and Prussia over the rest of Germany.)

However, the negotiations were disrupted by the crisis over the related issues of Poland and Saxony. Prussia, as subordinate ally to Russia, did not resist the loss of former Polish territories to Russia. Naturally, Prussia expected compensation and demanded the whole of Saxony, which had remained an ally of Napoleon until after the Battle of Leipzig. There was nothing new in such a policy; Frederick the Great had occupied Saxony during the Seven Years' War and contemplated its annexation. As for Maria Theresa then, now for Metternich this would mean an expansion of Prussia into central Germany and undermine his plans of exercising indirect influence over Germany. Metternich therefore engineered an agreement with Britain and France which threatened war with Prussia and Russia. Eventually a compromise was agreed: there would be a division of Saxony with a northern part becoming a Prussian province while the southern part remained an independent kingdom [83 *chaps 8–10*; 41 *especially p. 527*].

The crisis had two important effects, one European and one German. It brought France back into the arena of international relations as one power amongst others. It forced Metternich away from Prussia and towards agreement with the medium states for a much looser *Bund* with voting rights that ensured Austria and Prussia did not have a majority. At the same time, measures designed to weaken the medium states survived from the original plans. This was one motive for the otherwise strange insistence by Metternich that states should have constitutions with estate assemblies. Metternich assumed that these assemblies would be dominated by nobles (some of them former independent rulers from the era of the Holy Roman Empire) who would restrict the reforming ambitions of the princes. Here we have an interesting case of constitutions not being regarded as modern, liberal or national but the precise opposite. However, constitutions turned out very differently from Metternich's expectations.

Territorially, the relationship between Prussia and Austria within the *Bund* was skewed. Prussia had become more 'German' through the settlement, losing Polish possessions and making gains in western and central Germany, even if not as many as it had wanted. What is more, without realising it at the time, Prussia had acquired areas which were to be at the heart of later industrial and commercial growth (along the Rhine, in the Ruhr valley) which was oriented towards trade west and north with the economically most dynamic parts of Europe and the increasingly important Atlantic trade routes. (*See* map 3.)

Austria, by contrast, had become less German, regaining a few areas such as the Tyrol lost to Bavaria (but not its pre-1789 possessions in the Netherlands), losing the German imperial title and acquiring more territory in the Balkans and Italy. If a threat of war arose with France, it was Prussia rather than Austria which was in the front line of the defence of Germany on the Rhine. Austria aimed less at territorial gain and more at the maintenance of equilibrium, partly through influence over smaller rulers in 'intermediate' zones like Germany and Italy. This was fine in 1815 but such influence, in part based on the model of the Holy Roman Empire as a 'peace order', would become increasingly difficult to exercise.

Such a loose confederation of German states subject to external constraints but not truly unified suited the medium states and, for a time, Austria. It even suited Prussia which, following the crisis of 1814–15, retreated into a policy of cooperation with Austria. However, it was anathema to nationalists who insisted that the war against Napoleon had been fought for nobler objectives. These nationalists, along with those who criticised the peace settlement as restoring too much power to the old order of princes and the nobility, were much feared by Metternich and others in power.

CONCLUDING REMARKS

The main reasons for the recovery of Austria and Prussia from the despair of 1807–9 lay outside Germany, in Napoleon's failure to defeat Britain and his disastrous invasion of Russia. German nationalism played only a minor role in the subsequent revival of German military fortunes. The princes appealed to the German people but not as a political force or with any view of forming a national state. Some prominent figures such as Baron Stein did have a perspective extending beyond, even against, the Germany of princes, but they were only politically significant as servants of those princes. Less well-connected nationalists made much noise and have attracted attention subsequently but were of marginal importance at the time. Most of the ambitious reforms pursued by the *Rheinbund* states and Prussia either had purposes other than assertion of independence or were too flawed or slow to have such an effect by 1815. The 'German' state which mobilised the most soldiers against Napoleon and dominated the peace settlement was Austria, where Metternich opposed nationalism and reform.

However, we should not conclude that Napoleon's defeat was wholly the work of 'old' Europe or that this period did not see major changes. The capacity of Prussia and Austria to take decisive advantage of the opportunity provided in 1813 owed much to administrative and military reform, especially in the case of Prussia which was much smaller and weaker than Austria following her defeat of 1807. The appeals to the German people could be turned against the princes in the future. The consolidating reforms of the *Rheinbund* states helped ensure their survival and influence in postwar Germany. The Prussian reforms would have a long-term impact and, along with changed political geography which made Prussia 'more German' and Austria 'less German', could help change the relationships between Austria, Prussia and the other German states. Although the overriding concern in 1815 was the restoration of peace and stability, the Polish/Saxon crisis had shown that potentially Prussia and Austria could come into conflict over German affairs. In the years immediately after 1815 they acted cooperatively, with Austria as the more powerful state taking the lead. However, there were tensions right from the start which also need to be considered when we turn to the post-1815 period.

CHAPTER THREE

COOPERATIVE DOMINATION, 1815–48

INTRODUCTORY COMMENTS

This period is often dubbed that of 'restoration' or 'reaction' [as in title of 105]. In Germany it is also sometimes known as *Vormärz* (pre-March, before March 1848) although some historians take this to apply to the shorter period *c.* 1840–48 and 'restoration' to a decade and a half after 1815. Another term used is *Biedermeier*. The first three terms have negative associations. Restoration implies a return, or an attempt to return, to an earlier era. Reaction means a drive against progressive movements. *Vormärz* characterises the period by what brought it to an end rather than in its own terms. Taken together, these terms suggest that the period is marked by efforts to put the clock back while suppressing progressive forces which finally, in 1848, burst through the dams erected against change. Metternich, the individual with whom this period is most closely associated (see the titles of the document collections 3 and 15) himself took this view. By contrast, *Biedermeier* refers to a certain style and taste, characterised as vulgar, complacent and bourgeois, placing high value on security and comfort. This also suggests a dull era which turned away from the heroic values associated with war, nationalism and revolution. [For short sketches of Germany in this period, see essays by Clark and Friedrich in 51; for longer treatments, see 47; 52; 57a *chap. 3*; 59; 105.]

There is some truth in all these suggestions. After 1815 princes and statesmen wanted to run down armies, reduce state debt, settle matters diplomatically and avoid the twin threats of revolution and war. Only after mid-century were people who had no adult experience of the continual war and upheaval of 1792–1815 coming into positions of power and only then do we find a greater willingness to unleash large-scale violence as an instrument of policy. However, there were also important changes within this period, some beyond the control of governments, which altered the situation in Germany from what had been aimed at in 1815. This chapter moves from Europe to change within the German lands and then considers how Austro-Prussian relations within Germany developed from restoration to revolution.

EUROPE

Once the Saxon crisis was over, Prussia was content largely to follow Metternich. Prussia had few foreign policy ambitions, being preoccupied with military and financial retrenchment and consolidating control over her territories. The end of the military occupation of France in 1818 contributed to the first objective. Prussia did not have entanglements with Russia as did Austria (e.g., in relation to the ailing Ottoman Empire) and steered clear of issues in southern Europe. Metternich sought to contain Russia through a 'restraining alliance' (a term used in 41 *chap. 14*) rather than direct confrontation, rather like the line he had taken towards Napoleon between 1810 and 1813. This was part of his general policy of alliance diplomacy to avoid great power conflicts getting out of control. This cool conservatism was more important than the alliance of Christian states ('Holy Alliance') cherished by Tsar Alexander, something about which Metternich always expressed scepticism.

Although avoiding great power confrontations, Metternich had no scruples about intervening in the affairs of minor states to prevent radical changes. A series of international conferences accompanied this diplomacy until 1822, although France and Britain increasingly distanced themselves from such coordinated policy-making. Britain especially, after Canning had succeeded Castelreagh as Foreign Secretary, tended to a more unilateral policy based on maintaining a balance of power in Europe irrespective of the internal politics of various states. Thereafter cooperation was less formally organised. It was put under strain, for example with Russian involvement in the Greek rising against Ottoman rule in the late 1820s, but this did not seriously affect Austro-Prussian cooperation [41 *chaps 13 and 14*].

The July revolution in France, and further unrest which followed within and beyond Germany, strengthened this cooperation. The overriding fear of both Austria and Prussia was the threat posed by a revolutionary regime in France. There was specific Prussian concern about the Belgian revolt against Dutch rule, because of the weakening effect this could have in relation to France. The *Bund* prepared for military intervention in Luxemburg. More alarming was an uprising in Congress Poland, the kingdom established at the Congress of Vienna (hence the name) which was ruled by the Tsar under a personal union. There was little either German power could do about most of these issues except stand troops on its borders and present a united front against any extension of troubles into the German lands [41 *chap. 15*].

As it was, despite symbolic attempts by Louis Phillippe to lay claim to the prestige of Napoleon, France posed no threat to the Vienna settlement or the German states until 1840. It was only then, with the combined

British and Russian exclusion of France from influence in Ottoman affairs (including a treaty of 1840 which Austria and Prussia also signed), that the French Prime Minister Thiers reacted by making threatening noises over German territory on the left bank of the Rhine. When it was clear that the other major powers would oppose any such action, Thiers was removed from office. Thereafter, until 1848, the restoration settlement continued to work effectively [41 *chap. 16*].

Less dramatic but arguably more important in altering the nature of the German question was economic change over the period. Britain rapidly emerged as an industrial power, moving decisively ahead of her continental rivals in the factory production of textiles (especially cotton), mining of coal, smelting of iron and the building of railways, steam engines and machinery. Britain's demand for food and raw materials stimulated commercial advances in German regions, especially eastern areas, with plentiful grain and timber and good river access to the Baltic. Britain paid for these imports by increasing its exports of manufactured and semi-finished articles, as well as colonial wares like tea and coffee which, under the terms of the Navigation Acts which remained in force until mid-century, had to pass first through Britain, carried by British ships, on their way to Europe. [Generally, see 119 *chap. 3*.]

The German lands found themselves falling behind the economies to their west, which were more integrated, for example, operating without any internal tariff barriers. In turn, the beginning of industrial growth in a few German regions (the Rhineland and Westphalian provinces of Prussia, Saxony, Bohemia, the regions around Berlin and Vienna) as well as other parts of Europe set in train a dynamic based on regional disparities and relationships. Increasingly, a challenge was posed to the German lands as to how they would respond to this dynamic [119 *chap. 4*; 135; *Doc. 16*].

This sense of western European superiority was seen not just in economic but also political and cultural terms. While German conservatives railed against modern constitutions and commerce, many professional and business people looked with envy at British industrial growth, at the political reform of 1832 in Britain which enfranchised the middle class and secured the dominance of the House of Commons. More radical figures looked to France and the 1830 revolution, even if this had turned out disappointingly. British fashion and literature, French music and art, were widely influential amongst educated circles in the German lands. For others, the USA or Belgium or Switzerland provided economic or political models to emulate. This admiration for foreign institutions and achievements could, of course, provoke a nationalist reaction but as yet that appeared less important than a form of nationalism which argued that one had to imitate more advanced societies in order to strengthen and improve Germany.

GERMANY

The German Confederation was supposed to coordinate policy while retaining sovereignty in the individual states. Some German statesmen saw in the Confederal constitution possibilities for constitutional harmonisation, common defence policy, customs and commercial agreements. However, little was achieved by 1819 and then reaction against radical movements turned the Confederation into a coordinating instrument of repression.

The specific occasion of this was the murder of a conservative writer Kotzebue by a student radical (Sand). Metternich and other conservatives had already been alarmed by noisy student festivals and excesses in favour of Germandom and constitutional restraints upon government. Bypassing much of the Confederal machinery and overriding state powers, Metternich convened a ministerial conference which approved repressive measures against university autonomy and press freedom, set up a political policing system and completed the *Bund* constitution [*Doc. 15*]. The principal criticism of such policies did not come from Prussia, where an increasingly conservative regime was largely in agreement with Austria, but from medium states like Baden which had implemented constitutions out of step with the Confederal model, in which suspect journals were published and where political festivals took place.

These vague aspirations for a liberal and national Germany were forced underground in the 1820s by repressive measures. They could only express themselves in displaced forms, for example through support for the Greek uprising. Cooperation between a dominant Austria and a supportive Prussia to repress such opinions was the main response [59 *chap. 7*].

Following on from the July revolution in France in 1830 disturbances extended into Germany, leading to constitutional concessions in Brunswick, Hannover and Saxony. Some Prussian statesmen regarded this unrest as arising from reactionary domestic policies and proposed reform as the cure. (It was noted, for example, that the unrest was found in states which had not responded positively to Prussia's customs union proposals.) Metternich took the simpler view that repression was the only way to deal with such threats. His view prevailed as new repressive measures were implemented throughout the Confederation [*Docs 22, 23*]. Given anxiety over a liberal nationalist demonstration in 1832, the Hambach Festival, as well as an attack upon a police station in Frankfurt am Main, the medium states went along with such interventions. This policy continued into the 1840s, including controls on movements by foreigners and artisans, increased restraints imposed on associations and publications, and attempts to influence neighbouring states such as Switzerland which were seen as havens and models for radical opponents of German states.

However, it was increasingly difficult to carry through such repression.

Underground movements formed, political opposition developed and formed links across state boundaries, smaller states proved unwilling to act along the lines precribed by Austria and Prussia; exiles in Paris, Brussels, Switzerland and elsewhere maintained links with Germany. Some statesmen argued the case for continuing reform – economic and political – as the best way to counter these limited and disparate oppositions. Metternich continued to favour repression, although not too savage and systematic [59 *chap. 7*; 95 *chaps 9 and 10*].

Two developments in particular indicated the limits on such a policy. First, there was a resurgence in popular nationalism in 1840. This was sparked off by the French threat to the left bank of the Rhine and was accompanied by the writing of popular songs and poems defending the 'German' Rhine. Some of these reached circulation figures of hundreds of thousands. It was not so easy to prosecute a nationalism directed against France rather than against the *Bund*. Furthermore, Prussia and the south German states most directly threatened considered military reforms as a necessary response, something boosted by the national indignation. This initiative was blocked by Metternich who had no desire to see Prussia and the 'third Germany' acting independently of Austria, but it had the effect of dividing the states and reducing the level of coordinated repression [*Docs 25, 26*].

This popular nationalism directed at foreigners was reinforced by growing tensions between Germans and Danes in the Duchies of Schleswig and Holstein [98]. By virtue of its geographical position, Prussia could be seen as the obvious defender of the 'German' interest here as well as on the Rhine. Although generally nationalism was seen as a liberal or even radical sentiment which existing monarchical states should oppose, this suggested to some prospects of a convergence between Prussian state power and German nationalism with Austria as an obstacle to a national policy [*Docs 21, 24, 27*].

However, the main initiative for reform of the *Bund* came from oppositional elements within the medium states. Paradoxically, the more effectively Austria and Prussia manipulated *Bund* institutions to repress liberal and national movements in other German states, the more this led those active in such movements to see that reform at state level was only possible if there was also reform at a national level. In this way arguments about constitutional advance and national reform went together. In the couple of years before 1848 like-minded radicals and liberals across state boundaries had taken up links with one another and begun to formulate programmes of national political reform [*Docs 29, 30*]. These would be crucial for the taking of initiatives on the national question once the revolution broke out in 1848.

AUSTRO-PRUSSIAN RELATIONS

Cooperation within the Bund

By 1819 Metternich was backing away from his 1815 agreement with the medium states against Prussia stimulated by the crisis over Saxony. With the major concern now the threat of liberal and national movements, his preferred method was to secure informal agreement between Austria and Prussia, negotiate secretly with the medium-sized states, and then bring matters formally to the *Bund* for a decision. Austria and Prussia agreed that *Bund* laws should prevail over (other) state laws. So long as the major concern of Austria and Prussia in Germany was to prevent constitutional government and to repress radical, liberal and national movements, this cooperation would prevail [95 *chap. 10*; *Doc. 23*]. This was the pattern both after 1819 and after 1830. The reformers had declining influence in the Prussian government, especially after the death of Hardenberg in 1822. In the 1830s the resignation of Bernstorff in 1832 signalled another step back from any reforming forward policy in Germany [129 *pp. 321–28*; *Doc. 24*].

Frederick William III did not act on his promises of a constitution but confined himself to creating provincial assemblies based on the traditional social estates. Although there were disagreements (e.g., on coordination of military matters in 1840), generally the period was marked by cooperation between Austria and Prussia. However, the loose and federalist organisation of the *Bund* meant this often had to be done informally and secretly. There were disputes as to whether some of the interventions Austria and Prussia organised under the auspices of the *Bund* were really legal. Britain, for example, in its role as one of the guarantors of the *Bund*, queried the use of federal troops in the city-state of Frankfurt following the 1832 attack on a police station, as this was undertaken against the wishes of the Frankfurt government.

However, this story of cooperation with Austria leading and Prussia following does not apply to tariff policy and the formation of customs unions.

Competition in tariff matters

The idea of a tariff free zone is modern. In eighteenth-century Germany there were so many obstacles to the notion of 'free trade' that it was difficult to have a clear idea of what this might be. First, there was the obvious impact of division into hundreds of states all levying charges on imports and exports. This could mean a commodity being subject to numerous such charges. There were also transit charges on stretches of rivers and roads. [See 152 *chap. 1* for this and following paragraphs.]

Second, different parts of the 'same' state had their own tariff barriers. By the late eighteenth century enlightened rulers and officials were seeking to dismantle these but progress was slow. It was not until 1818 that Prussia abolished the fifty-seven tariff barriers that still operated within its six central and eastern provinces. Austria in the eighteenth century had been more active, getting rid of barriers between Bohemia and its Austrian territories. Nevertheless, Austria only abolished such barriers generally in the western half of its territories (excluding Lombardy-Venetia) in 1829. It was not until 1850 that tariff barriers between the western and the eastern half of the empire were removed.

Third, privileges for different economic groups amounted to a further set of tariffs. For example, goods coming from the countryside into the town were often charged, in part to protect urban guilds. The mercantilist view that a state should aim at a surplus of exports over imports encouraged the charging of tariffs not merely to raise revenue or protect branches of domestic production but to produce a favourable balance of trade, and was also associated with the granting of monopolies or other producer privileges which in effect amounted to a tax.

The Napoleonic period changed much of this. Even before 1789, France had moved towards internal free trade, for example in grain. French-dominated Germany consisted of fewer states which in part signalled the unity of their new creations by removing internal tariffs. Abolition of guilds meant an end to economic barriers between town and country. Even Napoleon's protectionist policy aimed against Britain implied the construction of just one single external tariff wall. However, his simultaneous erection of tariff barriers against German territories east of the Rhine made clear how important it was to have tariff agreements. The Prussian reform movement after 1807 was keen to dismantle internal tariff barriers as well as restrictions on land ownership and guild trades. So the moves towards large tariff-free zones go back at least to the Napoleonic period.

Article 19 of the *Bund* constitution hinted at the possibility of moving further in this direction [*Doc. 14*]. The fact that Britain and France were tariff-free zones, combined with the mass influx of cheap manufactures from Britain after 1815, led manufacturing groups to demand both internal tariff freedom (to create a larger German market for their products) and a high tariff against external competition (to protect this German market against cheaper foreign goods). It was becoming natural to think of the economy like a human body, of trade as the flow of blood and to visualise tariffs as restrictions on that flow [*Doc. 16*].

However, there were many obstacles to such German-wide reforms. Internally there was a concern to protect state sovereignty and local interests worried about superior competition from other German states. Austrian Germany, which traded less with other German states than with more backward parts of its own empire, was anxious about the threat to its manufacturers from Rhenish or Saxon producers, both in Austria and other imperial regions. There was a strong tension between free trade interests (e.g., grain-exporting farmers of north-eastern Germany) and protectionists (e.g., south German textile producers). Faced with little chance of success at a national level, trade regulation lobbies after 1819 turned away from the *Bund* towards individual states, mainly Prussia or regional associations of medium states [152 *chap. 2*].

Even before 1815 Prussia had moved towards freedom of trade in the sense of freedom to practise a trade with laws on peasant emancipation and the abolition of guilds before 1815. In 1818 it abolished internal tariff barriers. This created a single internal market and drastically cut collection costs by reducing the length of frontier to be regulated. Furthermore, the commercial liberal beliefs of key reformers, combined with the interests of grain producers, meant this law included many low import tariffs and the abolition of export charges. High tariffs of around 30 per cent continued to be levied only on luxury and colonial goods, and that primarily to produce desperately needed state revenue, not to protect domestic producers.

Prussia still faced the problem of a physical division between its two western provinces and the rest of the state as well as the existence of a number of enclave states which were wholly surrounded by its central provinces. The next logical steps were to incorporate these enclave states within the Prussian customs zone and to bring some of the states which bridged the east–west division into a customs union agreement. Between 1819 and 1828 Prussia, by a mixture of bullying (e.g., charging high transit charges) and inducements (e.g., in revenue division) had incorporated the enclave states.

Stimulated by Prussian moves, the failure of national reform initiatives, and economic and fiscal needs, south German states began from 1820 to negotiate on a customs union. The problem was that some states, such as Baden with its wine exports and extensive through-trade (it was physically very narrow from west to east), wanted low tariffs while manufacturing interests in Bavaria pushed for high tariffs. Württemberg interests took up an intermediate position. There were many political differences, for example between Bavaria, which expected to dominate a regional association, and other states determined on a federal arrangement amongst equals, or with territorial disputes between Württemberg and Baden. The most that could be achieved by 1828 was an agreement involving just Bavaria and Württemberg. Nevertheless, this, not any arrangement involving Prussia, was the first customs agreement between two genuinely sovereign German states. Furthermore, this agreement embodied creative ideas, such as preserving separate state customs services but ensuring that these were operated on unified lines, and dividing customs revenue on the basis of population size.

Bavaria had been keen to secure agreement also with Hesse-Darmstadt as this would have bridged the division between its Rhenish territory and the rest of the state. However, Hesse-Darmstadt left these negotiations and by 1828 had concluded an agreement with Prussia [*Doc. 17*]. This virtually completed the land bridge Prussia needed and meant there would be intense pressure on other intermediate states such as Hesse-Cassel to join this union. Agreements with Thuringian states in 1829 opened up a link to the south, leading to a customs agreement with the south German states and the start of work on a tariff-free road from Prussia to Bavaria. A number of alarmed central German states sought to form their own customs union but this was too little, too late. In 1831 Hesse-Cassel joined Prussia, thus completing the land bridge [*Doc. 20*]. 1833 saw a customs union agreement between the Prussian-led union and the south German one, with the addition of Saxony and soon joined by Baden, Nassau and Frankfurt. The coming into operation of these agreements on 1 January 1834 is the conventional dating for the start of the German Customs Union (*Deutsche Zollverein*) [152 *chap.* 3; 117; 127].

Many of the medium states were worried about the lack of protection for domestic producers both against producers elsewhere in the *Zollverein* (no tariff protection) and beyond (often only low tariffs), but their fiscal needs and the declining capacity for states to hold out once their neighbours had come to agreement with Prussia meant that these concerns were overridden.

It is easy to see tariffs and custom union politics as a crucial area of competition between Austria and Prussia and to present a picture of a nationally oriented Prussia leading the way to unity with a modernising policy of free trade based on its own powerful economy. By contrast, Austria can be seen as backward and unable to involve itself in nationally progressive developments. Some key contemporary figures made comments supporting such a view [*Docs 18, 19*]. In the dramatic and influential account provided by Heinrich von Treitschke [60], the *Zollverein* signalled a breakthrough towards a progressive and national policy, led by Prussia, followed reluctantly by the smaller princes, and obstructed and castigated by Austria. Even before 1848 some liberal nationalists regarded the *Zollverein* as providing the base and model for moves towards a national state, rather as in our time a European customs union has been seen as the basis for European political unity.

However, it is important to distinguish short-run intentions from long-run results. The 'nationalist' view of von Treitschke saw the process in terms of deliberate national policy which combined economic modernisation with the extension of Prussian power over the rest of non-Austrian Germany, thereby laying down the foundation for the subsequent political unification. However, the customs union agreements were in the first instance oriented to the interests of individual states, not the national arena. Furthermore, although there were some like Motz who saw the matter in terms of economic development or political influence, many more state officials were concerned above all with the fiscal aspect. The simplification of tariff barriers reduced enormously collection costs, above all by drastically shortening the total length of tariff borders. Prussia's generous treatment of the revenue (to be distributed on the basis of population rather than the *per capita* imports and exports for the different states) meant a significant addition to revenue for other states. Given that some of these states had encountered difficulties with their constitutional assemblies on budgetary matters, this could free princes from such constraints. (This was why some south German liberals, otherwise in favour of greater national coordination, were critical of the *Zollverein*.) Finally, some of those who were concerned with economic development, like Friedrich List, while approving the abolition of internal tariff barriers, deplored the Prussian policy of low tariffs on manufactured imports. He argued that only protectionist policies would enable infant German manufacturing industry to develop. Thus at the level of intention the main concerns were state and fiscal, not national and developmental, and some with national and developmental concerns opposed the *Zollverein* [107; 117; 127; 135].

More difficult to assess is the economic significance of the *Zollverein*. It is possible that certain regional economic flows (e.g., between Baden and France, Rhenish Prussia and Belgium) were disrupted by arbitrary 'national' tariff boundaries. High tariffs on colonial goods caused hardship where poorer people had acquired a taste for tea, coffee or sugar, and may have depressed consumer demand for domestic products. Some economic historians have argued that contemporaries greatly exaggerated the importance of tariff policy (then and later), perhaps because it was the only significant economic instrument available to governments. The reduction of costs within the tariff-free market was probably more important than the level of tariffs applied to foreign goods. Even more significant was the growth of a belief that this tariff-free zone was here to stay and that people could more easily predict the costs of moving goods around this zone. This in turn would encourage investment in larger units of production because entrepreneurs could feel more secure than before about their access to markets in other German states. But this was a long-term consequence, difficult to pinpoint and not central to the concerns of policy makers. Again, what precisely the relationship was between the customs union and the railway building boom which began in the late 1830s and had become significant by the mid-1840s is difficult to establish [149; 150; 152 *chaps 3 and 4*].

The *Zollverein* only removed internal tariffs; it did little about harmonising currencies, weights and measures, commercial law and taxation, or extending freedom of movement from goods to capital and labour.

Nevertheless, improvements in transportation (canals and roads as well as railways) and communications (the multiplication of periodical and book publishing, the telegraph) allied with the customs union to spread a notion of Germany as a cultural and economic zone. This popularised the idea that small states represented a form of backwardness. (There is a cartoon from the time which shows policemen and soldiers blocking the way to merchants and carters and coach-drivers at every state boundary. Treitschke's description of huge queues of people as midnight approached on 1 January 1834 conveys the same view.) Yet at the same time such visions and developments put many people on the defensive. The sense of threat was intensified by the economic problems of the mid-1840s when there were financial failures, and poor harvests saw sharp increases in food prices which in turn hit manufacturing by decreasing demand. People called for restrictions on free trade (e.g., to keep food in poor regions) and blamed 'capitalism' for many of their problems. Even the commercial liberal tendency within the Prussian government was weakened [52 *chap*. 10; 59 *chaps 8 and 10*; 105 *part I*].

CONCLUDING REMARKS

By 1848 the customs union had not yet become a significant element in Austro-Prussian conflict over supremacy in Germany even if concerns were starting to be expressed. At the level of confederal policy Austria continued to take the lead with Prussia following in a policy of mild repression both within their own states and those of the rest of Germany. Metternich did sometimes worry about Prussia breaking from this policy [*Doc. 27*]. However, he was equally concerned about signs of change or weakness in the Prussian position, for example with the accession of Frederick William IV or when in 1847 Prussia convened a United Diet (made up of representatives from the eight provincial assemblies) to discuss a loan for a railway project and, at the insistence of deputies, constitutional reform. At the same time figures such as Radowitz pushed for Prussia to take the lead on confederal reform [*Doc. 28*]. However, reformers soon lost hope in Frederick William, especially when he refused to negotiate with the United Diet [130 *chap. 5*]. As it was, the next chance of national reform would not come from any change of government policy but with revolution and the temporary breakdown of Austro-Prussian control.

CHAPTER FOUR

AUSTRIA AND PRUSSIA LOSE CONTROL, 1848–49

INTRODUCTORY COMMENTS

In this chapter the distinctions I make elsewhere between Europe, Germany and Austro-Prussian relations become difficult to operate because revolution shattered them. Above all, there was no real relationship between Austria and Prussia as both become self-absorbed in their own internal crises until early 1849. Instead I focus on the national question during the revolution, above all as seen from the perspective of the German National Assembly meeting in Frankfurt am Main. At the end of the chapter I consider how 1848–49 had altered the European, German and Austro-Prussian dimensions of the national question. This lays the basis for understanding how Austria and Prussia related to one another on German affairs after the revolution.

Revolution broke out in early 1848 for reasons which had little to do with the national question. There was a background of long-term economic difficulties for artisans and peasants and short-term problems caused by harvest failures in the 'hungry forties'. There was the frustration of those seeking liberal political reform in the face of repression. There was the expectation that revolution in France would trigger upheavals elsewhere, as in 1789 and 1830. Governments were uncertain and weak in their handling of challenges from popular movements and political opponents. [Generally on 1848, see 43; for a short overview, see 97; specifically on Germany, 57a *Chap. 5*; 124.]

These were common patterns throughout most of Europe. In the German case a special feature is that some people advocated national unity as a way of dealing with the economic and political issues which had brought about revolution. Some liberals and radicals had come to the view that only national unity would enable reform at the level of individual states [*Docs 21, 29, 30*]. They now called for a national parliament to replace the *Bundestag* and to push through such reform [*Doc. 31*]. In the political vacuum of March–April, steps were taken which led to the election of the German National Assembly which convened in Frankfurt in mid-May.

For a few months the German National Assembly had the field to itself so far as the national question was concerned. In Prussia, Frederick William IV, in response to the initial outbreak of revolution, talked of 'Prussia going forth into Germany', but with insurrection in Berlin, the removal of soldiers from the capital, the appointment of liberal ministers and the election of a Prussian National Assembly, such a policy was shattered. In Austria, the rapid loss of control in Italy and Hungary, coupled with popular challenges in various parts of the western half of the empire, including Vienna itself, meant those in power were fully engaged simply trying to prevent territorial breakup. All the other German states had capitulated to popular unrest and political opposition in March and had appointed liberal ministers and convened elected assemblies to enact constitutions.

WHAT WAS THE NATIONAL QUESTION IN 1848?

[The best overall study of the German National Assembly which should be referred to for all of the following sections on the national question in 1848–49 is 102.]

The only 'national' authority the members of the German National Assembly had experience of was the *Bund*, which they opposed and had now replaced. How could they both build on the pre-existing national framework but also devise something new which was 'really' national?

First, they had to define the 'nation'. Until one knows who belongs to the nation, one cannot decide how it will be united and free. More practically, decisions about the membership of the nation were needed immediately in order to determine where national elections should take place and who could vote in them.

Possible criteria were ethnicity, culture and language. The German nation was seen as the bearer of German culture which in practical terms meant native speakers of German. When Ludwig I of Bavaria had a national monument – the Valhalla – built at Regensburg, the pantheon of German heroes represented within it included Swiss and Dutch figures, reflecting this linguistic conception. It was natural for representatives of the national movement – overwhelmingly upper-middle-class professionals, academics and state officials who had been educated in a common high culture at various German universities – to discuss the national idea in these terms. This was also the idea of Germany which had been celebrated in popular pamphlets and songs written in 1813–14 and again in 1840 [*Docs 7, 26*].

However, taken literally the principle would have entailed radical territorial alterations to the *Bund*, surrendering non-German-speaking areas within the *Bund* (e.g., Bohemia and Moravia) and claiming German-speaking areas outside the *Bund* (e.g., in the Prussian Grand Duchy of Posen, Schleswig, and Baltic regions under Russian rule). Furthermore, language never yields clear-cut territorial divisions. In Bohemia and the Grand Duchy of Posen, German speakers dominated urban centres while native speakers of Czech and Polish respectively made up a majority of the surrounding rural population. Then there were bi- or multi-lingual groups who could not easily be classified nationally by language at all. Finally, any such proposals would encounter enormous opposition – from threatened states, non-German-speaking populations (and sometimes even German speakers), and the international community. The idea was never practical; no one seriously pursued it; hardly anyone even thought about it.

Furthermore, the liberal majority in the German National Assembly were reluctant revolutionaries, beneficiaries rather than makers of the March revolutions. They were anxious to work with rather than against individual states, especially Austria and Prussia, and wished to preserve the monarchical form of the state, even if modified by constitutionalism. It was within this framework that they sought to construct a stronger national authority. They also tended to think of Germany in territorial rather than cultural terms. Germany was the sum of the German states, not the home-lands of the German nation.

Consequently, 'Germany' was defined by the various assemblies which laid the basis for elections to the German National Assembly as the ter-ritory of the *Bund*. There may have been nationalists harbouring fantasies of a much larger national state, but they were in a minority. The only additions made to the pre-1848 territory of the *Bund* were the Prussian provinces of East and West Prussia (this had already been decided by the *Bundestag* in early 1848) and Schleswig. It was within 'Germany' so de-fined that elections to the German National Assembly were held in April.

Further boundary issues soon arose in the east and the south. In July 1848 the Assembly approved Prussia's decision to partition the Grand Duchy of Posen and incorporate the German part into Prussia. Originally the national movement, both at Frankfurt and Berlin, had considered Posen as part of a restored Polish state. However, the rapid growth of a Polish national movement, the backlash from German speakers, growing concern about the strategic implications of surrendering all of Posen, and fear of conflict with Russia led the Prussian government to revise its initial policy. Without a com-plete renunciation of that policy, the only solution was one of partition. In the German National Assembly harsh views were expressed about the inability of a degenerate Polish nation to form a healthy state [*Doc. 32*]. Justifications were put forward for German rule over Poles by virtue of a higher culture and superior power instinct. As it was, strategic concerns, the difficulties of neatly separating language groups, and aroused German national sentiment all meant that the line of partition was drawn one-sidedly in favour of Germans.

Similar sentiments of superiority, power and expansion were expressed in reaction against a Czech boycott of the elections in Bohemia and

Moravia. Palacky, the leading Czech national spokesman, declared that the majority Czech-speaking population of Bohemia did not consider itself German although it was a loyal segment of a multi-national and federal Habsburg state. Many German National Assembly deputies, by June 1848, welcomed the Habsburg repression of a Czech uprising in Prague, even though the man who led it, Windischgrätz, hated German nationalism too and would subsequently repress the revolution in Vienna, ordering the execution of Assembly deputies present in the city.

The constitution drawn up by the Assembly incorporated minority-protection clauses for non-German speakers, recognising that a German citizen was not necessarily a German speaker. One might interpret that either as a liberal principle or as proof of the unprincipled use of the cultural nationality principle; cited when it justified territorial expansion, ignored when it implied surrender of territory [*Doc. 38*].

Taking together the views expressed on Schleswig, Posen, Bohemia and elsewhere, one could make it appear that the Assembly had no principled or consistent national view but simply wanted to expand 'German' power as far as possible. Such arguments have been used to establish connections with the expansionist ambitions of the Second Empire and the Third Reich. However, they fail to take account of many things [contrast 102 and 118].

First, the Assembly never led the way in any territorial claim. The *Bundestag* had already decided on East and West Prussia and agreed the case for Schleswig. Bohemia and Moravia were already part of the *Bund*. The Posen issue arose because of the way in which the Prussian government sought to reverse an earlier policy of territorial surrender.

Second, such issues always divided the Assembly. When one analyses these disputes, no consistent 'national' view emerges. Left-wing deputies who favoured the incorporation of Schleswig opposed the partition of Posen. Conservatives who accepted the Posen partition in support of the Prussian state were equally quick to accept the Malmø armistice with Denmark which effectively surrendered Schleswig.

Third, one can point to contrary tendencies. Sympathy for Polish national demands did decrease in 1848 because of the Posen question. Yet there remained considerable sympathy for Italian and Hungarian national claims and the view that the Habsburg Empire would have to break up, even if a Habsburg Emperor remained titular head of the various parts. There was less sympathy for Slav demands. However, this was a view common to many liberals (including in Britain and France) who saw only in the 'historical' or culturally dominant nations (Germans, Magyars, Italians, Poles) the basis of statehood and regarded 'historyless' nations such as Slavs and Rumanians as no more than cultural groups which might be given limited rights (e.g., on the language of local administration and elementary education) but did not have a legitimate claim to their own states.

In any case, debates over territory took up only a small amount of the time of the Assembly. Admittedly, in the case of Schleswig such debates were bound up with issues of war and peace, and plunged the Assembly into a crisis which marked the beginning of its decline. Yet its debates and decisions continued to be of importance from September 1848 through until April 1849. I will focus on three themes which were crucial to an understanding of the national question: the nation and the German people; the nation-state and individual states; the relationship between Germany, Austria and Prussia.

THE NATION AND THE GERMAN PEOPLE

Democracy

In early 1848 the decision was taken in principle that all adult males were entitled to vote in elections to the German National Assembly. The country was divided into constituencies of roughly equal size and candidates winning the most votes were returned. The parliament thus had a democratic mandate.

However, this did not happen because political elites, even from the pre-1848 opposition, accepted democracy. Rather, under the pressure of the initial revolutionary outbreak, it was not considered possible to implement an anti-democratic franchise. Indeed, one concern was to divert the popular movement into taking part in elections rather than insurrections. However, it was difficult to make an abrupt transition from a world which at most had only known elections on a restricted franchise for advisory assemblies to one with democratic elections to a sovereign parliament. Various qualifications to this democracy immediately came into play. The insistence that voters must be 'independent' was sometimes used to exclude those without work, even those who worked for wages. In most cases, as in Prussia, elections were indirect, in two stages. In the first stage the voters chose members of an electoral college which in turn chose the parliamentary representatives. The hope was that this would filter out the worst excesses of democracy. It went without saying for all but a tiny radical minority that only men could vote.

There were many instances of intimidation or corruption, especially where ballots were not secret. However, in a society much more unequal, hierarchical and deferential than our own, many voters *wanted* to be guided by those above them. It required a considerable leap of the imagination for a small-town artisan or an agricultural labourer who had never travelled outside his locality and had never been asked his opinions on 'political' issues to work out the significance of voting for something as remote and abstract as a 'national' parliament. That did not mean that many people were incapable of very quickly adapting. Indeed, contemporaries constantly remarked upon the appetite for political debate which rapidly developed. Nevertheless, there were no mass political organisation or loyalties to shape and direct this newly emerging popular politics. Radicals did try to form political associations, distribute pamphlets, put up posters and call public meetings, but they were starting from scratch. Existing institutions and authorities such as churches, landowners and employers often filled the vacuum. Well-known individuals were supported by competing political groups and stood in a number of constituencies, often being nominated for election without their consent or even knowledge. In some places the original electoral committee saw its task simply to inform the electorate about the candidates and only the election contest itself generated clearer political divisions. [For a good regional study see 126.]

Nevertheless, millions of German men who had never before voted did so in April 1848. The Assembly which met in May had a democratic mandate which gave it considerable moral authority. One should note the limits: the exclusion of women; the continued importance of established authority; the lack of democratic institutions such as parties to maintain links between deputies and voters; the restricted reach of print media which alone could ensure regular and extensive mass political debate. However, we should not judge 1848 by the standards of our day. We must appreciate just how radical a break the popular movements of March and the mass elections of April represented. It certainly appeared so to contemporaries.

However, the idea of democracy was neither clear nor secure during 1848. Many radicals had other ideas of democracy than that secured through parliamentary elections. They favoured direct action such as mass petitioning, demonstrations and, most ominously of all, insurrection. Such people could not adjust to the delays and uncertainties of elections, parliamentary debates and the culture of compromise which accompanies parliamentary democracy. (Indeed, right across the political spectrum it was difficult to accept the idea that 'politics' was a permanent and healthy condition, rather than a transitional phase one passed through before the 'right' form of government and society had been established which would render political conflict obsolete.) The threats these radicals posed to the old order and the new parliaments helped discredit the idea of democracy and led many parliamentarians to consider how they could constrain and limit the power of a mass electorate, shifting their attention to that problem and away from the task of ensuring that the old authoritarian and monarchical order had safely been removed.

The German National Assembly did not actively foster a democratic politics. The deputies, mostly strangers to one another, acting in an institution and with objectives that had no precedent, devoted most of their energy to establishing the procedures and authority of the parliament, organising into parliamentary political groups and concentrating on the political and constitutional tasks which confronted the Assembly. Except for radicals who would appeal to the 'people' against parliament, the deputies did not do a great deal to keep the electorate in touch with their work. This problem was compounded by the sense that the electorate had much more definite ideas of what it wanted from those it had elected to state assemblies compared to the National Assembly. For example, elections in Prussia to the Prussian National Assembly and the German National Assembly were merged into the same process; voters gave two votes – one for Berlin and one for Frankfurt. Yet whereas artisans and peasants were elected to Berlin (as later they were elected to an Austrian National Assembly), the voters chose only professional, educated people to go to Frankfurt. Clearly, the feeling was that the state assemblies would be considering 'practical' matters like guild and land reform and one should send people who knew about these issues and could be trusted to represent 'their' people, whereas the 'national question' was a more abstract, difficult one which should be left to people who specialised in such matters.

There was a minority within the German National Assembly which wanted to realise the democratic idea in the new constitution in the form of a republic, if not for every constituent state, at least for the national state. The majority of the parliament, however, favoured constitutional monarchy and restrictions on both the franchise and powers of an elected parliament. The constitution adopted in early 1849 accepted constitutional monarchy, offering the hereditary emperorship of the nation-state to Frederick William IV of Prussia. However, it also included democratic provisions. The lower house of the national parliament was to be elected on the basis of universal manhood suffrage. The Emperor could delay but not permanently block the will of parliament. (This was known as the 'suspensive veto' in contrast to the 'perpetual veto'.) The reason for this was because the moderate majority had split and, in key votes in the spring of 1849, those wishing to offer the crown to Frederick William IV could only obtain a majority by wooing the democratic minority. [For these constitutional provisions, see *Doc. 38*.]

The rights of the German people

Apart from political democracy, the parliament also debated and finally agreed the 'Basic Rights' (*Grundrechte*) of the German people. Some historians have seen these debates, which continued over the summer of 1848, as a distraction from the important political issues, revealing the impractical, intellectual bent of the 'Professors' Parliament'. To a degree this is true, although the phrase is misleading. A high proportion of the deputies had been to university and then into the professions or government service for which such education was necessary. There were far fewer academics. In authoritarian monarchies ruling over largely agricultural populations these were the main routes, for those outside the court and landed nobility, to the exercise of power. The Frankfurt deputies were not obviously more intellectual or less versed in politics than, for example, those who met at the Estates-General in Paris in 1789.

The Assembly felt it had to wait until the dust settled down from the initial revolution before tackling key issues about where power should reside in the new nation-state. Most deputies considered it neither possible nor desirable to work without cooperation from state governments, especially Prussia and Austria. Revolution had made it unclear just what policies would be adopted and which forces would effectively exercise power in the various states. Debates on basic rights clarified issues about how a structure of national rights and obligations would replace one based on privilege and particularism. The debates and decisions made clear what national unity would mean for most Germans and set limits on how far the Assembly was prepared to concede to demands for social and economic change.

Liberal values predominated, for example, the separation of church and state, the independence of the judiciary, the institution of *habeas corpus*, the abolition of capital punishment. The debates display vividly resentment against regimes which meddled with the law or people's religion and which arbitrarily inflicted punishments upon their subjects. Most of the decisions in favour of civil and religious liberties appear to have been well, or at least not badly received, although powerful groups did insist that education should be under church control. [See 20 for an English translation of the final version of the constitution.]

More contentious were decisions on social and economic rights. Much of the substance and detail of such questions as the completion of peasant emancipation or guild reform were regarded as state affairs. Nevertheless, there was a national dimension. The Assembly considered that people should be free to move across state frontiers, settle in new places, choose their occupation and acquire property. Such liberties meant abolishing the powers of guilds and local and state governments to enforce restrictions in such matters. These rights could be defended as essential civil liberties within a national society, that is, as political rather than economic, but they were understood by many interests as an interference in traditional economic and cultural practices. Such interests were not simply 'conservative' or 'right-wing'; there were democrats who defended the right of communities to protect themselves against outside forces, often depicted as cosmopolitan and capitalist. Such hostile responses contributed to a loss of popularity for the Assembly and a shift of attention back to the state level. In response, state governments, and especially princes, were already cultivating corporatist and communal sentiments, as well as taking the credit for popular reforms such as peasant emancipation. (A good example was the acceptance by the Austrian Emperor of the measure on peasant emancipation passed by the Austrian National Assembly, even after the assembly had been dissolved.) By the time the parliament entered into its critical political phase with the Malmø armistice in September, it had lost much of the popular support it had possessed in May.

NATIONAL AUTHORITY VERSUS STATE AUTHORITY

How was the Assembly to enforce its decisions? Should it act as a provisional government as well as a constituent assembly? In the new nation-state what should be the division of power between the national authority and the member states?

In the individual states governmental and parliamentary institutions remained distinct. The prince appointed ministers, even if compelled to accept liberals. Civil servants and the army continued to work for the state, even if it was unclear whether loyalty was owed primarily to the new ministers or the prince. The various constituent assemblies focused on the issue of drafting a constitution. This rough division of labour did not operate at the national level because there was no prince, no ministry, no judiciary, no civil service and no army. If it was not to fall completely into the hands of state governments the National Assembly needed to develop such institutions. However, these could not simply be plucked out of thin air, against the resistance not only of princes but liberal ministries and state parliaments with their own reform agendas.

The ingenious solution devised by the Assembly was to establish a Provisional Authority presided over by a Habsburg archduke of liberal tendencies, Archduke Johann, the *Reichsverweser*. He appointed parliamentary deputies to a cabinet which was responsible to him, not the Assembly. The hope was that this distinction between parliament and Provisional Authority and the choice of a man who had a foot in both liberal and Habsburg camps would mean that an effective, if fragile, authority could be created. [*Doc. 33*]

The difficulty came when the Assembly tried to invest this Provisional Authority with some of the attributes of a real state. Only two governments, Switzerland and the USA, recognised the Provisional Authority. There was no time to form an imperial civil service. The Provisional Authority decreed that soldiers should swear an oath of national loyalty but Austria and Prussia prevented this happening. Where soldiers did act on behalf of the Assembly, for example repressing the September riots in Frankfurt sparked off by the Malmø armistice, they did so to restore order, further alienating the Assembly from popular support. Later, when the rump of the Assembly struck out on its own, pressing for the Imperial

Constitution against the major powers, it soon found that armies (except in Baden) remained loyal to their princes.

The constitutional position of the parliament was federalist. Sovereignty resided with the national state but many powers devolved to member states. However, this is different from modern conceptions of federalism. Although the princely states were more authoritarian and illiberal than today's democracies, those monarchies lacked many of the powers of a modern state. For example, the only 'social' benefit of any importance was that of poor relief which was a communal affair, even if subject to state regulation. There was no state welfare or health system to administer, little in the way of a state education system, no national media to control (apart from censorship of private publishers), no detailed regulation of economic activity or family affairs, no massive public sector to finance.

The *Bund* had helped establish ideas of shared authority on such matters as military and constitutional questions, even if it had largely failed to realise such ideas. The German National Assembly sought to strengthen national authority by transferring powers such as declaring war and making peace, and setting and collecting tariffs, to the national level. At the same time it weakened the existing arbitrary powers of states by insisting on accountability to parliament, the rule of law safeguarded by an independent judiciary, and entrenching many individual liberties into both national and state constitutions.

All this helps explain why the Assembly took so long to appreciate what strikes the modern observer as the obvious 'problem of sovereignty', that is, where does ultimate power reside? With the later formation of nation-states the issue of sovereignty becomes clear-cut, affecting not just issues of war and peace and enforcement of the law but also powers of taxing and spending, economic and social policy, immigration control and much more. Many of these issues were unimportant or non-existent in 1848. Most of the smaller states had already ceded many powers of policing, diplomacy and control of armies to the *Bund*, which meant in effect Austro-Prussian domination, so the theoretical transfer of sovereignty to the national authority did not signify much change for them. It was less this which mattered and more the question of what type of national state was envisaged (republic or monarchy, restricted or democratic franchise) and how far common constitutional provisions would be imposed upon individual states. Here the liberal constitutionalism of the Assembly was opposed by many princes in the smaller states but they felt unable to come out in open opposition until they could be sure that Austria and/or Prussia would be able to restore order. In practice, therefore, the issue of sovereignty was really a question of the power relations between Frankfurt, Berlin and Vienna. This brings us back to the main concern of this book.

AUSTRIA OR PRUSSIA?

This was not a question which in territorial terms troubled the national movement before or even during 1848. As we have seen, it was agreed that Germany was the territory of the German Confederation, with a few additions. This meant that the parts of Austria which belonged to the *Bund* should continue to be a part of Germany. Rather the question – Austria or Prussia? – was one of power. How could these two powerful monarchies be persuaded either to surrender their authority to a new national state or for one to subordinate itself to the other? The National Assembly only explicitly confronted this question in debates and decisions from the end of October 1848.

For democrats there was no principled problem. Monarchy was to be replaced by democracy. Therefore there was no question of having to gain the consent of either or both the Habsburg and Hohenzollern princes to the establishment of a national state. The problem instead was how could democrats force their project through the Assembly and mobilise a popular movement to force this constitution on the princes. Minority status within the Assembly, internal divisions amongst themselves and limited success in mobilising mass support all ensured that this democratic route to national unity had no chance of success.

The liberal-constitutional majority wished to preserve the monarchical form of the state and regarded cooperation with Austria and Prussia as essential to success. But how could one include the Austrian part of the German Confederation in a nation-state and exclude the rest of the Habsburg Empire without destroying the Empire? Even if this could be done, would not this strengthen the position of Prussia within Germany to a degree which most Germans would find unacceptable? The other alternatives, either excluding or including *all* of the Habsburg Empire, appeared completely unacceptable. The former would mean a truncated Germany under Prussian domination; the latter would contradict the principle of a national state and mean Habsburg domination. Although these issues had never been sharply posed or even appreciated prior to 1848, by that autumn they could no longer be evaded.

For many deputies within the German National Assembly what policy to pursue depended upon the course of revolution in the two states. During the summer of 1848 it appeared that the Habsburg Empire was breaking up. Its Italian army had virtually been expelled from Lombardy and Venetia; it was powerless to help smaller Italian states; it had conceded control in the Hungarian half of the Empire; it faced demands for federal autonomy in Bohemia and for democracy in Vienna. It seemed unlikely to many observers that Habsburg authority could ever be restored in Italy and Hungary and, even if recovery was possible in its core Austrian territory, that the regime would be much weaker than before. All this suggested one particular solution to the national question. The Habsburgs should continue to rule both in German (i.e., *Bund*) territory and whatever non-German territory over which it managed to regain control. However, these two territories would be ruled by the Habsburgs in 'personal union'. That meant that the German and non-German territories would have separate constitutions and be separate political entities, having in common only the person of the monarch. Habsburg German territory would be subject to the same constitution as the rest of Germany. First drafts of Article 1 of the constitution drawn up by the Constitutional Committee defined Germany as the territory of the *Bund*. Article 2 stipulated that no part of the *Reich* could be united with any external state. Article 3 declared that the principle laid down in Article 2 would not be breached by personal union, and outlined in practical terms (e.g., concerning command and movement of armies) just what that meant.

This was not regarded as a pro-Prussian policy but as one which took account of Habsburg fragmentation and tried to ensure that the German territories of the Empire remained integral to a future nation-state. The policy was especially identified with the Austrian deputy Anton Schmerling, who in October 1848 was Prime Minister in the Provisional Authority. (We will encounter him again as Austrian Chancellor in 1860.) Schmerling envisaged a loss to the Habsburgs of Italian and Polish territories and a Habsburg personal union between the western, 'German', and the eastern, 'non-German', halves of what remained. He also wanted the Habsburg Emperor to be titular ruler of the new German state. Even a reduced Habsburg Empire was seen as able to command the leading position in Germany. After all, the population of the Habsburg part of this new Germany would be about the same as that of Prussia.

However, from the outset problems with this policy were recognised. A minority clause was attached to Article 3 which stated that if Austria could not subscribe to such an arrangement, there should instead be a treaty of close alliance between Germany (excluding the Austrian part of the *Bund*) and the Habsburg Empire. This minority view became important as the plenary debate on the first articles of the constitution got under way in late October. This coincided with a decisive moment in the restoration of Habsburg authority. Windischgrätz had put down unrest in Prague in June; Radetzsky was well on the way to restoring Habsburg authority in northern Italy following victory over Piedmont at Custozza in July. In the last week of October the rising in Vienna was suppressed. Robert Blum, a democrat and deputy of the German National Assembly who had gone to Vienna to 'observe' events (though he was clearly sympathetic to the insurgents) was deliberately and provocatively executed by the military authorities on 9 November. In early November Polish opposition was crushed in Galicia.

On 21 November Schwarzenberg, brother-in-law of Windischgrätz, was appointed Minister-President. On 2 December the feeble-minded Ferdinand abdicated in favour of his young nephew Franz Joseph. Hungary still remained under insurgent control but it was clear that the Habsburg Empire was not going to break up into three or four parts, that strong central authority was being imposed, and that new, younger and harder men than those of the pre-March era were now at the helm. In the following March the government would dissolve the Austrian Constituent Assembly, decree its own constitution, which it immediately suspended (and never subsequently put into effect), thus restoring absolutist rule [131].

These new men in Vienna made it clear in December 1848 that they would not accept a weakening of Habsburg authority envisaged by the idea of personal union between their German and non-German territories which was now proposed by the German National Assembly [Docs 34, 35]. Prussia now also moved in a counter-revolutionary direction with the removal of the Prussian National Assembly from Berlin in November, followed by its dissolution and the unilateral issuing of a constitution by the king in December. This met some liberal demands, giving considerable powers to a parliament which included a lower house elected on a democratic franchise [130 *chap. 7*]. All this encouraged liberal opinion in the German National Assembly to switch towards a more pro-Prussian policy, though still adhering to the idea of a close 'inner link' between the German state and the Habsburg Empire. The switch of policy was marked by the resignation of Schmerling as Prime Minister in mid-December and his replacement by Heinrich von Gagern who had for some time advocated the idea of a *kleindeutsch* state with special and close links to the Habsburg Empire, sometimes known as the 'inner' and the 'outer' circles.

By January 1849 a pro-Prussian, even *kleindeutsch* position was developing, but it was by default, associated with the forging of special links to the Habsburg Empire, and regarded as the first stage of a process which would lead eventually to a 'greater Germany' [Doc. 36]. There was still a consensus that Germany was basically the territory of the *Bund*. This pragmatic *kleindeutsch* position appealed primarily to Protestant liberal deputies, both from Prussia and the medium states. By contrast, deputies from Austria and more generally Catholic deputies were alarmed by this shift away from Austria towards Prussia. Within the territory of the whole *Bund* Catholics were in a majority; the exclusion of Austrian Germany would reduce them to a minority. To many Catholics a combination of minority status and the liberal provisions for a separation of church and state (including secular education) made the proposals of the Assembly unacceptable.

A minority of democrats in the Assembly was more concerned to utilise divisions between pro-Prussian and pro-Austrian factions to press for a constitution with parliamentary sovereignty and a democratic franchise. It was the alliance forged between the *kleindeutsch* group and the radicals (helped by some pro-Austrian deputies who voted for a democratic constitution in order to make it unacceptable to the Prussian king) which finally produced small majorities for a constitution which included the suspensive veto and democratic franchise, along with the offer of the hereditary emperorship to Frederick William IV.

In this halting, unintended and compromise form the German National Assembly had arrived at a *kleindeutsch* position. Vienna made it clear that this was unacceptable: the Habsburgs would neither accept proposals for inclusion in Germany (the personal union idea) nor any solution which excluded it (the *kleindeutsch* option) [*Docs 37, 39*]. Prussia indicated that it was prepared to discuss proposals which would involve it leading a *kleindeutsch* Germany, although the signals were unclear.

The deputation which travelled from Frankfurt to Berlin to offer Frederick William the hereditary emperorship at the beginning of April 1849 soon encountered difficulties. Prussia regarded the constitution as too radical but it was difficult for the parliamentarians to revise that constitution given the fragile basis of the majority on which its acceptance rested. In any case, some of the deputies thought that the parliament still had popular support which gave it bargaining power. Others suggested that accepting the constitution as it stood and actually putting into effect all its provisions were two separate issues. Prussia was also worried about the opposition Austria would raise to its acceptance of the offer from Frankfurt. These various considerations, combined with Frederick William's personal antipathy to the offer, led to the rejection of the hereditary emperorship in early April. That rejection was made official and public on 28 April [*Doc. 40*; 130 *chap. 8* for the king's views].

With that rejection the days of the Assembly were numbered. Austrian deputies had already left the parliament on instructions from their government. Soon members of the *kleindeutsch* group also were leaving, often obeying instructions from their states. The radical rump which remained moved the parliament to Stuttgart. Some of the deputies were involved in the wave of second revolutions which took place in the spring and early summer of 1849 in Saxony, Württemberg, the Rhineland province of Prussia and Baden. These revolutions, fuelled mainly by a determination to preserve democratic gains, were ostensibly in defence of the Imperial Constitution of 1849, although they can be better understood in terms of local political traditions and socio-economic conditions. [See 124 for a general treatment; 126 for a regional one.]

With the failure of the German National Assembly initiatives on the national question shifted back to Austria and Prussia. The revolution had made plain just how difficult it was going to be to move from a confederal

Germany dominated cooperatively by Austria and Prussia to a real national state. It was now recognised by most people that there was no prospect of achieving this by means of a popular movement. Even amongst those who wanted a national state, there were insuperable divisions between Catholics and Protestants, democrats and liberals, Austrians, Prussians and those from the 'third Germany'. It seemed impossible to construct an arrangement which offered acceptable roles to both Austria and Prussia in a German state yet equally to dispense with one or other of these powers. At the same time the revolution had laid bare the weaknesses and inadequacies of the pre-1848 arrangements and the sharply opposed positions of Austria and Prussia. The national question needed addressing urgently but with the failure of the revolutionary approach by early 1849 it was quite unclear how this was to be done. Very rapidly Austria, Prussia and the medium states came forward with new but opposed proposals which are the subject of the next chapter.

CHAPTER FIVE

COUNTER-REVOLUTION, COOPERATION AND CONFLICT, 1849–58

INTRODUCTORY COMMENTS

For a brief moment in 1848–49 it had appeared that the construction of a German national state was possible through popular movements and a national parliament rather on the basis of state initiative and power, whether from Prussia, Austria or the medium states. However, the rapid recovery of old regimes, especially in Prussia and Austria, the divisions within the national parliament and its growing isolation from waning popular support meant that by early 1849 the initiative was returning to the princes.

Their priority was the restoration of order. This was a European-wide concern and brought international and domestic politics together, most obviously with Russian assistance to the Habsburgs in crushing revolution in Hungary. Insofar as national movements had been a part of the revolution, the restored monarchies were anti-national. Frederick William IV refused the imperial crown offered by the German National Assembly in part because it was tainted by association with revolution and was embedded in a democratic constitution [130 *especially pp. 188–96; Doc. 40*]. The new Habsburg Emperor, Franz Joseph, and his Chief Minister, Schwarzenberg, were determined to crush breakaway movements in Hungary and Italy and to reimpose strong central control from Vienna. [See 43 and 124 for counter-revolution in Germany and beyond respectively.]

The two states responded differently to the national issue in Germany. Austria opposed any moves towards a national state whereas Prussia was interested in such moves if it could control them [*Docs 36, 37*]. The different opportunities the two states perceived in the first phase of counter-revolution, from early 1849 until the end of 1850, were to bring them into sharp conflict of a kind that had not been seen since the dispute over Saxony in 1814–15. This time the conflict ended with a clear retreat by Prussia. For the next eight years the policy was one of cooperative domination within the restored German *Bund*, mainly to clamp down on demands for political change. At the same time Prussia extended its influence over non-Austrian Germany through the expansion and development of the *Zollverein*. However, this duality of political cooperation and economic competition did not just repeat the situation from before 1848, partly because of the impact of the revolution itself but also because of other significant changes in Europe, Germany and the two German powers. These changes in turn laid the foundation for the public re-emergence of the 'national question' after 1858 in a very different form from that it had assumed previously.

EUROPE

The policies of the major powers played an important part in bringing revolution to an end in the German lands as elsewhere. Britain and Russia supported Denmark in the Schleswig-Holstein affair which led to Prussia ending its war there, even if it did not formally renounce its claims until the end of 1850. Austria appealed to Russia for military assistance against Hungarian insurgents. Revolution in Italy was crushed by a multi-national combination of Austrian, French, Papal and Neapolitan soldiers.

When Prussia continued to pursue a forward policy in Germany in 1849–50, Russia saw this as continuation of revolution and backed Austrian opposition to it. For a brief period there was a revival of the conservative alliance between Prussia, Austria and Russia (1850–54). Once again it appeared that the prime purpose of foreign policy was to restore and maintain domestic order. [84 remains the best general diplomatic treatment for the period after 1848.]

This emphasis came to an end with the outbreak of the Crimean War. The war brought Britain into alliance with the 'old enemy' France and against its old Napoleonic ally, Russia. This was the first war between major European powers since 1815 and signalled a new readiness to use war as an instrument of policy without worrying about possible domestic instability. The war was the first in Europe marked by new industrial conditions, for example the use of steam ships to bring men and material from western Europe to the Crimea. [Generally, see 78.]

The war placed Austria in a difficult position. It was beholden to Russia for assistance in 1849–50 in repressing revolution and confronting Prussia. Some policy makers in Vienna considered it essential to maintain this conservative alliance. However, Austria was worried about Russia's drive against the Ottoman Empire, its claims to defend the interests of the Christian subjects of the Ottoman state, its appeals to Balkan nationalities, its search for access from the Black Sea to the Mediterranean, and specifically its attempt to take control of the semi-autonomous Danubian principalities of the Ottoman Empire, Moldavia and Wallachia. Austria decided upon armed neutrality but one which was effectively anti-Russian with troop mobilisation on its borders and eventually the military occupation of the Danubian principalities. This policy deprived Austria of Russian support in later years and cost a good deal of money. On the other hand, the outcome of the war did temporarily put an end to a forward Russian policy in the Balkans. However, the financial and military weakening of Austria and its subsequent diplomatic isolation would come to take on major significance after 1858 [58 *chap. 6*; 67 *chap. 3*; 131 *chap. 5*].

GERMANY

Political repression after 1848 was more effective than before. State police forces now communicated directly with one another about suspect individuals and organisations rather than going through ministerial and diplomatic channels. The restored *Bund*, under Austro-Prussian domination, intervened in internal state affairs over constitutional provisions and laws on freedom of association, assembly and expression. Although censorship did not play a major role, a whole battery of controls such as caution money and liability of printers and publishers to prosecution muzzled the expression of dissent. [Siemann: 124 and 161 *pp. 400–1* is especially good on this, having earlier written specialised studies of the subject.]

However, while Austria was preoccupied with its own internal problems of restoring order in early 1849, Prussia played an active role in ending revolution elsewhere in Germany, for example in Baden. Counter-revolution also took different forms in the two states. In both cases constitutions drafted by democratically elected assemblies were aborted or set aside and the assemblies dissolved. However, Prussia imposed a constitution which, although modified in anti-democratic ways in 1850 and later, continued to operate until 1918. Austria, by contrast, imposed but immediately suspended a constitution (permanently it turned out) and the regime went back to absolutist rule. Thus there was provision for participation in elections and parliamentary debate in Prussia, even if restricted in many ways, unlike in Austria. [From the perspective of the two rulers, see 130 *chap. 9*; and 131 *chap. 6*.]

In the rest of Germany, the counter-revolution destroyed democratically elected parliaments and many of the freedoms the revolution had created. However, many parliamentarians had never been happy with democratic politics. Radical political figures were arrested and imprisoned, forced underground, driven into exile. The moderate liberals who remained were anxious to cooperate with restored regimes, whether on a constitutional or neo-absolutist basis, especially if offered suitable economic or national policies.

From a liberal or democratic perspective Germany presented a bleak picture through most of the 1850s. There was no scope for open political debate and organisation, whether on the national question or anything else. After the brief period of intense Austro-Prussian conflict in 1849–50, there was very effective cooperation between Austria, Prussia and the medium states to enforce counter-revolution throughout the German lands.

However, there are other aspects to consider. The period of the 1850s was one of rapid economic growth, much of it in the modern forms of coal, iron and steel manufacture and railway building. This was linked to liberal economic policies pursued by Prussia and Austria, for example the Prussian liberalisation of mining laws and joint-stock companies and the removal of tariff barriers between Austria and Hungary. Such liberalisation was in tension with official policies of clamping down on free communication. Economic growth was generally more rapid in the areas of the *Zollverein*, now covering most of non-Austrian Germany with the accession of Hannover in 1851, than it was in Austria. However, recent research has suggested that Austria was not as economically stagnant as was once commonly believed, and therefore one cannot easily draw a conclusion about the rapid falling away of Austrian strength compared to that of Prussia. [For Prussia and the *Zollverein*, see 100; 106/I *part I*; 111; 119 *chap. 4*; for Austria, see 104; 109; 112; 119 *pp. 222–9*; 156.]

AUSTRO-PRUSSIAN RELATIONS

Open conflict, 1849–50

On the same day (28 April 1849) [*Doc. 40*] that Frederick William IV formally refused the offer of the imperial crown, he initiated a forward policy in Germany developed by his minister, Joseph Maria von Radowitz, inviting the other German governments to a conference in Berlin to consider the way ahead on the national question. Some have seen in Radowitz anticipations of Bismarck with his concern for Prussia to confront Austria and to appeal to national opinion in doing so [130: *chap. 8*].

Internationally, Prussia could see no major obstacle to its pursuit of greater influence in non-Austrian Germany, provided this was on monarchical lines. Many other German princes owed their survival to Prussian support. Austria was still fighting revolution in its Italian and Hungarian territories.

The policy was two-pronged. First, the other German kingdoms (Saxony, Hannover, Bavaria and Württemberg) were invited to form a 'League of Kingdoms' which would draw up a constitution to replace the old *Bund*. Bavaria and Württemberg declined to join such a league but Saxony and Hannover did, though under duress and setting conditions on the completion of a move towards an effective union between Prussia and many of the smaller states.

Second, Prussia sought to secure liberal support. Elections were held to a parliament which met in early 1850 in Erfurt. Many leading figures from the German National Assembly which had offered the imperial crown to Frederick William were members of this parliament, which quickly accepted the constitution worked out by the three states. This constitution itself, minus many democratic features, leaned heavily upon the Imperial Constitution agreed by the German National Assembly. Prussia appeared to be leading the way towards a north German state [*Doc. 41*].

This policy was challenged by the medium states, led by Saxony and its chief minister Beust. He formed a 'four kingdoms' league' which envisaged a restored and reformed *Bund*, now with a central executive, national representation and a court, all of which would have provided it with far more unitary and national features than the pre-1848 *Bund*. Whether this was more than a riposte to Prussia's 'Union policy' is difficult to say. Certainly it was accepted by Austria tactically as one way of blocking Prussian policy. [*Doc. 42*]

Finally, the Austrian Finance Minister, Bruck, proposed yet another policy. The whole of the Habsburg Empire should join the *Zollverein*, creating a great central European zone of seventy million people. This went well beyond any 'national' framework. It is difficult to see how it could have been put into practice given the much lower level of economic efficiency and performance in the Habsburg Empire (especially the eastern half) compared to the *Zollverein* region (see Chapter 8 below). One could interpret this move also as a riposte to the Prussian union policy rather than a seriously considered policy in its own right. [*Doc. 45* comes from the following year but contains similar views to those of 1849. See also 64.]

These options for Germany – Prussian-dominated, Austrian-dominated, based on the 'third Germany' – were mutually incompatible. Meanwhile, by the middle of 1850 Austria and Prussia had agreed to the establishment of a provisional *Bund* commission to consider ways of coordinating counter-revolutionary policy. However, until the other, new and conflicting policies were settled, it would not be possible just to return to the pre-1848 arrangements.

Matters came to a head in late 1850 in Hesse-Cassel. A liberal ministry had aligned the state with Prussia's Union policy. This was reversed when the Grand Duke dismissed the ministry, suspended the constitution and withdrew from the Union. His actions were disavowed by the *Landtag*, many civil servants and the army. Schwarzenberg declared that Austria would support the prince if he appealed to the *Bund*. The prince did just this on 15 October. Based on a military agreement of 12 October between Austria, Bavaria and Württemberg, Bavarian troops were to intervene in support of the prince, to be reinforced if necessary by Austria and Württemberg. Prussian troops entered the state to defend the 'constitutional' Union policy.

Schwarzenberg made it clear that Austria was prepared to go to war on the matter and had the backing of Russia. In Berlin opinion divided between Radowitz, who was prepared to risk war, and more conventional conservatives who were not but wished instead to conclude an agreement with Austria and clamp down on liberal and constitutional initiatives at home. Bismarck loudly championed this course [*Doc. 44*], although at first, along with many other Prussian conservatives, he had hated the idea of backing down in the face of Austria. After various crises and ultimata this view prevailed. In the Bohemian town of Olmütz, Prussia agreed to abandon its Union policy and withdraw its troops from Kurhesse [*Doc. 43*]. It also abandoned the pursuit of claims in Schleswig-Holstein. A conference was subsequently organised in Dresden in early 1851 at which plans for a reformed *Bund* (whether based on the Beust or Bruck proposals) were abandoned. The *Bund* was restored with the same territory, institutions and competences as before 1848. Prussia and Austria now concentrated on using the *Bund* as an instrument to enforce counter-revolution throughout the German lands. [On Olmütz from the Austrian perspective, see 64 and 131 *chap. 4*; from the Prussian perspective, see 130 *pp. 206–13*; more generally, see 59 *pp. 710–15*.]

There are different views on the 'humiliation of Olmütz'. For some it was a decisive check on Prussian ambitions and meant that Prussia's drive for domination in Germany came to take on a very different form in the 1860s. For others, such as the Bavarian First Minister, von der Pfordten, what mattered was that Austria had not acted more decisively and ended up withdrawing its own plans for confederal reform as well as forcing Prussia to do the same. He declared: 'The fight for control of Germany has been settled and Austria has lost' [131 *p. 66*]. Perhaps a more reasonable opinion is that the two powers had cancelled out each other's plans for a forward policy in Germany, leaving the conflict to be taken up again at a later time.

Uneasy Cooperation, 1851–58

The years between 1851 and 1858 are perhaps the least well researched for the whole century as historians skip forward from the revolutionary period to the opening up of politics again at the end of the decade. Both Austria and Prussia combined political repression with economic liberalism. Economic growth, increasing social mobility and migration from one state to another, the publishing of more popular magazines, expansion of the railway network, the formation of many new associations (though not overtly political and not allowed to affiliate on a state- or nation-wide basis) meant that actually there were many social and economic links that governments could not control. However, the very fact that governments were unable to do very much means that such activity is not reflected in governmental sources. We can only guess at how far such developments permitted and encouraged informal discussions of political matters [57a *chap. 6; 59 pp. 710–29*].

Attempts by Austria to move closer to the *Zollverein* were blocked. Although economic growth in Austria was quite rapid (indeed, some historians argue that certain regions, especially in the western half of the Empire, effectively entered upon a process of industrialisation from the late 1820s into the 1850s [112], this lagged behind the *Zollverein* in key respects. For example, coal and iron production expanded at about twice the rate in the *Zollverein* compared to Austria in the 1850s. Austria's share of European trade in 1860 was about one-third the level of that of the *Zollverein*. The customs union concluded between Austria and Hungary in 1850 made links to the *Zollverein* even more difficult. It has been estimated that, while *per capita* production in the *Zollverein* was about twice that of the western half of the Empire, it was something like six times greater than the eastern half. It is difficult to see how Austrian manufacturing interests could have easily surrendered their privileged access to Hungarian markets.

Meanwhile Prussia expanded the *Zollverein*. Its success in getting Hannover to join in 1851 was of major importance as this had been the last sizeable German state outside the union. Prussia had been prepared to make substantial concessions to achieve this goal and demonstrated its own increasing authority over the *Zollverein* by imposing these changes upon the other members [107, 143, 152]. The effect was to lower further import tariffs (making it even more difficult for Austria to come into the union) and effectively to cover all of northern Germany and its major river and road routes to the Baltic and the North Sea. That made it possible for Prussia to contemplate moving to a purely north German union if the south German states would not go along with its policy. At the same time, economic growth and increasing customs revenue in the 1850s ensured an ever greater dependency of the other states on membership. Even when princes sought to oppose Prussia, the latter could mobilise business opinion in those states against their own government policy. Austria, which tried to support the opposition of these states to the Hannoverian accession could, by contrast, bring very little effective pressure to bear. The other states came into line; Hannover was accepted; the *Zollverein* was renewed for a further twelve years in 1853 [*Docs 45, 46*]. Yet the matter was not closed. Austria and the *Zollverein* concluded a more liberal commercial treaty in 1853 and it was agreed that from 1860 negotiations on a possible future membership of Austria in the *Zollverein* should begin.

At the same time Prussia did not challenge Austrian pre-eminence in the *Bund*. It did not actively support Austrian policy during the Crimean War but instead formed an 'offensive-defensive' alliance with Austria which was extended to the Confederation [130 *chap. 10*]. However, this was on the basis of strict neutrality in relation to the warring powers, a policy which in turn constrained those in Austria who wanted to come out on the side of Britain and France. Bismarck, who was at this time the Prussian ambassador to the *Bund*, complained that the policy would enable Austria to pull Prussia into an anti-Russian direction [133 *chap. 3*]. He urged instead that Prussia exploit Austria's difficulties in order to expand in Germany. He continued to do so once the war was over [*Doc. 47*].

Prussian conservatives in power in Berlin were, however, more worried about the threats from the new imperial regime under Louis Napoleon in France and the potential for instability if Austria and Prussia came into conflict openly with each other. Only dramatic changes in the situation in both Austria and Prussia were likely to alter the policies of these two states. These changes came in 1858–59.

CHAPTER SIX

FROM COOPERATION TO WAR, 1858–66

EUROPE

By the early 1850s the European economy had largely recovered from the crisis of the mid-1840s and had entered a period of rapid growth [37; 38]. The aftermath of the Crimean War left France, Britain and Russia reluctant to pursue potentially destabilising policies in central Europe for some time. By 1858, however, Louis Napoleon in France was interested in supporting liberal and national movements, starting with Italy, especially if France could make territorial gains. This could compensate for failing popularity at home. International relations were also favourable for such an initiative. Since the end of the Crimean War Louis Napoleon had moved closer towards Russia. Both had interests against Austria – France in Italy and Russia in the Balkans. Furthermore, Britain, although generally a supporter of Austria, was less concerned about preserving Austria's Italian sphere of influence than that in the Balkans. The Prime Minister in Piedmont, Cavour, was anxious to expand his state into the core of a kingdom of north Italy against Austria. He met with Louis Napoleon in 1858 and came to an agreement on common action against Austria. [For diplomacy from 1856 until 1859, especially Austro-French relations, see 72 and 79.] The direct result was the war of 1859. Rapid and bloody defeat in northern Italy, coupled with threats of national opposition being fomented in its eastern territories, persuaded Austria to conclude a peace and to give up the rich province of Lombardy to France which passed it on to Piedmont.

French success here (the newly established Kingdom of Italy handed over Nice and Savoy to France) emboldened Louis Napoleon in other spheres. In the early 1860s he determinedly pursued a free trade policy which led to agreements with Britain, Belgium and Italy. He also negotiated such an agreement with Prussia which Prussia in turn imposed on the *Zollverein* with the full support of the French. These low tariff agreements helped maintain the exclusion of Austria from the *Zollverein* when the matter came up again for negotiation in the early 1860s. The inclusion of a 'most favoured nation' clause in many of these treaties resulted in the commercial liberalisation of much of Europe [116]. (This was a provision in a trade treaty between two states which automatically extended to each other any lower import tariffs negotiated subsequently with a third state.)

The opening up of gold fields in the USA and Australia provided the underpinning to the credit and monetary expansion involved in this growth, while the closing down of some American markets and supplies with the Civil War probably focused attention on developing markets within Europe. Large banking operations were involved internationally with investment schemes throughout western and central Europe, especially in the field of railway construction. The hope of many liberals was that commercial liberalisation and the internationalisation of economic activity would promote middle-class influence and reduce the possibilities of war between states. What the 1860s showed was that such economic developments actually combined with warfare to bring about dramatic changes in the political geography of Europe. [Generally on economic development, see 37 and 38; on finance 103.]

The war of 1859 led by 1861 not merely to the formation of a north Italian kingdom but unexpectedly to the unification of most of the peninsula under the Piedmontese monarchy. Only the Papal States and Venetia remained outside. To German liberal nationalists this provided a compelling model of what determined state action could achieve, even if they were ambivalent about this success coming at the expense of Austria, a German power. The war also made clear the need for military innovation in a way that the Crimean War had not. Troops were moved by rail, new mass-produced weaponry played a key part in French success. Finally, the war led to internal political crisis and change in Austria. This in turn altered the balance of power with Prussia. When Bismarck, already well known for his view that Prussia must act against Austria in order to provide an adequate sphere of influence for itself in Germany, was appointed Prussian Prime Minister in September 1862, it was clear that he would be working out how to exploit these changed conditions.

From this point the major diplomatic attention moves towards the policies of Austria and Prussia in relation to the German question. I will only consider the policies of the other European powers in terms of how these influenced Austro-Prussian relations.

GERMANY

Authoritarian rule and economic liberalism characterised politics in Germany through most of the 1850s [48 *chap. 4*; 52 *chap. 14*; 59 *chap. 12*]. There were, however, tensions between these two. Economic growth strengthened the position of middle-class interests which felt stifled by continuing political restrictions and divisions between many small states.

More generally, such growth was accompanied by new associations, reading habits, and better communications and transport which undermined authoritarian control. The German lands shared in the rapid economic growth after 1853 which was only briefly set back in 1857–58. For the first time the industrial labour force started to grow more rapidly than that in agriculture, the urban population in relation to the rural population. Investment in railway building reached over one-quarter of all manufacturing investment by 1860. This was linked to the formation of larger banks which concentrated investment in industrial ventures. Certain urban regions were taking shape – in the Rhineland/Westphalia provinces of Prussia (most notably the Ruhr district), Saxony, parts of Silesia, in Bohemia, as well as round large cities such as Berlin and Vienna [106/II *part I*; and see Tables II.1 and II.4 at the end of Chapter 8].

With the relaxation of state supervision from 1858–59 such conditions helped sustain a sharp increase in the formation of all kinds of associations – professional and occupational, cultural and political. One of these was the *Nationalverein* (National Association), formed in 1859, which pursued the objective of a national state formed under Prussian auspices (its programme of 1859 is published as document 3 in 26). The *Nationalverein* established a network of branches across the German states, although with higher levels of support in Protestant areas. As an organisation of upper middle-class elites, the *Nationalverein* did not seek to become a mass organisation (its membership never exceeded 25,000), although it was able to draw upon the support of a variety of cultural and educational associations with lower middle-class and skilled working-class memberships [106/I *chap. 8*].

Some of the leaders of the *Nationalverein* had been active in 1848–49. From that experience they had concluded that one had to work with, not against, established political authority and that Austria was resolutely opposed to national unity. They were themselves uneasily divided between moderates who quite liked the restricted constitutional Prussian system and radicals who wanted to create a popular basis for the new nation state, albeit in a non-revolutionary manner. They were prepared to see the smaller and even medium states subordinated to a more powerful central authority but at the same time they believed that Prussia itself must be considerably liberalised both in order to pursue a forward national policy and to be acceptable as the dominant element in a national state. These liberal nationalists believed that economic growth, constitutional reform and the deepening of institutions such as the *Zollverein* would provide the basis for success. The general support for peaceful and liberal progress towards national unity was vividly expressed in November 1859 with the celebrations of the centenary of the birth of Schiller, the great poet and dramatist. All over Germany there were processions, festivals and speeches, with Schiller presented as a man of the people, the embodiment of a vigorous German cultural identity.

The views of the *Nationalverein* stood in a complicated relationship to that of the smaller and medium German states. Where liberalism was a powerful force, as in Baden by the end of the 1850s, there was a willingness to consider surrendering much state sovereignty to the right kind of national authority. In other states, such as Bavaria, conservative as well as Catholic sentiments inclined the government against any moves towards Prussian, liberal and Protestant domination. The medium states were acutely aware of their great dependence upon Prussia through the *Zollverein* and tended to look to Austria to provide a balance to this within the *Bund*. There was support for more effective *Bund* action on such matters as currency reform and also for constitutional changes which would strengthen the national authority, but within a federalist framework which would ensure autonomy for the medium states. However, the varying interests of the different states (e.g., the suspicion of the others against Bavarian assertion, the Protestant/Catholic tensions) made it difficult to unite around any distinct programme. The response to the *Nationalverein* was the *Reform Verein* which insisted on the continued membership of Austria in any national state but which is better understood as a negative reaction to the *Nationalverein* than as an organisation with a positive agenda of its own. [See 108 for the politics of the medium states; 159 for their links to the *Bund*.]

What all these groups – states or political movements – had in common was a dislike for joint Austro-Prussian domination. Perhaps their main opportunity for influence was in exploiting situations where Austria and Prussia came into conflict with one another. However, both Austria and Prussia would in turn seek to use these German interests against each other. Especially between 1861 and 1866 there was a complex alternation between different combinations of Austrian, Prussian and German alliances which only came to an end with the military defeat of Austria in the Seven Weeks' War. It is, above all, through the prism of Austro-Prussian relations that the German question must be considered over these years.

AUSTRIA AND PRUSSIA

Developments within the two states, 1858–63

Austria

In many respects Austria had a good decade until 1859. The Crimean War had created problems but the main result was the defeat of Russia and the temporary end of its expansionist aims in the Balkans. The policy of economic liberalisation had paid off with rapid economic growth, including some industrialisation. The confidence of the regime was expressed in an ambitious rebuilding programme in Vienna. Austria began to trade and engage in other transactions on a more intensive basis with other parts of Germany than before 1848 and that in turn strengthened the movement for a closer link to the *Zollverein*. [Generally, see 57 *chap. 4*; 58 *chap. 6*.]

However, the war of 1859 created a political crisis. Austria had hoped for Prussian support and was bitterly disappointed that Prussia was only prepared to grant this if allowed to dominate the German military arrangements, especially along the Rhine. This looked like an attempt to exploit the Italian problem to achieve greater control in Germany. Austria refused to make such concessions and fear of its position in Germany was one reason for bringing the war to a rapid conclusion [131 *chap. 5*].

Defeat left the Austrian state in massive debt [103 *chaps 3 and 4*]. By 1865 this amounted to 1,670 million Thaler. By comparison, Prussian state debt then stood at 290 million Thaler. (Chapter 8 considers the implications of this comparison at greater length.) Two things were crucial: to reduce state expenditure and to rebuild political confidence. Both required an avoidance of risky policies which might lead to war or require extensive preparations for war.

First, reduced expenditure was most easily achieved by cutting back on the army. From 434,000 in 1850 it had been reduced to 306,000 in 1860 and stood at only 275,000 on the eve of war in 1866, the military budget having been slashed by half between 1860 and 1865. (See Chapter 8, Tables III.2 and III.3.)

Second, rebuilding confidence meant moving back to constitutional government. In early 1860 the regime experimented with an aristocratic federalist arrangement, depending on the support of conservative Hungarians, Bohemians and Poles. However, this was anathema to the economically and culturally dominant German elite which had been central to the neo-absolutism of the 1850s and, although willing to move down the constitutional path, wished to do so in a more liberal and centralist framework. In December 1860 Anton Schmerling, former Prime Minister of the German Provisional Authority in 1848 and a leading exponent of this German constitutionalism, was appointed Chief Minister. In February 1861 he introduced a new constitution with a dominant role for central institutions. The problem was that this was opposed not only by Bohemian and Galician nobles but by the much more powerful Hungarian nobility, leading to the suspension of their Diet in August 1861. The Emperor only half-heartedly identified with Schmerling's policies and by the end of 1864 was inclining back towards the aristocratic federalist line. The major domestic political weakness was conflict between the dominant German elite in the west and the Hungarian elite in the east, exacerbated by the continued growth of Slav nationalist pressures, especially amongst the Czechs of Bohemia. [See 58 *pp. 176–83* for constitutional issues 1859–64; 131 *chap. 6* for the views of the Emperor.]

These domestic political weaknesses and conflicts throw some light upon Austria's German policy. The German elite saw itself as part of Germany and was resolutely opposed to any weakening, let alone exclusion, of Austria from the rest of Germany. Indeed, for Schmerling, a central role for Austria in Germany was essential to maintaining a central position for Austrian Germans in the Empire. Coming from economically the most advanced parts of the Empire and supporting liberalisation, it was interested in closer links with, if not membership of, the *Zollverein*. Tactically, it veered between a policy of seeking to dominate Germany through agreement with Prussia against the interests of the medium states and liberal national opinion, and of appealing to precisely those interests against the threat of Prussian hegemony. Schmerling supported the more forceful reformist policy; Rechberg, who shaped foreign policy for much of the early 1860s, the dualist approach. That approach also tended to be associated with a less forceful, centralist and constitutional line within the Empire. The result was a certain inconsistency in policy-making [*Doc. 48* expresses the more negative line; *Doc. 51* the more positive line. See also 67 *chap. 3*; 75.]

Thus, in 1862–63 the Schmerling line led to the floating of ideas of reform of the *Bund*, culminating with a meeting of the German princes to agree such a plan [*Doc. 51*]. Only the refusal of the Prussian king, which Bismarck had to work hard to achieve, to attend the meeting undermined the scheme [133 *chap. 5*; 134 *pp. 230–2*]. However, in 1864, with the war against Denmark over Schleswig-Holstein, Rechberg steered Austria back towards cooperation with Prussia and the exclusion of the rest of Germany from influencing policy. This policy reached its peak in August 1865 when the Convention of Gastein divided the occupied duchies with Prussia taking control of Schleswig and Austria of Holstein [*Doc. 57*]. This was bitterly condemned by both the medium states and the national movement which had wanted to see a new state established within the *Bund* under the rule of the Duke of Augustenberg. However, early 1866, and with the threat of approaching war, saw Austria changing tack yet again, now taking up the cause of Augustenberg. Indeed, it was the decision of Austria to allow demonstrations in support of Augustenberg in Holstein which provided the pretext for the Prussian ultimatum which led to the war itself [69 *chap. 3*].

There was also an economic reason for these contradictions. The German elite was at the forefront of industrial development in the Empire. Liberalisation of trade across the Empire (e.g., the removal of tariff barriers between Austria and Hungary in 1850) suited these German interests. *Politically* there was much to be said for closer links to the *Zollverein* as part of the policy of ensuring Austrian dominance in Germany. *Economically*, however, these German interests were well aware that they were inefficient compared to *Zollverein* competitors. Aristrocratic and bureaucratic elements within the German elite were perhaps prepared to pay the price of import penetration for the sake of political gains, but the German business community was not. Before 1860 it might have been possible for the dynasty to override that opposition, especially as interests such as Hungarian landowning magnates in turn were attracted to the prospect of cheaper manufactures, inward German investment and greater markets for their foodstuffs. However, the constitutionalist path was designed precisely to attract support from the Austrian German business community, in order to be able to raise loans, and that had given those business interests the political power to block such a policy. Just as these Germans politically favoured reform and integration in Germany but opposed *Zollverein* membership, Hungarian interests opposed closer political ties but were more positive about the economic links. Policy-making as a consequence fluctuated and probably made a determined pursuit of entry into the *Zollverein* impossible [57 *chap. 4*; *Doc. 55*].

This ambivalence makes Austrian policy difficult to follow. A further complication is that Austria had to balance concerns about Germany with those about Italy and the Balkans. It suffered from the condition of major powers which Kennedy has termed 'imperial overstretch' [34] to a much greater degree than Prussia. What complicated matters further was that the two policies of reforming centralism and stand-still dualism could be linked rather than opposed, with one serving as tactical leverage in support of the other. Thus support for national reform against Prussia might serve as a way of forcing Prussia back into a policy of cooperative domination. All these contradictory pressures meant that Austria had little clear idea about asserting itself in any decisive fashion in Germany (whether through territorial claims or constitutional reform or subordination of Prussia or closer economic links) but was more bent on the negative goal of preventing Prussian domination. The clarity with which Schwarzenberg had acted between 1849 and 1853 had disappeared. When war finally came in 1866 Austria embarked on it more as an escape from the dilemmas of policy-making than as an instrument of a particular policy.

Prussia

In 1858 William became Regent in place of his brother. New elections to the *Landtag* produced liberal successes and William appointed moderate liberals to the government. The hopes of liberal nationalists that Prussia would now lead the way to a reformed and national Germany were raised by these events. This pointed to one vital difference between Prussia and Austria: Prussia had a constitution and a nationally elected parliament which provided a basis for a liberal direction of policy before any major crisis; Austria only moved in such a direction as the result of such a crisis. [Apart from general studies such as 48; 52; and 59, on the 'New Era' see 106/II *part I*.]

The Prussian government had never completely followed Austria since 1850, although this was an impression that Bismarck later cultivated in his reminiscences in order to highlight the difference his appointment made from 1862 [16; 133; 134]. During the Crimean War, Prussia refused to go beyond an alliance based on strict neutrality with Austria. Since 1856 it had quietly allied itself with Russia rather than Austria on matters where there was conflict. Prussia's trade policy had determinedly kept Austria out of the *Zollverein* and had involved close links to France, a policy opposed by principled conservatives. [See 127; 143; 152 on customs union policy; 130 *chap. 10* has some details on conservative criticisms.] Indeed, when Bismarck in 1864 suggested a weakening of this policy as part of his then dualist cooperation with Austria, ministers with financial and trade responsibilities, along with Rudolf Delbrück who shaped tariff policy, ensured Bismarck was overruled [133 *chap. 6*].

Prussian population growth was about twice that of Austria. Its booming economy and lack of international commitments compared to Austria meant a low state debt. Army reforms were tilting the balance of power between the two states. [See Chapter 8 below for further analysis.] Generally, however, the preference of the conservatives who shaped policy in these years was to follow an independent course from Austria but to avoid direct conflict so far as possible and certainly not to provide any support to liberal nationalism. Thus the liberal hopes raised in 1858 through a turn-around in domestic politics were doomed to disappointment in the foreign policy sphere.

This pragmatic conservative line continued in 1859, steering between principled conservatives who wanted Prussia to ally with Austria against France (seeing the war in anti-French rather than in pro-Italian terms) and principled liberals who looked sympathetically upon the Italian liberal nationalist cause and wanted Prussia to take up such ideas. Then there was the eccentric position of Bismarck, who urged the government to use Austria's difficulties to expand its own position in Germany, seeing this in dynastic and Prussian, rather than liberal and national, terms. [*Doc. 47* outlines Bismarck's ideas more generally and a little earlier.] Some of these differences were reflected in the policy-making elite of the time [*Doc. 49*]. What in fact the Prussian government did, much to the dismay of Austria and Franz Joseph in particular [131 *chap. 5*], was to insist that it could only provide assistance if put in charge of all non-Austrian *Bund* troops. This, along with Prussian mobilisation on the Rhine in case Louis Napoleon extended the scope of his actions, appeared to Austria as a bid for leadership in Germany. It was one reason Austria went on rapidly to conclude a peace with France; while the mobilisation also made Louis Napoleon anxious to bring the war to an end [79 *chap. 9*].

The end of the war, however, clearly had greatly weakened Austria and stimulated the national movement which looked to Prussia for leadership.

However, it had also revealed Prussian weaknesses. Partial mobilisation had shown just how weak the army was, a matter of acute concern to William who was especially concerned about an increased threat from France. After all, the original Napoleon had started with military success in northern Italy and then turned his attention to the Rhenish region. After a review William ordered a radical reform of the army, expanding its numbers, increasing the length of service from two to three years and marginalising the role of the territorial reserve army, the *Landwehr*. [26 deals with some of these matters. See also 68; 73 and 87.] These reform plans, however, offended the new liberal majority in the *Landtag*, not because of the additional expenditure (state finances were healthy and the liberals recognised the need for a strong army) but because the increased length of service and diminished role for the *Landwehr*, coupled with the insistence of the king that he alone had complete power of command over the army, made them fear that the army could be used as an instrument of the monarchy against parliament.

The two bills to reform the army and to pay for this were put before the *Landtag* in early 1860. William refused to accept that the parliament could alter anything in the army reorganisation bill though he could not deny the budgetary powers of the parliament. The *Landtag* in turn made it clear it would only provisionally grant extra monies. This was a fateful decision because it meant that the army reforms could be set in hand, even if their cost had not been firmly approved. In an attempt to improve the situation William dissolved the parliament and called for new elections. The result, and this was repeated over the next couple of years, was the return of a larger and more determined liberal majority. The combination of liberalisation, a more mobile and organised society, and crisis was generating political forces beyond the control of the regime. In early 1861 a new party, the Progressive Party, was formed which took the liberal lead. Subsequently, branches of the Progressive Party were formed in other states, pointing up the national implications of the conflict. [See 93 for the period of the constitutional crisis.]

One possible way out of the crisis was for the government to try to take the lead on the national question as liberal politicians demanded (See, for example, document 4 in 26). It is no coincidence that in December 1861, just as there was a new round of elections, the Prussian government floated a new version of the Union policy of 1849–50. It resembled the *Nationalverein* programme (document 3 in 26) except that it did not make provision for any elected national assembly. In part this was a response to yet another initiative by the Saxon minister Beust for a federated Germany with an executive authority, court and national representation but also more influence for the medium states [*Doc. 50*].

Neither domestically nor beyond Prussia did the policy initiative work. Austria and the medium states rejected the idea, just as they had done in

1850. The Progressive Party registered electoral victory. In the new *Landtag* it decided against voting any more provisional budgets for the army reforms. William dissolved the *Landtag* yet again in March 1862 but elections in May returned an even more determined liberal majority. In the meantime, Austria – well into its constitutional policy under Schmerling – decided also to take up the issue of national reform in conjunction with some of the other German states.

It was at this juncture that the decision to appoint Bismarck Minister-President was taken by the embattled William on the advice of his War Minister, the architect of the army reforms, von Roon. As the book by Williamson [26] already published in this series deals with Bismarck from 1862 until the end of his career, I will not spend much time on biographical detail but just note some key points. [See 133 and 134 for studies of Bismarck. There are other good English language studies not listed in the bibliography.]

Bismarck had long advocated confrontation with Austria in order for Prussia to expand in Germany. Subsequently, he suggested that previous Prussian governments had subordinated themselves to Austria and it was only with his appointment that this policy was reversed. This is at best a half-truth, tending to make policy appear as a function of personality and contributing to a one-sided 'great men make history' view. As we have seen, Prussia steered a confrontational course in foreign policy in 1849–50 and took an independent line from 1854, including a determinedly anti-Austrian line in the key area of trade policy and *Zollverein* membership. What it did not do, until December 1861, was revive the Union policy which had brought it into direct conflict with Austria in 1850. However, Bismark had loudly condemned that policy and supported the Olmütz agreement that brought it to an end [*Doc. 44*]. Indeed, his own appointment as ambassador to the restored *Bund* in 1851 arose directly out of that agreement and his support for it. It also had the effect of bringing into the diplomatic service a man who had failed to complete his probationary period as a civil servant, resigned from office, retreated to run his estates in Brandenburg, and had only come back into politics with the constitutional crisis of 1847 and then by taking a hard counter-revolutionary line in 1848–49.

Indeed, it was that reputation as a determined defender of royal pre-rogative at a moment of crisis rather than his rogue opinions on Prussian foreign policy which accounts for Bismarck's appointment in September 1862. His immediate objective, we must recall, was not to lead Prussia into Germany but to assert the royal will over the liberal majority in parliament, a majority which was the most important force agitating for such a forward national policy.

This domestic challenge was to be Bismarck's major preoccupation for the first year or so after his appointment. Bismarck argued that the budget already granted to the government should continue to operate at a time when the executive and the upper house (*Herrenhaus*) of the legislature failed to agree with the lower house (*Landtag*), on the grounds that those drafting the constitution had surely never meant government to break down in the event of such a disagreement. This dubious 'constitutional gap' theory worked because the *Landtag* was not for its part prepared to pursue active sanctions against the government such as leading a tax boycott or some other kind of civil disobedience.

As for any national policy, Bismarck was at a loss. The revived Union policy of 1861 had been rejected by liberals, the medium states and Austria. He took a firm free trade line in 1862 to ensure agreement with France and the exclusion of Austria from the *Zollverein*. He continued with this policy up until the renewal of the *Zollverein* in 1865 (though as we have seen, he contemplated diluting the policy in 1864), making it clear that, if necessary, Prussia would leave the customs union and negotiate separate agreements with non-German states. Faced with such a threat the other German states had no option but to fall into line [*Doc. 55*].

Bismarck also strengthened the positive relationship with Russia. At the heart of this was the Polish question. When a new insurrection broke out in Russian Poland in 1863 Bismarck quickly and demonstratively signalled Prussian support for its repression. However, the main effect was to alienate him even further from liberal nationalists who supported the restoration of a Polish state and who saw Russia as the main obstacle to German unity. It also alienated France. It is difficult therefore to see how this would actually help Bismarck make any decisive policy change in the German question. The liberal opposition was also not greatly impressed by Bismarck's famous 'blood and iron' speech when he declared that the way of solving the national question was not through parliamentary resolutions (the 1848 method) but through the use of power [see 26 *document 9*]. As Bismarck was not actually challenging Austria in this way, this phrase looked more like an oblique reference to the crisis in Prussia than a signal of a possible change in foreign policy. Yet the liberals never seriously believed that Bismarck was going to send soldiers into parliament and try to cow it into submission. Indeed, they could not see him remaining in office for very long given the weight of public and parliamentary opinion against him.

They were right to believe that Bismarck was not prepared to take the line of a coup and the return to non-parliamentary government. Bismarck was well aware that in the long run, without parliamentary support, above all without the support of the business and professional middle classes on which the liberal majority was based, his could be little more than a stop-gap administration. That support was needed above all for the credit-worthiness of the state. For all his harsh rhetoric Bismarck had no intention of going down the path of *coup d'état* and a return to absolutism which some conservatives envisaged. He would try to bribe and intimidate deputies, buy up newspapers to express pro-governmental views, have discussions with radical labour leaders like Ferdinand Lassalle about the possibility of basing monarchical rule on popular consent, thereby under-cutting the liberal parliament elected on a weighted franchise. He also 'indiscreetly' insinuated to deputies that he really wished to govern with their support but that the king had to be persuaded and this would only happen if parliament would be a little more forthcoming on its side. All these measures and rhetorical tricks were intended to push liberals towards agreement with Bismarck, not to replace the present constitution. Further-more, Bismarck was aware that his value to the king was precisely that he was overriding but not abolishing parliament. Once things had gone that far government could be handed over to bureaucrats and soldiers. Bismarck was a creation of the very constitutional politics he opposed. [See 133 and 134 for detailed support for this interpretation of Bismarck.]

However, none of these tactical twists and bewildering array of half-promises and veiled threats proved successful in Bismarck's first year or so in office. Poised between parliament and the hardline conservatives at court, dependent almost entirely on the personal support of the ageing king, blustering about radical new policies but actually governing in a traditional authoritarian manner, it appeared to many that Bismarck was an inter-esting, unprincipled politician who would not be able to retain power for very long. His successes were negative ones. He persuaded the king not to attend the princes' congress Austria had organised in 1863 as part of its bid to take the lead on national reform. In return, he had suggested that a reformed *Bund* should have some nationally elected assembly but one could hardly take such an idea seriously from a man ruling in defiance of the one such assembly that existed in Prussia. In 1863 a shrewd contemporary might well have judged that Austria was making the running in German matters and that Prussia was paralysed by internal conflict. [See *Docs 51–54* on these reform proposals in 1863.]

The Schleswig-Holstein affair changed everything.

THE STRUGGLE FOR SUPREMACY IN GERMANY, 1864–66

We have already encountered Schleswig-Holstein and the ways in which it brought about conflict locally between Danish and German nationalism and war between the *Bund*, Prussia and Denmark in 1848. The matter had finally been subject to international regulation under the terms of the Treaty of London of 1852. Neither side was happy: Danish nationalists wanted to incorporate Schleswig directly into Denmark while German nationalists wanted to bind it to Holstein and form a new German state out of the two Duchies. [See 98 for the longer-term background; 69 *chap.* 2 and 89 for the origins of the war of 1864.]

In 1848 the attempt to alter the *status quo* had come from the German side and the major European powers, especially Britain and Russia, had taken the Danish side. One major difference in 1863, when the problem re-emerged, was that now the initiative was taken by Denmark. Denmark had drawn up a charter in March 1863 which laid down that the successor to Frederick VII would succeed to rule over Schleswig as well as Denmark. Frederick died on 15 November 1863. His successor, Christian, claimed Schleswig and signed a constitution to that effect. This went against the 1852 treaty.

This enraged German nationalists who insisted instead that the two Duchies be formed into one state under the Duke of Augustenberg and this state should become a member of the *Bund*. (The Duke's father had resigned his claim and had been compensated for that as part of the preparation of the 1852 treaty. The Duke now declared that he was no longer bound by that resignation, given the action of the Danish monarchy.) The *Bund* decided upon a military intervention against Denmark and in November federal troops from Saxony and Hannover occupied Holstein. The difference from 1848 was that Denmark could not be presented this time as a victim, France was more active, Britain was less interventionist, and Russia was concerned to maintain good relations with Prussia and Austria because of the Polish issue. The powers also became impatient when Denmark refused to negotiate any compromise on its new position. Denmark was under pressure from its own nationalist opinion and did not think that ultimately the major powers would abandon it [69 *chap. 2*].

Thus when Austria and Prussia determined bilaterally upon an invasion of Schleswig in January 1864, insisting that they were doing so in defence of the Treaty of London and not to advance any German national cause, this was not opposed by the other powers. Bismarck had found a way of Prussia acting decisively on a matter dear to German nationalism but the manner of action, with Austria, independently of the *Bund* and avowedly to restore the 1852 arrangement, actually had the effect of uniting the medium states and nationalist opinion in condemnation of the policy. [*Doc. 56* puts Bismarck's dualist line clearly.]

The advantage for Austria was that it distanced Prussia from nationalist support, ensured that the Prussian government remained locked in conflict with the liberal majority in parliament and seemed well on the way to restoring the double hegemony the two states exercised over German affairs. There was also the hope that such cooperation in north Germany might lead on to cooperation elsewhere, for example in undoing some of the results of the 1859 war. The disadvantages were that at the same time Austria undermined its own policy of bidding for liberal and national support in Germany and became entangled in an affair in distant northern Germany in which it had no direct interest and which it could not control.

Denmark was no military match for Austria and Prussia. [See 69 *chap. 2* for the war generally; 68 *chap. 4* for Prussia's role.] The war gave the Prussian Chief of Staff, von Moltke, an opportunity to test the efficacy of the army reforms. Many people in Prussia were simply proud as Prussians to see their army winning battles and taking control of new territory. The intransigence of Denmark and its unfounded faith in international intervention led to the loss of the two Duchies. Now the idea began to grow in Prussia, and certainly in Bismarck's mind, that the final outcome might be Prussian annexation of the two Duchies. He had already broached the subject at a Crown Council meeting as early as February 1864. For Bismarck this was vastly to be preferred to a return to pre-1864 arrangements or the formation of yet another small German state which, in Bismarck's view, simply added to the nonsense of all other such states.

At what point the matter could also be used to engineer a direct conflict with Austria over the relative position of the two states in Germany is less clear. Already by May 1865 the possibility of war had arisen. The Gastein Convention settled that crisis and made quite clear the impotence of the other German states or nationalist opinion [*Doc. 57*].

Moltke declared in his memoirs that the war of 1866 was deliberately planned by the Prussian government. Certainly Bismarck had long insisted that Germany must be divided into a Prussian and an Austrian sphere of influence and that the arrangements of a shared hegemony over the *Bund* were not tenable [*Doc. 47*]. Such a policy of regional expansion within a 'national' zone was, after all, what Frederick the Great had pursued suc-cessfully in Silesia, what Prussia had aimed for over Saxony in 1814–15, what Radowitz had sought in 1849–50, and what Manteuffel had briefly outlined in 1861. Furthermore, there was nothing new about claiming that this was in the interests of Germany; Frederick the Great had justified his policy in just this way. The big difference was that there was now a much more popular and powerful national movement which would insist that reality matched such rhetoric and that expansion could not simply be dynastic annexation.

Before the war broke out, however, the key point to note was that this was a high-risk policy. Frederick had only succeeded in taking Silesia after two long wars involving all the major powers. Prussia backed down in 1815 and 1850 when faced with the prospect of war against Austria and other powers, a war which there was no clear likelihood of it winning quickly. Was Bismarck taking a gamble in 1866 as Frederick had in 1740, a gamble which his immediate predecessors had refused to take? Or was there some essential difference this time?

The road to Königgrätz

There were important differences from earlier conflicts between Austria and Prussia.

The first was the possibility of isolating such a war from broader international complications. Britain was very reluctant to become involved in another European war. Earlier interventions (1740–48, 1756–63, continually from 1793 to 1815) had been aimed mainly against France, still seen as the major threat to a balance of power on the continent. Prussia had been an ally in 1756–63 and 1813–15. There was sympathy for Prussia as a Protestant culture, close links between the royal families (Victoria's daughter was married to William's son, Frederick), sympathy for the liberal and national cause and, above all, no strong sense that Prussia could become a threat to the general balance of power. Russia was close to Prussia because of Polish matters and in conflict with Austria since the Crimean War. Especially as Prussian policy since 1864 actually seemed to go against the liberal movement and was firmly in a dynastic tradition of state aggrandisement, this policy did not raise the fears that the Union policy of 1849–50 had created in Russia. In any case, Russian influence since the Crimean War was not nearly as great as it had been before 1848 or in the counter-revolutionary period from 1849 to 1854. [See 84 for a general diplomatic background.]

The biggest potential problem was France [85]. After his success in the Italian theatre, Louis Napoleon was interested in advances on the Rhine. However, for him the best policy was to wait and see how a conflict between Austria and Prussia developed before exploiting this to best advantage. This was the line he took when he and Bismarck met at Biarritz in October 1865; there was nothing more than vague allusions to possible territorial alterations to French advantage in the event of remaining neutral during an Austro-Prussia conflict. Louis Napoleon leant towards Prussia in the sense that he had tended to an anti-Austrian policy since 1856, found the Habsburg dynasty repellent, wanted to complete his Italian policy with the detachment of Venetia from Habsburg control and recognised that it was Prussia that would take the initiative in bringing about a confrontation. [See 79 for the period to 1864; 85 thereafter.] Nevertheless, ambiguous neutrality was his principal policy and he took this line also in negotiations with Austria. His encouragement for the Prussian–Italian alliance of April 1866 further suggests that his main policy was to bring about conflict between Austria and Prussia and exploit the outcome. It may be that his secret treaty of 6 June 1866 with Austria signalled a turn away from that policy and a belated awareness of the danger of a rapid and decisive Prussian victory, although it could also be interpreted as just another way of ensuring conflict by strengthening Austrian resolve.

Certainly, then, for a short period one could anticipate the non-involvement of the other three major powers. It needed little ability on Bismarck's part to secure this diplomatic situation. The second question was the prospect of winning such a localised war.

We have seen that between 1860 and 1865 the military balance of power between Austria and Prussia shifted rapidly in favour of Prussia. Whereas in 1860 army strengths on paper stood at about 300,000 and 200,000 respectively, in 1866 they stood at about 275,000 and 215,000. However, this Austrian numerical superiority was itself undone by the Prussian–Italian agreement of 1866, an agreement supported by Louis Napoleon. Both Prussia and Italy had an interest in using the other one in a conflict with Austria in order to make territorial gains. Equally, each was worried that the other, having used this leverage successfully, would abandon its ally. The agreement, formally commencing on 8 April 1866, was limited to just three months. Italy agreed to go to war against Austria if Prussia did, and both states agreed not to bring war to an end until each had made territorial gains. The ball was in Prussia's court but it needed to start the war soon. Italy's army had a paper strength of 230,000 although this was an unrealistic estimate and the Italian army performed woefully in 1866. However, it meant that Austria had to divide its army, sending 100,000 troops south. In theory, Austrian soldiers were boosted by the entry of Saxony, Bavaria, Württemberg and Hannover into the war on its side. However, only 33,000 Saxons succeeded in joining up with Austrian troops in Bohemia, bringing the strength up to a little over 200,000. The other states were rapidly defeated by Prussia and hardly delayed the mobilisation and movement of Prussian soldiers into northern Bohemia. Numerically there was rough parity between the two sides in the German war zone in Bohemia. [See 68; 74; and 91 for the 1866 war.]

When the war started many informed observers believed it would be prolonged, possibly indecisive, and that Austria was more likely to emerge the winner. [On the public war aims of the two states, see *Docs 58 and 59.*] Austria had the advantage of a central position. Moltke opted for the very high-risk policy of dividing his army into three to bring them over the mountains into Bohemia, providing the Austrian commander Benedek with the chance of concentrating his force on to one of these armies and then picking off the other two. In the event Benedek failed to do this, the Prussian armies were brought together on the eve of (indeed, even during) the decisive battle. Part of the reason for this was that Moltke fully exploited railway networks (far superior for his troops coming south to the Austrian border than for Austrian troops coming north from Vienna) and the division of his forces to move much more quickly than Benedek had expected. The telegraph also, at least in the initial stages of movement, enabled better coordination of widely dispersed forces. Nevertheless, this did not go like clockwork; there were many breakdowns in communication and bottlenecks in transport, and once in Bohemia route marching and mounted couriers took over.

Second, when troops closed on one another, the needle-gun used by Prussia (a breech- rather than muzzle-loading rifle which could be fired more rapidly and from the prone rather than standing position) inflicted devastating casualties on Austrian troops who tried to close in for hand-to-hand combat. Broadly speaking, these elements – rapid movement of divided forces, concentration at the point of battle, and superior infantry – were the key to Prussia's rapid success. At the same time military historians do point to missed opportunities and mistakes by the Austrian command. The war had been a huge gamble; the Prussian leadership had not expected so dramatic a triumph.

However, it is not enough to point to such military factors. One also has to explain why they existed. Why did Prussia have the needle-gun and not Austria? Why did Prussia plan for war in a more effective way? Why was Prussia able to use railways more effectively? To answer these and other such questions we have to go beyond conventional military history and that is the purpose of Chapter 8 below.

What also needs to be explained is why one lost battle, however calamitous, should lead so rapidly to the end of the war. The defeat of Sedan in 1870 did not bring the war with France to an end; why should Königgrätz do this in 1866? Austria had been successful in the Italian theatre. It could have transferred troops from the south (this operation was actually started), fallen back in defence of Vienna and raised more troops. France was now regretting its previous policy and shifting in favour of Austria. Russia was not happy about the imminent destruction of various German monarchies and the massive expansion of Prussian power. It would not have been unreasonable to anticipate the other major powers becoming concerned about Prussian success, bringing pressure to bear for a negotiated settlement and pushing back hoped-for Prussian gains [84 *chap. 8*; 69 *chap. 3*].

One reason Austria did not take this line was that it was concerned about its remaining territories. Bismarck in 1866, just like Louis Napoleon in 1859, had established contacts with Hungarian radicals linked to the 1848 leader Louis Kossuth, who wished to use Austria's weakness to revive the 1848 drive for independence, or at least much greater autonomy. Austria had, in the secret treaty of June with France, already agreed to concede Venetia to France, which intended in turn to pass it over to Italy. (Thus Italy was secure of Venetia whichever way the war turned out!) Also important is that Austria lacked positive war aims in Germany. It was not clear whether it aimed to deprive Prussia of territory, reorganise the *Bund*, destroy or join the *Zollverein* or whether it would simply have used victory as a way of restoring a confederal Germany in which Austria was preeminent and Prussia followed its lead. These fears and lack of a positive set of war aims help explain Austria's capitulation. Finally, public opinion even amongst Austrian Germans, the section of the population which was most committed to the German connection, was against continuing a war which could be debilitating. [See *57 chap. 4*; *131 chap. 6*. I consider this further in Chapter 8 below.]

Bismarck was equally concerned about the consequences of continued war. In his reminiscences he describes vividly the emotionally exhausting arguments with his king and military advisers who wanted to march to Vienna (though one always has to be aware of exaggeration in order to make Bismarck's own role more central) [*16 chap. 20* 'Nikolsburg'].Once those arguments were won, Bismarck had made it clear that Austria would not be asked to surrender any territory in Germany but simply to give up its influence over other German states by allowing the *Bund* to be destroyed, as well as to pay an indemnity. He also hinted at territorial gains to France after the war. Consequently, there seemed to be no good reason for Austria continuing with a war which would probably not improve on such a settlement and might easily lead to something much worse. [On Prussian peace policy, see *26 document 17*; for the peace agreement, see *Doc. 60*.]

The Consequences of Prussian victory

The biggest losers were the medium states in northern and central Germany (see map 4). North of the River Main Bismarck followed the traditional policy of annexation, creating new Prussian provinces in Schleswig, Holstein, Nassau, the northern part of Hesse-Darmstadt and Hannover, while forcing the remaining states into a Prussian-dominated North German Confederation. The German states south of the Main, principally Bavaria, Baden and Württemberg, were deprived of Austrian protection, still dominated by Prussia through the *Zollverein* and now forced into secret military alliance with Prussia. Whether they could resist for very long a more complete incorporation into a Prussian-dominated Germany was a matter of debate [*69 chap. 4*].

The national movement was plunged into disarray by the rapid course of events. Although some liberal nationalists by 1864–65 had begun to look more positively on Bismarck as providing a way towards national unity, most deplored the unconstitutional and military path he pursued. The outbreak of war between Austria and Prussia was greeted with dismay; this was a civil war between the two major German powers which would lead either to one of these powers dominating Germany or to a debilitating conflict which would weaken Germany and expose it to outside interference, especially from France. [*59 pp. 899–912* calls this section of the book 'the German civil war'; see also *26 document 12*.] Bismarck's sudden conversion to national reform, for example calling for a democratically elected German parliament, was not taken seriously.

Nothing, however, succeeds like success. Prussian victory changed the situation utterly. Furthermore, from his new position of strength Bismarck sought reconciliation with Prussian liberals and the national movement more generally. New elections to the Prussian *Landtag*, held on the day of Königgrätz (but before news of its outcome), had stimulated Prussian patriotism and led to victory for conservative candidates. Much to everyone's surprise, Bismarck did not use this opportunity to put a seal of approval upon his policy against the parliament, but instead placed before the *Landtag* an indemnity bill which was designed to return to normal constitutional rule [*Doc. 61*]. The liberals split between those who considered that it was better to work with Bismarck than against him, in the hope that such cooperation would impart a liberal and national character to Prussian success, and those who could not set aside four years of unconstitutional rule, harassment and the refusal to accept that in a future crisis such conduct could not be repeated. The pro-Bismarck faction formed the National Liberal party which in turn established branches in the new Prussian provinces and other German states. [See 114 and 122 on the development of liberal parties.]

Bismarck sought to work with the National Liberals in his German policy too. He convened a democratically elected constituent assembly for the new North German Confederation and the National Liberals emerged as the largest party. The constitutional draft Bismarck put before this assembly and which was agreed with some significant changes (such as the introduction of a secret ballot and a limited accountability of the Chancellor to the elected lower house, the *Reichstag*) was hardly a model of liberal constitutionalism. Military expenditure was exempted from normal, annual budgetary control. Key powers remained with the individual states (especially Prussia). At the national level the upper house, the *Bundesrat*, which, like the old *Bund*, was made up of state envoys, was intended to be the institution in which legislation was drafted; the *Reichstag* was seen as a body which could just say yea or nay to laws laid before it. However, the national constitution did provide the National Liberals with an instrument for liberalising reform which they were to use to full effect over the next few years. Furthermore, liberal politicians from the annexed provinces could join with counterparts in 'old' Prussia to exploit the constitutional provisions of Prussia. In these ways Bismarck effected a partnership of sorts between the Prussian state and German liberal nationalists. [See 139 for a study of such a liberal politician.]

The story of the North German Confederation and Bismarck's policy up to the Franco-Prussian War is dealt with by Williamson's book in this series [26] which in turn relates that to Bismarck's career as the first

German Chancellor up to 1890. Another book in the series by Mason [21] looks at the domestic politics of Austria-Hungary after 1866, beginning with the new constitution of 1867 which conceded autonomy to Hungary. I will not go over ground traversed by these authors. The focus of this book is upon the conflict between Austria and Prussia for supremacy in Germany. With the benefit of hindsight we know that, in effect, that matter was settled in 1866. However, contemporaries could not be so sure about this until after the defeat of France and the formation of the German Second Empire. The Austro-German alliance of 1879 finally made clear the Habsburg acceptance of Austria's exclusion from Germany and subordination to the more powerful Second Empire in a very different kind of cooperation. This last phase, from 1866 to 1871, needs brief consideration.

CHAPTER SEVEN

THE DEFINITIVE EXCLUSION OF AUSTRIA FROM GERMANY, 1867–71

Not everyone in Austria immediately accepted that the outcome of the war in 1866 was irreversible. This was signalled by the appointment of Beust as chief minister. Beust had been chief minister in Saxony and the architect of various plans for reform of the *Bund* which would give a prominent role to medium states. An attempt still to appeal to the 'third Germany' against Prussian domination and to use favourable international situations to undo at least some of 1866 could be anticipated [66 *chap. 2*; 120; 131 *chap. 7*.]

However, the first step necessary was to ensure internal political stability. Even before the war, in order to secure Hungarian support, Franz Joseph had promised constitutional concessions. In 1867 a new constitution conceded internal autonomy to Hungary. Spokesmen on behalf of Slav nationalities were unhappy with a failure to implement federalist measures below the level of the two halves of the Empire; the result appeared to be German dominance in the west and Magyar dominance in the east. More important in the short term was that the conservative Hungarian nobility also now had greater influence over the remaining powers of the imperial centre, including military and foreign policy. Any risky policy of trying to reverse Austria's setbacks in Germany was likely to be opposed from this quarter [21 *chap. 2*; 58 *pp. 187ff.*].

Beust's hopes instead had to be focused on the other major powers. How far would they accept what Bismarck had created? British opinion was not too concerned. Bismarck's return to constitutional politics was reassuring and a stronger Prussia appeared a more reliable bulwark against France than the weaker and divided *Bund*. More generally, there was a Protestant preference for Prussia over Austria, royal connections, and some admiration for what was seen as an efficient and non-corrupt regime. [For British policy, see 65 *pp. 113–21*.] Russia had offered mediation in August 1866 but was more positive about the defeat of Austria than any of the other major powers. A weakening of Austria offered more chance of success for its Balkans and Black Sea policies. However, Austria, shorn of its Italian territory and excluded from the rest of Germany, was more determined than ever to defend its position in south-east Europe [84 *chap. 9*].

The best chance lay with France. Louis Napoleon's German policy had been ruined by the unexpectedly quick and comprehensive Prussian victory. Bismarck quickly disavowed any of the vague promises made at Biarritz and indeed deliberately made public French demands for territorial compensation as the price for its 'support' in 1866. By doing this Bismarck unleashed a storm of nationalist protest which he could then claim prevented him from making concessions [134 *chap. 9*].

Precisely such a reaction made it impossible for Beust to conclude any agreement with France because it could be presented as anti-German. All that he could do was seek to maintain good relations with the south German states and to encourage elements within those states which opposed taking up closer links with Prussia. The best hope of such a policy was political Catholicism. There were other oppositional groups – for example, the supporters of the deposed Hannoverian king, democrats who saw Prussian constitutional concessions as just the 'fig-leaf of absolutism' (a phrase used by the radical and later socialist leader, Wilhelm Liebknecht), and the liberal groups who could not accept Bismarck as a partner. Certainly, these groups made life difficult for Bismarck. For example, one device he used to form closer links to the south German states was to arrange for a *Zollverein* parliament, made up of delegates from the North German Confederation and popularly elected deputies from south Germany. The plan backfired when anti-Prussian candidates won a majority of the south German seats. There was also indignation in Bavaria and Württemberg when the secret military agreements Prussia had concluded with them became public knowledge, especially when the state governments sought to introduce the Prussian system of conscription and three-year service. Some historians have suggested that these setbacks to Bismarck's attempts to incorporate the south German states was one reason for his preparedness to go to war with France [69 *pp. 161–78*].

The story of the origins and outcome of that war has been told elsewhere. [For a range of studies, see 26; 69; 80; 81; 90.] Temporarily at least, it stilled German opposition in a mood of anti-French feeling. Bavarian soldiers fought alongside Prussian soldiers. Austria did not dare support France. As with Louis Napoleon in 1866, the only chance lay in exploiting French victory or a prolonged and indecisive war. As in 1866, this did not happen. Although the war dragged on into 1871, with Prussia making much heavier demands than in 1866 and France raising new armies, the early battlefield victories had already made clear who was to be the eventual winner.

On 18 January 1871 William was declared German Emperor and the German Second Empire was founded. Some of the innovative features of the North German Confederation, such as a democratically elected *Reichstag*, were extended to the new empire but at the same time the south German states were wooed with federalist provisions for significant internal autonomy. [See 20 for the text of the constitution; 133 *chap. 8* and 134 *pp. 364–77* for Bismarck's thinking.] Austria now recognised that there was no prospect of altering its 1866 exclusion from Germany [66 *pp. 51–9*; 131 *chap. 7*].

Beust, ever the realist in search of a way of securing enduring links between all the different parts of Germany, was quick to adjust policy accordingly. Through the 1850s and until 1866, as Saxon minister he had tried to secure federal reform through the 'third Germany' of the medium states, a reform which would bind Austria and Prussia to a German political system. From 1866 to 1870, as Austrian first minister, he had tried to work out ways in which some of the results of the Austro-Prussian war could be undone [120]. Now he recognised that there was no way in which Austria could be included as part of a federal German state. Rather, the Austro-German link could only be secured at the diplomatic level. In May 1871, in a report to Franz Joseph, he summarised the main element of such a policy:

> ... the achievement of the dominance of central Europe in the balance of Europe's future through an agreement between Austria-Hungary and Prussian Germany embracing all current affairs with the declared aim of preserving world peace. [Quoted in 131 *p. 178*]

Beust himself did not usher in such a policy; he was dismissed following the setback of 1871. However, Austria soon concluded a conservative alliance with Russia and Germany, to some extent returning to a pre-1848 policy. In 1879 Austria concluded an alliance with Bismarck which turned it into Germany's subordinate ally [57 *chap. 5*]. It was the most enduring alliance into which both states entered. However, it did not have the ultimate outcome Beust had hoped for. Rather, it bound the two states together into their entry into war in 1914, a war which would lead to the defeat of both states and the final destruction of Austria-Hungary.

PART THREE | ANALYSIS AND ASSESSMENT

CHAPTER EIGHT

COMPARING AUSTRIA WITH PRUSSIA

INTRODUCTORY COMMENTS

Around 1800 Austria appeared the more powerful of the two major German states. Until 1812 it more often and effectively opposed revolutionary and Napoleonic France than did Prussia. Austria committed more soldiers in the war of 1813–15. At the 1815 peace settlement Austria was confirmed as a power with wide-ranging European interests and the leading state in Germany, symbolised by the office of Presidency of the German Confederation. Prussia followed Austria's political lead in the 1820s and 1830s, despite taking the initiative in the formation of the *Zollverein*. Prussia briefly pursued an assertive policy in Germany in 1849–50 but abandoned it when directly confronted by Austria. At that time (Table III.3) Prussia had an army strength on paper of less than one-third that of Austria.

Between 1850 and 1866 it seems that Prussia 'overtook' Austria. A confrontation, avoided by Prussia in 1850 as likely to end in defeat, was sought in 1866 and resulted in decisive triumph. However, were contemporaries, even such well-placed ones as Bismarck, aware of the changes which underlay such a presumed and rapid shift in the relative power of the two states? Indeed, can the historian, even with the benefit of hindsight, provide persuasive evidence for such changes? Might it not be the case that success was more the result of chance and individual skill than the probable outcome of crucial superiorities? (One could certainly argue such a case for the eventual success of Frederick the Great's Prussia in war against Austria.) Might historians be projecting back such superiorities from the mere fact of success?

Here I will consider the problem of measuring the relative power of two states in order to explain the outcome of conflict between them. Included are some tables which provide statistical comparisons. This analytical chapter takes a different approach from that of the earlier, mainly narrative chapters. There is nevertheless a good deal of overlap. The two approaches are intended to complement one another. Accompanying tables are placed at the end of the chapter.

THE RESOURCES OF A STATE

Population

The most basic resource of a state is its population (Table I.1). In 1820 the Austrian and Prussian populations within the German Confederation were roughly the same. Austria, however, had much more territory and population outside the German Confederation. Consequently, even with a less productive economy, Austria could collect more state revenue and support larger armies than Prussia (Tables III.2 and III.3). However, the population of Prussia grew at roughly twice the rate of that of Austrian Germany over the next fifty years. By 1866 there were seven million more Prussians in the German Confederation than Austrians. This had at least two implications.

First, assuming that people living in the German Confederation, whether in Prussia, Austria or the rest of Germany, were more positively inclined to greater German unity than people living outside the Confederation, the balance of such inclination had shifted heavily towards Prussia.[1] Furthermore, non-German populations were generally hostile to greater German unity unless it advanced their own interests. In the Habsburg Italian provinces this led to support for Prussian-led national unity because that helped bring about independence from Vienna. In Hungary it stimulated opposition to risky policies promoting German interests.

Such attitudes relate to the political loyalties of different segments of the population. Many 'Italians' or 'Hungarians' were not especially concerned with or even aware of national issues. This was especially so amongst peasants and agricultural workers who made up the majority of the population. However, it also was the case amongst higher social classes, especially the nobility of landowners, civil servants and military officers where a combination of regional and dynastic loyalties predominated over that of nationality. The greater mix of nationalities in the Habsburg Empire would only be a source of weakness relative to Prussia if national identity and loyalty itself increased in importance. There is some evidence that this did happen in the Habsburg Italian provinces and Hungary and amongst some Slav groups such as Czech speakers, partly related to key events like the 1848–49 revolutions and partly in conjunction with urban growth and the development of commercial manufacturing and agriculture. (There is not space here to divert into important debates about what causes national

---

[1] Obviously one cannot simply equate inhabitants of the German Confederation with German speakers or pro-German national sentiment, as the existence of Czech speakers in Bohemia and Polish speakers in eastern Prussia, many of whom were hostile to incorporation within a German nation-state, makes clear. But broadly speaking, the correlation works with the major exceptions of these two examples.

identity to increase in extent, intensity and political importance. See the surveys of such debates in 40 and 42.)

Also important is the political influence of various groups. Austria and Prussia began to develop constitutional politics between 1848 and 1860 and only for restricted groups. For a brief moment in 1848–49 the opinions of peasants and artisans mattered, but this was exceptional. The views of Magyar magnates or, increasingly, Rhenish bankers, counted for much more. There was roughly an inverse relationship between the obedience and usefulness of different kinds of subjects. A rich taxpayer or a highly trained army officer was of greater value to the state than a pauper or an illiterate infantryman, but also was less submissive. These considerations of loyalties and influence require us to move from a state's population as a quantitative matter to judgements about its qualities.

Economy

Quantitative comparisons

The first such judgement concerns economics. In the early 1850s statisticians were clear that Prussia and the other *Zollverein* states were economically far superior to Austria, even leaving aside the backward eastern half of the Empire.[2] Furthermore, Prussian economic growth after 1850 was faster than in Austria as well as qualitatively distinct. However, the contrast between a backward and stagnant Austria and a dynamic and modernising Prussia has been exaggerated. One problem lies in the way the statistics are often presented. Long-run statistical series constructed after 1871, for example covering the period from 1815 to 1914, take the territory of the German Second Empire or the German Customs Union as it was by 1865 and compare this with the territory of the post-1867 Habsburg Empire [166; 169]. This is reasonable for measuring long-term trends but has the effect of projecting back the outcome of German unification into the earlier period. The whole point of 'snapshot' comparisons is that Prussia and Austria in 1850, 1860 and 1866 have both changed a good deal and it is the differences these short-run changes have made to their relative power that we are trying to grasp.

---

2   See, for example, Albert Kotelmann, *Vergleichende Statistische Übersicht über die landwirtschaftlichen und industriellen Verhältnisse Oestreichs und des deutschen Zollvereins so wie seiner einzelnen Staaten* (Berlin, 1852). This statistical comparison of the Austrian and Prussian/*Zollverein* economies was intended to contribute to the discussion about Austria joining the *Zollverein* or signing a trade treaty with it. Kotelmann uses official statistics to document that Austrian agriculture was less productive than that of the *Zollverein* while also forming a much larger part of the whole economy and that the main competitive advantage of Austria in less technically advanced branches of manufacturing was much lower wages.

No one seriously denies Prussian economic superiority in 1850 and in growth rates in the two decades following [see Tables II.1, II.2, IV.1 and IV.2]. However, economic historians have recently argued that not only was there considerable growth in the Austrian economy over the period 1825–70, but that its extent has previously been badly underestimated [112]. Also, the picture is modified by taking into account regional variations. Figures for urbanisation, manufacturing, per capita income or formal schooling fall dramatically as one moves eastwards from the Austrian to the Hungarian half of the Empire. There were regions in Bohemia or around Vienna which were economically advanced and which compared favourably to the more backward provinces of Prussia.

Qualitative comparisons

Also important is qualitative economic comparison. If one compares cotton spinning, production in mid-century Austria was well ahead of Prussia. The opposite is the case when comparing railway construction or iron and steel production [Tables III.1, IV.1 and IV.2]. This shifts the perspective from the economy generally to specific ways in which the economy conditions the power of the state.

Bucholz has argued persuasively that the wars of German unification represent the 'beginning of the modern' in military history [68]. Superior rail transportation enabled Prussia to move its armies into northern Bohemia quickly, throwing the Austrian army leadership off balance [74; 87; 91]. The right combination of precision engineering and mass production had only come about in the early 1860s. Only on this basis was Prussia able to re-equip the army with the breech-loading rifle in time for the war of 1866 and then again to mass produce improved and expanded artillery by 1870. [See 92, including the importation of US precision engineering techniques, though this was more important for 1870 than 1866.] Faster movement of troops and supplies and superior firepower (rifles in 1866, artillery in 1870) were crucial to Prussian success and these possibilities had only emerged in the decade before the actual wars of unification on the basis of specific economic and technological capacities. Yet the existence of a superior rail network, coal, iron and steel industries, and techniques of precision engineering were not the result of state military planning; rather they were functions of independent economic development which could then be exploited for military purposes. (The needs of the army did influence the location of specific railways and the establishment of particular engineering works but only on the basis of a more general, prior development.)

The very recent and innovative nature of these technologies helps explain why contemporaries had little appreciation for what had changed. It is striking, for example, that one finds nowhere in Bismarck any sense that in the reformed Prussian army he controls a new kind of war-making enterprise which will dramatically change the art of warfare. [This important 'negative' observation is made in 68.] In a memorandum written in February 1860, Moltke, Chief of the Prussian Army General Staff and the individual with the deepest insight into what was changing, had not thought there could be any decisive and quick victory over Austria, even if it was possible to keep the war isolated from any wider diplomatic entanglements. (Admittedly Moltke tended to put pessimistic scenarios forward, in part to buttress the case for more military provision.) No wonder the general opinion was that the war would be protracted and that Austria would be the probable winner.

Society and culture

I have considered economic comparison in two respects: the general level of development and growth and certain key technologies with military implications. Clearly the two are related. A more complex and advanced economy, with higher levels of urban and manufacturing populations, favours a greater development of new forms of transportation such as railways and has more capital as well as know-how to use for technically advanced forms of production.

Economic differences relate to social differences. Generally speaking, the role of formal education increases with the advance of urban living and manufacturing activity, although Prussia was noted for its well-developed elementary schooling system and high level of literacy even before such developments. Prussia was clearly well ahead of Austria at the levels of elementary, secondary and university education (Table II.3).

Under pre-modern conditions, such a difference would not necessarily favour the state with the better educated population. Indeed, when military force was primarily a matter of forcing illiterate peasants and workers into the army under traditional aristocratic leadership, in many respects the more educated, arguably civilised society was the weaker state. The Greeks could not withstand the Romans; eighteenth-century Saxony could not withstand Prussia. However, the 'beginning of the modern' in matters of war altered this relationship fundamentally.

First, the success of French armies in the revolutionary and Napoleonic period led to a serious questioning about the value of armies made up of forcibly conscripted peasants and workers or augmented with paid mercenaries. An army of citizens, it was argued, was more committed to the cause of the state because such soldiers regarded that state as their own. Committed and intelligent citizens showed initiative, could be trusted to act without constant surveillance by officers, provided a pool of talent for promotion by merit which raised the quality of officers. These lessons were taken especially seriously by the Prussian military reformers who acquired power following the disastrous defeat of 1806–7. In 1813 Prussia introduced the principle that all adult males were obliged to perform military service [*Doc. 8*]. It was the only European power which held to this principle after 1815. The British army was a volunteer force until 1916. The French diluted universal conscription by allowing wealthier men to purchase substitutes and only moved back to universal conscription after 1870. Russia and Austria followed the principle of selective conscription which focused on the lower orders so far as rank-and-file soldiers were concerned.

That principle was admittedly diluted. University education entitled one to a reduced period of service. The demobilisation of the mass army after 1815, coupled with the failure of conscription to keep up with general population growth into the 1860s, undermined the idea of a *universal* obligation. The aristocracy re-established its hold over the officer corps [73]. Furthermore, Prussia did not grant the constitution promised by Frederick William III during the War of Liberation [*Doc. 13*] and so there was no mass citizenry. There did remain certain distinct qualities – for example, the use of a lottery to decide which of a particular age-class should be conscripted, and the continued existence of the reserve or territorial army (*Landwehr*) in which all men were supposed to serve after their two-year term in the regular army. However, the conservative leadership of the state regarded the *Landwehr* with intense suspicion as both militarily ineffective and politically unreliable. The reforms of the early 1860s which produced the triumphant armies of 1864, 1866 and 1870–71 included the marginalisation of the *Landwehr* and, for precisely that reason, were opposed by the liberal majority in parliament, thus leading to the constitutional crisis which brought Bismarck to power.

On the other hand, the expansion of the Prussian army in the 1860s restored meaning to the idea of universal obligation to military service. Furthermore, the granting of a constitution in 1848, even if arbitrarily altered in authoritarian ways in the early 1850s, did give the idea of political citizenship more substance. By contrast, Austrian constitutional experiments came much later (1860–61) and on a much more limited basis.

By the early 1860s there were two further important qualitative differences between the Austrian and the Prussian armies which relate to social differences and post-Napoleonic reform. The first, at elite level, concerns the rising influence of a relatively new institution, the General Staff, and will be considered in the next section. The second, at popular level, concerns education and the new technical demands of warfare. I will take one important example: the adoption of the needle-gun by Prussia shortly before 1866, coupled with the decision of Austria not to adopt this weapon. [See 87 *part 2* for this whole section.]

The idea of a breech-loading rifle had been around for some time before the Prussian army decided to re-equip with one particular model, the Dreyse. The Austrian authorities also knew about the weapon and in principle could have also acquired it. Some reasons for not doing so (and these were considerations shared by all armies apart from that of Prussia up to 1866 and were even expressed by some Prussian officers) were purely military [91 *pp. 21–5*]. There were doubts about the reliability of the weapon, as breech-loaders had a propensity to jam or to explode, especially under conditions of mass production. The Austrians had observed French success with infantry hand-to-hand fighting and the use of the bayonet in 1859 and used this themselves to good effect in the war against Denmark in 1864. Other reasons are financial. The Austrian government was cutting back military expenditure in the early 1860s and such a massive re-equipping would have been very expensive.

However, there are also considerations relating to social differences. Re-equipping the infantry in this way was a challenge to basic military instruction and depended on how officers regarded their men. The breech-loading rifle was used in a completely different way from the muzzle-loader. With the muzzle-loader men had to stand or at least kneel in order to re-load. They could only fire one shot at a time. A drill developed whereby one row of men fired their rifles in a volley and then knelt to re-load while the row behind them fired a volley, and so on. The whole process could be regimented in a precise, timed fashion by officers.

The breech-loader, by contrast, could be loaded and fired by men lying down. Furthermore, one could fire off a number of shots before having to re-load. This raised two issues. First, there needed to be a re-training process. Obviously, if there was high literacy at the level of non-commissioned officers, then in part this could be achieved through the distribution of clearly written and short manuals. It also would help if one only needed to do that in one language. Both these requirements were fulfilled for the Prussian army; neither for the Austrian army. The widespread ability to read and write in one language gave the Prussian army a crucial advantage faced with such a technical challenge. Furthermore, the Prussian army was prepared to invest in much more intensive (and expensive) training than the Austrians, using five times the number of bullets per soldier [91 *p. 24*].

Second, there are the attitudes officers took towards their men. (There has been little study of this so far as I know and this section is therefore a little speculative.) The great danger of the breech-loading rifle was that men would fall to the ground more to avoid harm than to fight effectively, and then would waste their ammunition firing wildly in the general direction of the enemy. There was an especial fear that such soldiers would not be able to take part in second-phase movements. The drill of the muzzle-loader avoided this danger. Conversely, the great advantage of the needle-gun was that the rifleman could operate more effectively and independently. If one had little trust in the infantrymen, the danger would be emphasised; a greater level of trust stressed the advantage. The more educated, socially integrated, single-language Prussian army tended to trust; the less educated, socially selective and multi-language Austrian army to distrust. Armies have to be seen as cultural as well as purely military institutions and such variations in trust or distrust must be taken into account.

Interestingly, the French army – closer to the Prussian than the Austrian model – was also by 1870 equipped with an effective breech-loading rifle, the *chassepot*, which actually outperformed the Prussian needle-gun. Fortunately for Prussia, superior artillery now mattered more. However, that also had involved rapid re-equipping and an intensive and expensive re-training programme between 1866 and 1870. The revelation of inferiority in rifles in 1870 in turn led to another upgrade (to the Mauser) which again involved increased expenditure, highly technical production capacities and rapid and intensive re-training. This is the beginning of the modern arms race where economic resources, technology, education and training count for much more than before. The nature of Prussian society, still deferential to monarchical authority, but relatively well-educated and socially fairly integrated through the system of conscription, fitted Prussia better than Austria for meeting these challenges at the outset.

Other differences which have been suggested are less persuasive. The various nationalities of the Habsburg army may have presented problems in terms of training and coordination because of different languages but this does not seem to have reduced morale or combat-readiness significantly. That was much more apparent in the Italian army in 1866, where language as well as regional and political divisions (central and southern Italy had only just come under the rule of the Piedmontese monarchy) were apparent not just amongst serving troops but also in the decision not even to try to recruit soldiers from some areas. [See 91 *chaps 4 and 5* for some vivid examples.] Equally, Catholic soldiers and those who served in state armies which fought on the Austrian side in 1866 (Hannover, Hesse, Württemberg, Bavaria and, most effectively, Saxony) seem to have served just as effectively on the Prussian side in the war against France in 1870. It is not possible to make an easy correlation between 'nationality', confessional or state identity and conduct in war.

THE CAPACITIES OF THE STATE

It is not enough to have superior resources in demographic, economic, social and cultural terms, and to have broad support from key elites and large sections of the population. The state has to be able to use these resources effectively. I will briefly look at the issues of money, public opinion and military organisation.

Money

Austrian public finances were always in a poor state after 1815. There were numerous reasons for this. Austria had a much wider range of diplomatic commitments than Prussia which made it difficult to retrench. A less productive economy provided fewer resources for taxation. Added to that, the maintenance of fiscal privileges, especially in the Hungarian half of the Empire, blocked possible sources of revenue. Austrian state debt was much higher in both absolute and relative terms than that of Prussia (see Tables III.2 and IV.1) These financial problems were compounded by Austrian military mobilisation during the Crimean War. Between 1847 and 1859 Austrian public debt increased almost three-fold compared to a near-doubling in Prussia. The lost war of 1859 created a crisis for Austria. It had to pay much higher rates of interest on loans than Prussia and to offer to sell increasingly valuable securities such as state-owned railways. Around 26 per cent of Austrian state revenue was now servicing public debt, compared to 11 per cent for Prussia. Even then, by 1860 Austria was finding it almost impossible to find anyone who would lend it money [103 *chap. 4*]. This led to two policies: a severe cut-back in public expenditure and the adoption of a constitutionalist policy designed to increase public confidence and credit-worthiness.

Thus between 1860 and 1865 military expenditure was moving in opposite directions in Austria and Prussia. The most obvious result was in army sizes (Table III.3) where the superiority of Austria dropped from a ratio of 3.5 to one in 1850 to 1.5 in 1860 and 1.3 in 1866, the latter more than compensated by the involvement of the Italian army. Not only that, but Prussian military expenditure on each soldier by now was significantly higher, as evidenced in the scale and frequency of exercises or the use of live ammunition in training. We have already seen how this relates to the difference in the rifles used by Prussian and Austrian infantrymen in 1866.

This is not to say that Prussia did not have financial problems. However, they were of a different order. In the Prussian case it was the constitutional crisis which blocked the raising of extra taxes through parliamentary consent and which made bankers jittery about lending large sums. That was possibly one reason why Prussia avoided war with Austria in 1865. Bismarck was forced to resort to novel methods, involving the sale of railway and mining assets, in preparing for 1866 [103]. After that, however, victory brought with it reconciliation with parliament and the imposition of a large indemnity on Austria. The financial problems prior to 1870 were minor by comparison.

Public opinion

The war of 1866 was a 'cabinet war', that is, it was a result of decisions made by a small elite at the top of the state relatively independently of any broader opinion (unlike, for example, France in 1870). There had been some attempts to influence public opinion, for example in the various reform proposals which Prussia and Austria bandied about between 1861 and 1866. It is doubtful whether these had much positive impact. Few even in Prussia were prepared to believe that Bismarck, ruling in defiance of parliament, would really reform national institutions in a liberal direction. Austrian reform proposals did not even make such promises but were rather about giving more say to the princes of the medium states. When the war came, there was little enthusiasm and much hostility throughout Germany to both states.

The situation was different on the battle over the *Zollverein*. The same Prussian *Landtag* which opposed Bismarck on constitutional and diplomatic matters greeted the trade treaty of 1862 with France and the imposition of this agreement upon the other states in the *Zollverein* by 1865 with great enthusiasm. It was not difficult for Prussia to coerce the other members of the *Zollverein* into agreement, not just through exploiting their fear of lost state revenue but also by appealing beyond them to public, especially business, opinion which clearly felt that continued membership of the *Zollverein* was vital to their economic well-being. Conversely, the very same Austrian-German middle-class opinion and money which the Habsburg government was courting through constitutional concessions remained fearful of opening itself up to full-blooded competition from the *Zollverein* states.

Some historians conclude from this that the *Zollverein* issue prefigured the political outcome [the path-breaking work is 143]. The most important new economic interests in the 'third Germany' recognised their ties with Prussia while similar groups amongst Germans in Austria looked to a protected position within the Empire. Certainly this can help explain the sharp shifts in public opinion which occurred after Königgrätz. On the one hand, there was a sudden wave of enthusiasm in Prussia as well as amongst national and liberal groups in other north and central German states [114; 122; but see also 59 *pp. 909–11* for more negative responses]. It was partly on that basis that Bismarck could now implement some of the reforms he had promised. At the same time, in Austrian Germany public opinion was against any continuation of the war. Austrian Germans saw little to be gained by trying to assert Habsburg interests in the rest of Germany. Their main concern before 1866 had been that without that assertion through some policy of greater political and economic integration, German influence in the Empire itself might be endangered. However, they were not prepared to sacrifice economic interests which such a policy of integration required. After 1866 they pursued a different tack: agreement to allow Hungary much greater autonomy in the eastern, coupled with the pursuit of German domination in the western, half of the Empire [21; 57 *chap.* 5; 58 *chap.* 7].

However, although these features of public opinion can help explain why Austria so rapidly sued for peace *after* one lost battle, they do not explain that defeat itself. Our final comparison must be military.

Military organisation

The 'beginning of the modern' [68] displayed in the wars of German unification exploited new forms of transport (railways), communications (telegraph), and weapons technology and production (rifles, artillery). Prussia was well-endowed in these respects relative to its opponents and that was a key to success in 1866 and again in 1870–71. [See 68 and 87 for this whole section.]

However, the key word in the paragraph above is 'exploited'. It was not merely that Austria and France did not have these resources to the same degree as Prussia. Indeed, in the French case, arguably there was parity if not superiority in some of these things. Crucial was that they did not exploit them to the same extent.

The key to this difference was the Prussian Army General Staff. Set up by Napoleonic reformers, this organisation provided certain valuable technical services to the army: good maps, historical analyses of campaigns, the preparation of war games and summer manoeuvres. Yet it remained a marginal organisation until beyond mid-century. Its Chief, von Moltke, had had limited battlefield experience in the 1830s in the service of the Ottoman Empire. That and his humble origins, in a world which still stressed aristocratic and dynastic leadership and the virtue of physical courage (whether hunting or fighting), put him fairly low down the leading offices in court and army. He did not play as major a role in the army reforms of the early 1860s as did von Roon, the Minister of War. Yet, key changes in the early 1860s meant that by the opening stage of the Austro-Prussian War von Moltke was effectively in charge of the army when the king decreed that henceforth orders coming from Moltke be regarded as royal commands.

The main reason for this change was that the organisation of knowledge took on a new meaning under modern conditions. [This whole section is indebted to 68.] A combination of technical innovation and the increase in the speed and scale of military operations presented military planners with unprecedented challenges. Railways provide a good example. Their existence made it possible to bring together soldiers and equipment more quickly, in larger quantities and from a greater geographical area than had been possible before. These widely distributed resources had then to be channelled into a smaller and smaller area, culminating in their concentration upon a single battlefield. When the war with Austria started on 6 June 1866 military operations were taking place over an area of 40,000 square miles; by 23 June this had reduced to 2,500 square miles; on 2 July to 40 square miles; and on the afternoon of 3 July was concentrated on an area of four square miles. In effect a new dimension of military warfare – operational planning and its implementation – had interposed itself between the level of strategy (planning the war as a whole) and tactics (making decisions once battle was joined). A new method of organisation was required for this. As such an organisation became central, it also took in hand strategic and tactical planning.

Such operations could only be conducted by means of the effective collection, coordination and use of a huge amount of information. The timetable (an organised coordination of future time and space) took on a new significance. By early April 1866 the General Staff had constructed a precise timetable for future operations stretching forward seventy-five days. The timetable included the gathering of troops at their home stations; the entrainment of whole battalions (the lowest level at which one had a 'complete' unit combining the various military functions) and their equipment. It involved assuming train movements of constant speed, making allowance for single-track as well as double-track lines. Moltke built into this timetable a system of allowances for inevitable breakdowns and delays. The timetable required constant updating and the time calculations became increasingly short and precise as enemy troops closed in on one another.

The recognition that such planning would take on a new importance became clear with an analysis of the Franco-Austrian War of 1859 in which the French made effective use of railways. Also important was the experience of the botched Prussian mobilisation during that war. The General Staff began to move closer to the centre of decision-making. From 1862 to 1863 Moltke was also analysing the American Civil War which already displayed certain features of the 'modern', especially on the Union side. Yet at the start of the 1864 war with Denmark, von Moltke was still no more than a key adviser, some advance on five years earlier but still not at the centre of command. During that war the failure of top commanders, contrasted with Moltke's meticulous planning and implementation of a massive artillery barrage which led to the successful storming of the Danish fortress of Dybbol, made clear to the king what a valuable resource he had in the General Staff. At this stage much still depended on William making the decision to put the modern planner in command but conditions now made this a conceivable action. Once this decision had paid off so handsomely in 1866, the die was set not just for Prussia but generally. In Prussia the General Staff was expanded and developed more specialised branches.

Systematic experimentation and planning, as well as an intensive analysis of 1866, were accepted with far less resistance as the basis for future war-making. The army (including non-Prussian units) tripled in size between 1866 and 1870, presenting larger planning challenges. There was a complete modernisation of the artillery by 1870. This war was conducted on a much greater scale than that of 1866, mobilising a little over one million men in the first eighteen days, nearly half of whom were by then in France.

Other armies learnt the lesson and a powerful general staff had become the rule by 1900. Austria expanded and upgraded its General Staff immediately after 1867. By then it was too late. Austria had actually run down its fairly small and unimportant General Staff in the 1850s. The main lessons learnt from the 1859 war concerned tactics rather than operations. (The Austrians noted that their rifle fire had been ineffective and that the French had closed on them with bayonets to good effect. The Austrian conclusion was to emulate the French; von Moltke's conclusion was to improve rifle fire. The Austrians also improved their artillery which out-performed the Prussian artillery in 1866.) Franz Joseph resolved never to assume personal command again. However, the appointment of Ludwig von Benedek as commanding general in Hungary was based on Benedek's battlefield prowess (he had distinguished himself in a successful action at Solferino in 1859). Simultaneously making Benedek Chief of the General Staff was actually an indication of the low regard in which such planning was held.

Prussia was favoured by a conjunction of events: a planning staff inherited from the Napoleonic period; rapid technological progress in the 1855–65 decade which could only be handled effectively by such a staff; opportunities for learning about certain modern practices in wars involving others (the Crimean War, the war of 1859, the American Civil War); and non-crucial failures on the part of the Prussian army itself (the mobilisation of 1859; the early stages of the war against Denmark in 1864). This led to military modernisation and brought the hitherto marginal planning institution into a more central position. This culminated with the decision by the king to give command to von Moltke. Military historians may still debate whether, by the time battle was joined in both 1866 and 1870, there were chances for the war to go another way, but there is no question that by being the first to exploit so systematically the 'beginning of the modern' in warfare, Prussia created the necessary conditions for victory in those wars.

STATISTICAL COMPARISONS BETWEEN AUSTRIA AND PRUSSIA

I. *Population*

1. Snapshot population statistics for 1820, 1841 and 1866

	1820[1]	*1841*	*1866*
Habsburg Empire[2]	25.5	30.7[3]	34.8
German Austria[4]	9.5		12.0[5]
Prussia[6]	11.7	15.1	19.5
Germany[7]	13.9	16.4	18.3

[1] The figures for Austria and the Habsburg Empire were reckoned for 1821; for Prussia and the remaining German lands for 1822.

[2] This does not include the Italian provinces of Lombardy and Venetia.

[3] The figure is for 1850.

[4] By German Austria is meant that part of the Empire which belonged to the German Confederation. This excludes the whole of the eastern/Hungarian half, Galicia, Lombardy and Venetia.

[5] This figure is for 1869.

[6] This is the figure for all of the territories belonging to Prussia between 1815 and 1864. This includes territory which was never (Posen), or not until 1848 (East and West Prussia), part of the German Confederation. It does not include territory acquired by Prussia between 1864 and 1871.

[7] By Germany is meant the states belonging to the German Confederation other than Austria and Prussia.

[Compiled from a range of sources]

II. *Social and economic indicators*

1. Industrial production (measured in £ millions)

	Germany (1871 territory)	*Austria (excluding Hungary)*
1800	60	50
1820	85	80
1840	150	142
1860	310	200

[155 p. 89]

2. Per capita production *c.* 1840 (measured in Gulden)

Economic sector	*Zollverein*	*All Austria-Hungary*	*German and Italian Austria*	*Hungary and Galicia*
Agriculture	46.3	27.6	29.3	25.6
Handicrafts (*Kleinbewerbe*)	15.2	3.6	5.6	1.7
Industry	8.1	4.0	6.2	1.9
Total	70.0	35.0	41.0	30.0

[155 p. 89]

3.   Education

Figures in 1,000s	Primary school pupils	Secondary school pupils	University students
Austria[1] 1840	1365	20.5	8.6
Austria 1860	1656	36.7	8.0
Prussia 1840	2224	123.0	11.6
Prussia 1860	2778	172.9	12.4

[1] Excluding the Hungarian half of the Empire.

NB. It is difficult to believe that in 1860, when the populations of Prussia and cisleithian Austria were approximately the same (about 18 million each), Prussia had about five times as many secondary school pupils, and yet only about 50 per cent more university students. Two possible explanations are that the secondary school statistics for Prussia included *Gymnasien* (grammar schools) which are sometimes included in the figure for 'higher education', and that Austrian statistics badly undercounted secondary school pupils. Whatever, it is clear that a much higher proportion of Prussians than Austrians stayed in education beyond elementary school.

[For Austria, 169 *p. 396*; for Prussia, 166 *pp. 224–30*]

4.   Railways (kilometres in operation)

	Austria-Hungary	Prussia
1841	351	375
1847	1,048	2,325
1850	1,357	2,967
1860	2,927[1]	5,762
1865	3,698	6,895
1870	6,112	11,460[2]

[1] However, 155 *p. 328* gives a figure of 2,345 for 1851 and 5,393 for 1860. This would in turn mean correspondingly larger figures for 1865 and 1870. I cannot explain these discrepancies but if true, they are very important because Lutz's figures suggest near parity between Austria and Prussia, whereas the other figures suggest that Prussia is well in advance of Austria. I have not discovered any other authority which gives such high figures for Austria and cannot locate Lutz's source so am inclined to set aside this discrepancy.

[2] This includes areas annexed to Prussia in 1867.

[Compiled from: 168 *pp. 792–3* and 169 *pp.315–17*; plus data for Prussia from 166 *p. 80* and 163/I *pp. 69-70*]

III.   Political and military indicators

1.   Key industrial outputs in 1870 (millions of tons)

	Austria	Germany[1]
Coal	6.3	23.3
Steel	0.02	0.13

[1] Almost all coal and steel production in Germany was in fact on Prussian territory.

[169 *pp. 188–9, 223* and 166 *p. 64*].

2. Public expenditure

Millions of Thalers[1]	Austria	Prussia
1857	262.8	122.8
1867	668.0	171.0
1870	299.0	212.9

[1] The exchange rate was about 6.8 Prussian Thalers to 9.6 Austrian Gulden.

[103 *p. 123*]

3. Army sizes

	Austria	Prussia
1850	434,000	131,000
1860	306,000	201,000
1866	275,000	214,000[1]

[1] Prussia's ally, Italy, had in 1866 an army with a paper strength of 233,000.

[167 *p. 251*]

IV. A series of comparisons, 1865–66

1. Between Austria and Prussia

	Austria	Prussia
Population (millions)	37.5	19.3
Percentage labour force in agriculture	70	45
Grain production (million tons)	0.7	0.8
Fixed steam engines/millions horsepower	3,400/0.1	15,000/0.8
Coal production (millions tons)	5.7	12
Pig iron production (tons)	460,000	850,000
State revenue (millions of Thalers)	292	240
State debt (millions of Thalers)	1,670	290
Military spending (millions of Thalers)	51	45

[155 *p. 330*]

2. Between a number of states in 1850

	Rlys (km)	Raw iron (1,000 tons)	Cotton spindles	Steam power [1,000 PS]
Habsburg Empire	1,579	130	1,400	100
Great Britain	10,660	1,975	18,000	1,290
Germany [1871 territory]	5,839	215	900	260
France	3,009	525	4,500	270
Belgium	855	214	400	70
Russia	618	232	350 (1843)	70

[156 *p. 117*]

CONCLUDING REMARKS

Nothing is inevitable; it only appears so after it has happened. Even to contemporaries who noted the systematic development of superiorities on the part of Prussia compared to Austria, the rapid exclusion of Austria from the rest of Germany was unexpected. Furthermore, that very rapidity does suggest other possibilities. France and Russia soon regretted their failure to intervene more effectively. Even if Austria on its own was less powerful than Prussia by the mid-1860s, diplomatic coalitions and military alliances often can make up for such inferiority. (This is why estimates of success cannot just involve comparing states as isolated units.) Precisely because the novel changes to war-making were not appreciated, such coalitions were not formed. Equally, the rapid and unexpected triumph of 1866 provided the base for that of 1870, something quite impossible to predict before 1866. That, plus the continued failure to appreciate just what new forms of power the Prussian state had succeeded in creating, meant that in turn coalitions to prevent further Prussian success were not constructed.

Making comparisons as this chapter has done is therefore not to argue that Prussia was bound to win a struggle for supremacy in Germany with Austria. Rather it is to try to lay bare some of the necessary conditions for that success. In doing that I have tried to show how unintended and contingent were some of those conditions, how rapidly power balances could change, and how much depended upon the way leaders used those conditions. At the same time, without an analysis of those conditions, there is a danger either of making the whole process appear inevitable or of reducing it to the genius of Bismarck and Moltke.

CHAPTER NINE

CONCLUSION

For centuries Germany was a cultural and political 'zone', not a country with distinct boundaries and certainly not a state. Powerful states with their core territories inside the roughly defined German zone sought to expand their power and influence both in that zone and beyond. Equally powerful states with their core territory outside the German zone, such as Russia, France and Sweden (briefly in the seventeenth century) pursued certain interests within the zone, both in terms of territory and influence. Some contemporaries, for example during the period of the Thirty Years' War, bemoaned the weakness of the political arrangements within the zone (too many small states, a lack of unity amongst the larger states) and how this could make it the battleground for wider conflicts of a confessional or dynastic character. People living in sixteenth-century Italy and eighteenth-century Poland made the same points. A stress on nationality tended to express a concern for independence rather than unity.

However, the periods of being battlegrounds alternated with other periods of relative peace, stability and prosperity. Then some people hailed the advantages of many small states or decentralised political arrangements which promoted culture or good administration rather than glory and power. The Holy Roman Empire was praised as a peace and legal order, rather than criticised for not being a power order. Even those who called for more political and military cooperation did not envisage the construction of a nation-state but rather more effective inter-state coordination. Sometimes a 'protector' state would gloss its actions as conducive to national unity and dignity. Thus did Frederick the Great justify his anti-Austrian policies. Napoleon and those he placed as rulers of satellite states claimed to defend 'Polish' or 'Italian' interests against Russia, Austria, Prussia and Britain, and the Confederation of the Rhine conferred on Napoleon himself the title of Protector [*Doc. 1(a)*]. It is difficult to know how seriously such rhetoric was taken. Perhaps its real significance is as rhetoric; it did indicate a new way of talking about politics.

What gave this political language an added appeal was, by the late eighteenth century, the success of Britain and France as 'national' states. Their examples made the idea of bringing a cultural zone under one political roof both more credible and attractive. The French revolution and the changes and responses this evoked beyond France enhanced the significance of principles of national unity and governments deriving their authority from the will of the people/nation. The rulers of Austria (1809) and Prussia and Russia (1812–14) [*Docs 9 and 10*] flirted with such views in public declarations aimed against France. However, these were easily ignored in the peace settlement of 1815, suggesting not only that they were not taken seriously by rulers but that they had not much influenced the political beliefs of subjects. In the German zone three rather different – but equally non-national and undemocratic political landscapes – took shape: the multi-national power of Austria with extensive non-German territories and concerns; the restored and more tightly organised state of Prussia with few non-German subjects; the enlarged, often new and constitutionally inclined medium states. These were all brought together in a loose political framework, the *Bund*, although how this would function in practice was unclear in 1815.

The struggle between these three elements, especially through attempts to manipulate the *Bund*, can in part be studied in terms of changing balances of power both between them and in relation to the broader European setting. One also has to build into the story the impact of social, economic and cultural change. These changes both conditioned and altered the balances of power and helped make the idea that national unity was advantageous and achievable more and more important. This happened first with the increasing intensity of communications and frequency of movement across regions and state boundaries. Second, there was, especially after 1850, an increase in the scale of capital investment and production and the development of regional divisions of labour which worked to make small state sovereignty appear increasingly obsolete or even a hindrance. Third, the same processes gave rise to new social groups (educated bureaucrats, modern entrepreneurs, skilled workers) who were directly interested in bringing about closer links across state boundaries. Finally, these processes also directly conditioned the power of states, most obviously with the 'beginning of the modern' in warfare which exploited new transport, communications and weapons technology.

All this made it increasingly likely that some or all of the German zone would be unified, economically and politically, under a system which explicitly took account of nationality and public opinion. From one point of view this was part of a more general European and later global story. However, what remained unsettled was how much of the German zone would be more effectively coordinated, which activities would be most affected (economic, cultural, political) and by what means this would happen. This book has focused on what emerged as the most important single conflict over this process, namely that between Austria and Prussia. The other possible instruments of unification – the medium states and a popular and powerful national movement – at different times had opportunities to take the lead but did not manage to do so. The medium states were too divided amongst themselves and too powerless in relation to either Prussia or Austria, let alone both of those states when they cooperated. The national movement was internally divided on confessional, state and political grounds and had limited popular appeal. Consequently, only one or both of the two major states had the potential to bring sufficient power to bear upon the forces tending to unification.

In this book I have sketched out how Austria and Prussia related to one another over the German question, how this relationship varied over time, how policy fluctuated in both states, and how these changes have to be related to both domestic and international politics. At first, Austria and Prussia worked together to use the *Bund* to produce a more streamlined and unified German political system but principally to repress unifying tendencies. Paradoxically, insofar as the two states made a reality of a national political system, they did so in order to prevent explicit moves towards national unity. Instead, Austria and Prussia tried to manipulate such unifying tendencies when they came into conflict with each other. Whichever state succeeded in this conflict would, therefore, have in part based its success on appeals to the nation. As it was, the 'solution' to the 'national question' came about through war, Prussian triumph and the division of the German cultural zone between the new state of Germany and the German part of the Habsburg Empire. To that solution was applied a national justification.

There was nothing inevitable about that result. There were moments when it seemed that Austria might extend its influence over much of Germany (e.g., in 1850) or when Prussia chose to work through a policy of dualism. Different military results could conceivably have led to a separation between a south, largely Catholic, and north, largely Protestant, section of Germany under the respective dominance of Austria and Prussia.

Equally, however, the actual outcome was not an accident. Certain modernising trends did favour Prussia over Austria. This was most evidently the case in the way in which the *Zollverein* anticipated the later German state. The advantages to medium states of membership in such a union were so great that eventually the rulers of those states were unable to break away, even if they were alarmed by the political costs involved. The significance of the *Zollverein* was not so much that it made Prussian-led unification inevitable as that it revealed the powerful economic and social forces tending towards unity, provided a model for the way forward, and gave Prussia important leverage. Increasingly, the probability was that if a unitary national state was created, it would be one which excluded Austria and was dominated by Prussia. However, this was only a probability. One can have economic coordination without political unity; political unity itself can take loose, confederal forms rather than involving the domination of one state over others. Certainly there appeared nothing inevitable about a Prussian-dominated *Kleindeutschland* until 1866.

It is people, operating under uncertain conditions without knowing what the future will bring, who turn probabilities into history. Only afterwards do historians make the mistake of thinking that once the probable has become the actual it can be regarded as inevitable. Bismarck himself expressed vividly an awareness of the way one has to balance the sense that one possible future can be brought about rather than others with the awareness that such a possibility can quickly appear and disappear and therefore that decisive action is required if it is to be realised. He often used the Latin phrase 'unda fert nec regitur' ('you can ride a wave, but not make it'). By the time Bismarck came to power the waves were starting to favour Prussia and Bismarck rode them well.

Documents are arranged in chronological order which is not always the order in which they are referred to in the text. Passages in italics are brief summaries of sections of documents. Where the title of a document does not make it self-evident I have added a brief characterisation of the document [in square brackets].

DOCUMENT 1   END OF EMPIRE AND FORMATION OF *RHEINBUND*

(A) ESTABLISHMENT OF *RHEINBUND*, 12 JULY 1806

His Majesty the Emperor of the French, King of Italy on the one side, and on the other side their Majesties the Kings of Bavaria and Württemberg, the Grand Duke of Baden ... [*there follow various German princes*] ... in order to secure internal and external peace for the heart of Germany, which both long experience and the most recent events have shown can no longer be guaranteed by the German Constitution, have drawn up the following agreement.

Article 1. The states of ... [*list of German rulers*] ... separate themselves in perpetuity from the territory of the German Empire and unite themselves in a specific association to be known as the Confederation of the Rhine ...

Article 12. His Majesty the Emperor of the French is proclaimed Protector of the Confederation.

[*Other articles stipulate titles and territories and transfer powers from Empire to* Rheinbund *states. Articles 35–38 detail how the states are to ally with France and commit soldiers to that alliance.*]

Huber, [10], pp. 28–34.

(B) *RHEINBUND* STATES LEAVE EMPIRE, 1 AUGUST 1806

... The events of the last three wars, which have disrupted Germany virtually without pause, and the political changes that have resulted, have made crystal clear the sad truth that the ties which presently link the various German states together no longer suffice, or more precisely have already been dissolved. ... Germany itself divided into a northern and a southern half in 1795 [*Peace of Basle between Prussia and France*] and from that moment all idea of a common fatherland and interest disappeared. ... The events of the last ten months have destroyed the last hopes [and] the princes of central and western Germany have decided to form a new association more fitted to the situation. ... The princes are secure of a powerful protector. ... His Majesty the Emperor of France ...

Huber, [10], pp. 35–6.

(C) EMPEROR FRANCIS II RENOUNCES IMPERIAL CROWN,
    6 AUGUST 1806

[*After chronicling recent events which have fatally undermined the Empire*]
... With this conviction that it is impossible any longer to discharge the
duties of our imperial office we are obliged ... to renounce a crown which
only has value in our eyes so long as we can fulfil the trust vested in us by
the Electors, princes, estates and other members of the German Empire ...

[*Declares Empire dissolved and with it any obligations between Austria
and other former members.*]

Huber, [10], pp. 37–9.

DOCUMENT 2　　PEACE OF TILSIT BETWEEN FRANCE AND
　　　　　　　PRUSSIA, 9 JULY 1807

Art. VII. The King of Prussia surrenders to the kings, grand dukes or
princes, as designated by the Emperor of France and King of Italy, all ...
territories ... as well as domains and landed property of every kind between
the Rhine and the Elbe which the King of Prussia ruled by whatever title at
the start of the present war.

　　Art. XIII. The King of Prussia surrenders in perpetuity all those
provinces which belonged to the Kingdom of Poland ... with the exception
of the Ermland and land to the west of old Prussia ...

　　Art. XXVII. Until peace is concluded between France and England all
Prussian territories without exception will be closed to English trade and
shipping. No ship may set sail for England from a Prussian harbour and no
ship coming from England or one of its colonies may sail into a Prussian
harbour ...

Demel and Puschner, [2], pp. 52–6.

DOCUMENT 3　　'A GOOD REVOLUTION': HARDENBERG'S RIGA
　　　　　　　MEMORANDUM

[Hardenberg, the future Prussian Chancellor, reflected in September 1807
on the reforms Prussia needed to introduce following its defeat by France.]

I. GENERAL CONSIDERATIONS

... The French Revolution, of which this present war is a continuation, gave
to the French, despite all the casualties and upheaval, a completely new
vitality. All slumbering forces were awakened, misery and weakness,
antiquated prejudices and crimes – admittedly along with some good things
– were destroyed. ...

The illusion that one can best combat revolution by holding fast to the old ways ... has actually promoted revolution. ... The power of the basic principles [underpinning the revolution] is so great ... that the state which does not accept them will either perish or be forced to adopt them.

Therefore, revolution in the good sense of the word ... that is our aim, our watchword. Democratic principles in a monarchical state seems to me to be the appropriate form for the spirit of the age. Pure democracy we must put off until the year 2440. ...

II. EXTERNAL RELATIONS

Independence is now an empty word.

How can we get it back? How can we avoid complete dependence?

As I see it Prussia must adopt the following principles.

Above all we must gather together forces to enable good organisation and effective planning of our internal affairs. Without delay we must arm again for struggle, insofar as we have the means, especially for our defence. Such a struggle could – probably will – come about quickly and it is urgently necessary to be ready. ...

We must not delude ourselves that we can remain neutral. ... It does not suit Prussia's circumstances and is completely impossible in the present situation. Only large and powerful states with a favourable situation can assert neutrality and avoid the entanglements which bring it to an end.

Above all we must show character. ... We have started to do this. Through its conduct in misfortune and true fortitude Prussia has won back something of the esteem it had lost and washed itself clean of the old political sins. ...

Avoid all conflicts so far as possible and give no grounds for conflict, so that we can win time during which we can strengthen ourselves.

Especially we must be extremely cautious in our dealings with Napoleon where there are still many issues to be resolved and he still holds the sword over us. Above all we must strive to get French soldiers off our land and be prepared for new sacrifices to achieve this.

III. INTERNAL ARRANGEMENTS

We must not flinch from granting the greatest possible freedom and equality. By this is not meant the anarchic and bloody horrors of the French revolution ... but rather the wise laws of a monarchical state which will not restrict the natural freedom and equality of its citizens any more than is required by their level of culture and for their own good. ...

The nobility

Every position in the state, without exception, is not restricted to this or that caste but must be open to all classes on the basis of merit and ability. ...

The exclusive privilege of the nobility to own noble manors ... is so damaging and so unsuited to our current time and condition that it must be abolished along with all other associated privileges.

The bourgeois estate

The bourgeois estate will gain much by having opened up to them access to all places, trades and employments and in turn must give up any practices which excluded members of other estates.

The peasants

This is the most numerous and important but also the most neglected and oppressed of classes and must now be the principal object of great care. We need a short and effective law as soon as possible abolishing serfdom. We also need to repeal all laws which prevent peasants from moving out of their own class. ... They must have the right to acquire property. ... It is not necessary to abolish compulsory labour services. They are often less onerous than money payments, according to local circumstances. Changes must be by agreement and only promoted by law to the extent of permitting peasants to buy out of services in kind or labour.

Uniting the nation with the government

... The idea of national representation ... is fine and appropriate. Amalgamating representatives with branches of the administration will be useful. ...

Creating the greatest possible freedom of action to subjects of all classes

There should be freedom to practise every trade or craft and the same taxation in town and country. ... We must also get rid of monopolies over such matters as milling and brewing.

[*Hardenberg declares against separate administrations for each province and the need to develop a national (i.e. Prussian) character. Indeed, the state should in future be known as Prussia.*]

IV. MILITARY MATTERS

It is necessary to assemble again as much military force as possible. So far as regular soldiers are concerned we need perhaps 45,000 infantry and

25,000 cavalry along with the necessary artillery, sappers, etc. I also recommend 80,000 infantry as reserve troops or provincial regiments. [*Also recommends volunteer forces in town and country for maintenance of internal order.*]

We must completely change the system of conscription, abolishing all existing exemptions. We must turn military service into an honourable calling. ...

Everyone must have the same chance of promotion. ... Non-commissioned officers should be chosen by the rank and file; the lowest officers by the NCOs.

V. INTERNAL POLICING[1]

[*Hardenberg declares for a laissez-faire policy in agriculture, trade, the arts and sciences and for as much press freedom as is sensible.*]

VI. RELIGION

The state ... tolerates all confessions which do not constitute a public threat or interfere with the beliefs of others. ...

IX. ADMINISTRATION

[*Hardenberg favours central appointment rather than local election of local officials.*]

Demel and Puschner, [2], pp. 86–97.

---

[1] By this term is meant general regulation, not the specific tasks of a modern police force.

DOCUMENT 4   PEACE OF SCHÖNBRUNN BETWEEN FRANCE AND AUSTRIA, 14 OCTOBER 1809

Art. III. The Emperor of Austria, King of Hungary and Bohemia surrenders [*the following territories*]:
Salzburg and Berchtesgaden.
[Territory on the Dalmatian coast, including Trieste.]
Land bordering Saxony.
[Land in western Galicia]

Art. XIV. His Majesty the Emperor of the French, King of Italy, Protector of the Confederation of the Rhine guarantees the integrity of the lands of the Emperor of Austria, King of Hungary and Bohemia as defined by this treaty.

Art. XVI. As the Emperor of Austria wishes to see peace restored at sea, he joins the prohibition system which France and Russia are applying against England in the present sea war. His Majesty will break off every link with England. ...

Demel and Puschner, [2], pp. 57–9.

DOCUMENT 5   STEIN TO COUNT MÜNSTER, 1 DECEMBER 1812

[Baron Stein insists on his national values.]

I have only one fatherland, and that is Germany, and because according to the old constitution I belong to that and not simply to any part of that fatherland, so am I committed with my whole soul to the whole fatherland and not any part of it. To me the dynasties at this moment of great developments are a matter of complete indifference. My wish is that Germany will be great and strong, in order to win back its standing and independence and nationality and assert itself in its position between France and Russia. That is in the interest of the nation and all of Europe.

From Gerhard Ritter, *Stein: eine politische Biographie* (Deutsche Verlags-Anstalt, Stuttgart, 1981), p. 408.

**DOCUMENT 6   CONVENTION OF TAUROGGEN,
30 DECEMBER 1812**

[The unofficial agreement made between the Prussian commander Yorck and the Russian army.]

[*Article 1 set out the territory occupied by Prussian soldiers. Article 2 declares that within this territory the Prussian army will be neutral and that even if the King of Prussia orders the army to rejoin the French army*] '...for a period of two months ... not to serve against the Russian army'. [*Further articles declare that other Prussian contingents should follow the same line.*]

Demel and Puschner, [2], pp. 60–2.

**DOCUMENT 7   ERNST MORITZ ARNDT: 'TO THE PRUSSIANS!',
JANUARY 1813**

[A pamphlet appealing to the Prussians to turn against the French.]

[*Arndt begins by outlining Napoleon's huge and corrupt power at the time he invaded Russia, his high hopes of bringing all Europe under his heel, and how this failed in the face of heroic resistance from the soldiers and ordinary people of Russia. ...*]

Prussians! You have a vivid example before you of what a people can do who fear God and love its fatherland and freedom above all else. ... You have this example; now give your own example. ...

You are fortunate to have the chance to be the first Germans to provide a fine model of the new life and power of the people. ...

A new age is beginning, a great and wonderful German age ... when the love and faith of the German people is thrown into the great struggle. Hatred of the foreigner, hatred of the French, of their baubles, vanity ..., their language, customs. ... Yes, hatred of everything about them ... this must unite all Germans. ... This hatred, as a safeguard of German freedom, must be passed on down to children and grandchildren, and must be planted on the river Scheldt, the Vosges mountains and the Ardennes as the best guarantee of German security. ...

Spies, [14], pp. 224–8.

| DOCUMENT 8 | **PRUSSIAN INTRODUCTION OF UNIVERSAL CONSCRIPTION** |

... We now command that for the duration of the war all exemptions from military service made by the existing cantonal constitution shall be removed by the following measures. All those between the ages of 17 and 24 who were formerly exempt can either volunteer for a mounted or foot rifle battalion or for the artillery. However, those who have not so volunteered within eight days following the publication of this order shall no longer have such a choice and will be placed in whatever branch of the army which the military authorities deem appropriate. [*Then follow exceptions listed on grounds of criminal conviction, sole support of family or government service.*]

Frederick William III, Breslau, 9 February 1813. Demel and Puschner, [2], pp. 392–9.

| DOCUMENT 9 | **FREDERICK WILLIAM III: 'AN MEIN VOLK', 17 MARCH 1813** |

[The Prussian king appeals to his people to rally against France.]

It is not necessary for my true people, as for Germans, to provide an account of the reasons for the war which is just beginning. The reasons are obvious to all in Europe who are not blind.

We suffer under the over-mighty power of France. The peace which tore away half of my subjects from me brought no blessings. Instead it inflicted further wounds upon us, even that of war itself. The marrow was sucked out of the land. The main fortresses remained occupied by the enemy.

Agriculture was ruined as was the prosperity of our towns. Free trade was strangled and thus the sources of wealth and welfare dried up. The country has fallen victim to poverty.

By means of the strictest fulfilment of the agreements we have made, I hoped to make things easier for my people and to convince the French Emperor that it was in his own interest to let Prussia have her independence. But my purest intentions were undermined by arrogance and faithlessness. We see clearly that the Emperor's agreements will slowly ruin us even more surely than his wars. Now the time has come when all misunderstanding of our situation must cease.

Brandenburgers, Prussians, Silesians, Pomeranians, Lithuanians! You know what you have suffered for seven years and what will be your tragic fate if we do not bring this new war to an honourable end. Think back to earlier times, to the great Electors, to the great Frederick. Keep in your minds the things for which your forefathers fought – freedom of conscience, honour, independence, trade, the arts and sciences. Think of the great example of our powerful ally, the Russians. Think of the Spanish and the Portugese, also small nations who have fought successfully for these same goals against a more powerful enemy. Think of the heroic Swiss and Dutch.

Great sacrifices are demanded from all classes, for we make a great start and equally great are the numbers and resources of our enemies. You will give that more willingly for your fatherland, for your own king, than for a foreign despot who has given countless examples that he will sacrifice your sons and all that is yours for ends which are utterly alien to you. Trust in God, endurance, effort, and solidarity with our allies will reward our virtuous efforts with success.

Whatever sacrifices are demanded of individuals, they are outweighed by the holy cause for which we make them, for which we fight and must win, if we do not wish to cease being Prussian and German.

This is the last and decisive struggle, for our existence, our independence, our welfare. The only choice is between an honourable peace or noble destruction. Even that can be faced with equanimity if it preserves our honour, for without honour no Prussian or German wishes to live. But let us trust that God and our firm resolve will bring our just cause to victory, with a secure and glorious peace and the return of a happier time.

Demel and Puschner, [2], pp. 414–16.

DOCUMENT 10   KALISCH DECLARATION OF MARCH 1813

[The Russian Tsar and the Prussian King appeal to Germans.]

Proclamation to the Germans!

... These armies, watched over by their monarchs (Tsar Alexander I of Russia and Frederick William III of Prussia), led by their commanders and trusting in the power of a just God, hope to finish for the whole world, and irreversibly for Germany, what they have so gloriously begun in the way of removing the most shameful of yokes. ... Their watchword is: honour and freedom! May every German still worthy of the name quickly and decisively join with us. May everyone, prince, noble or from the ranks of the people, support the liberation plans of Russia and Prussia, with heart and mind, property and blood, body and life. ...

Thus we demand true cooperation, especially from every German prince, and gladly we want to see that there will be none amongst them who will be unfaithful to the German cause, thereby laying himself open to a merited destruction through the force of public opinion and the power of just weapons.

The Confederation of the Rhine ... laid upon a defeated Germany, even removing the old name, cannot be tolerated as the result of foreign coercion and as the instrument of foreign influence.

... France, beautiful and strong in your own right, in future just concern yourself with promoting your own domestic fortunes. No external power wants to interfere with that, there will be no hostile violation of your just boundaries.

But France must know that the other powers intend to conquer a lasting peace for their peoples and will not lay down their weapons before the foundation of the independence of all the states of Europe has been laid down and secured.

Issued at HQ Kalisch, 13/25 March 1813, in the name of His Majesty the Emperor and Ruler of all the Russians and His Majesty the King of Prussia and Prince Kutusow-Smolenskoi, General-Fieldmarshal and Supreme Commander of the Allied Armies.

Huber, [10], pp. 81–3.

DOCUMENT 11   METTERNICH'S INTERVIEW WITH NAPOLEON, DRESDEN, 16 JUNE 1813

[The interview took place during an armistice and we have only Metternich's uncorroborated testimony.]

[*Napoleon asserts he will once more beat his enemies. Metternich replies.*]

'Peace and war ... lie in your Majesty's hands. ... The world requires peace. In order to secure this peace, you must reduce your power within bounds compatible with the general tranquillity, or you will fall in the contest. Today you can yet conclude peace; tomorrow it may be too late.'

[*Napoleon replies*] ... 'Your sovereigns, born to the throne, may be beaten twenty times, and still go back to their palaces; that cannot I – the child of fortune; my reign will not outlast the day when I have ceased to be strong, and therefore feared.'

[*There follows an account of military losses, current and potential strengths of each power. Metternich doubts the quality of the French soldiers now being mobilised or whether France will continue to support Napoleon.*]

Napoleon recovered himself, and with calmer tones said to me ... : 'The French cannot complain of me; to spare them, I have sacrificed the Germans and the Poles. I have lost in the campaign of Moscow three hundred thousand men, and there were not more than thirty thousand Frenchmen among them.'

'You forget, sire,' I exclaimed, 'that you are speaking to a German.'

Walker, [15], pp. 25–31.

DOCUMENT 12 MILITARY FORCES AT THE BATTLE OF LEIPZIG, OCTOBER 1813

Date	Sides	Forces in action	Forces in vicinity	Casualties
16 October	French	177,000	198,000	
16 October	Allies	257,000	340,000	
18/19 October	French	195,000	198,000	73,000
18/19 October	Allies	365,000	370,000	54,000

Adapted from Chandler, D. (1966) *The Campaigns of Napoleon*, p. 1120.

DOCUMENT 13 FREDERICK WILLIAM III PROMISES A CONSTITUTION, 22 MAY 1815

§.1 There shall be a representation of the people.

§.3 A national assembly (*Versammlung der Landes-Repräsentanten*) shall be elected by the provincial assemblies.

§.4. The National Assembly is to be consulted on all matters for legislation which concern the personal and property rights of citizens, including taxation ...

Huber, [10], pp. 61–2.

DOCUMENT 14   GERMAN CONFEDERAL ACT, 8 JUNE 1815

Art. 1 The sovereign princes and the free cities of Germany, including their majesties the Emperor of Austria and the King of Prussia, of Denmark and of the Netherlands ... unite themselves in a permanent league to be known as the German Confederation.

Art. 2 The purpose of the *Bund* is the maintenance of the external and internal security of Germany and the independence and inviolability of the individual German states.

Art. 3 All *Bund* members have the same rights; they all pledge themselves to hold constant and unswerving to this constitution.

Art. 4 The affairs of the *Bund* will be dealt with by a *Bund* assembly.

[*The number of votes for each state is listed. Austria chairs the assembly. There is a more proportional voting arrangement for changes to the* Bund *constitution which require a two-thirds majority. Then articles on procedures and immediate tasks follows.*]

Art. 11 All members of the *Bund* promise to defend Germany as a whole and every individual state against any attack. ... When the Bund is at war no member can engage in negotiations with the enemy or conclude any truce or peace.

[*Members of the* Bund *retain the right to form all kinds of alliance but commit themselves to refraining from any connections which threaten the security of the* Bund *or any of its members.*

Members also undertake not to wage war against each other or to use violence in any dispute amongst themselves but to bring such matters to the Bund *assembly.*]

Art. 13 All *Bund* states will have an 'estate constitution'.[1]

Art. 16 Confessional differences amongst Christians provide no justification for any differences in civil and political rights throughout the territory of the *Bund*. ...

Art. 18 The princes and free cities agree to secure to their subjects the following rights:

Any property acquired in another state shall not be subject to any more charges and burdens than would be imposed on subjects of that state.

(1) The right to move freely from one *Bund* state to another which is prepared to accept them as subjects; and (2) to enter into the civil and military service of that state; (3) freedom from any emigration tax when property transferred from one state to another. ... ; (4) the *Bund* assembly will at its first meeting draw up common measures on press freedom and the protection of writers and publishers against pirate publication.

Art. 19 The members of the *Bund* undertake that the first meeting of the assembly will consider the issues of trade and transport as well as shipping between the different states. ...

Huber, [10], pp. 84–91.

---

1 'Landständische Verfassung' means that governments must make provision to consult assemblies based on the estates of nobility, towns and peasants.

DOCUMENT 15   VIENNA FINAL ACT, 15 MAY 1820

[This 'final act' went into greater detail than the German Confederal Act of 1815, shifting the emphasis to rights of intervention in the affairs of member states.]

Art. 25 The maintenance of internal law and order in each member state is a matter for the government of that state alone. However, exception can be made due to any threat to the *Bund* as a whole and to the obligation of *Bund* members to help each other. ...

Art. 26 When in a *Bund* state internal order is threatened through the disobedience of subjects and there is fear of the spread of insurrectionary movements, or where there is an actual insurrection, and the government, having exhausted all constitutional and legal methods, appeals to the *Bund*, then the *Bund* is obliged to provide assistance as quickly as possible in order to restore order. If in such cases the government is clearly unable to repress such insurrections by itself and also is unable to call upon the *Bund* for assistance, the *Bund* is still obliged to intervene in order to restore order and security.

Huber, [10], pp. 91–100.

DOCUMENT 16   PETITION FOR A SINGLE CUSTOMS SYSTEM, APRIL 1819

... Thirty-eight tariff and toll barriers in Germany disrupt internal trade and have roughly the same effect as there would be on the human body if bound in such a way that blood could not flow from one part to another. To trade between Hamburg and Austria or from Berlin to Switzerland, one has to pass through ten states, to study ten sets of rules for tariffs and tolls, to pay ten transit charges. Whoever is unlucky enough to reside in a place where the boundaries of three or four states come together, has to live his whole life amidst hostilely competing customs officers and toll keepers, he has no fatherland. ...

Petition of the General Association for Trade and Manufactures, drawn up by Friedrich List and submitted to the parliament of the *Deutsche Bund* on 14 April 1819.

Hardtwig and Hinze, [9], pp. 147–9.

DOCUMENT 17   CUSTOMS UNION AGREEMENT BETWEEN PRUSSIA AND THE GRAND DUCHY OF HESSE, FEBRUARY 1828

Article 6. On the day of the implementation of this agreement all entry, exit and transit charges will cease to operate at the borders [of the two states]... Prussian harbours will be open to the trade of Hessian subjects subject to just the same levies as apply to Prussian subjects and Prussian consuls in foreign ports are charged to provide support and protection to Hessian subjects. ...

Agreement of 14 February 1828.

Hardtwig and Hinze, [9], pp. 150–1.

DOCUMENT 18   MEMORANDUM OF PRUSSIAN FINANCE MINISTER FRIEDRICH VON MOTZ, 1829

[Motz considers the significance of customs unions.]

Prussia with the Grand Duchy of Hesse on the one side and Bavaria and Württemberg on the other have committed themselves to a single customs and trading system, a system which makes its leading principle the freest possible mutual trade in all natural and manufactured products.

...This signals a new epoch for Germany. ... If it is true that entry, exit and transit tolls are only the consequence of the political separation of different states (and it is true), then it follows that it is also true that the coming together of states into a customs and trade union leads to the formation of a single and common political system.

Hardtwig and Hinze, [9], pp. 152–3.

DOCUMENT 19   METTERNICH'S REACTION TO PRUSSIAN CUSTOMS UNION POLICY, JUNE 1831

... This question [Prussian customs union policy] has its political aspect. States which are bound together by material interests and have as a result common tariff, trade and manufacturing laws, have powerful motives not to be separated from one another on political grounds. The influence of that state which provides the model and centre for such a common interest must steadily increase along with the number of smaller states which ... attach themselves to this common interest. Thus starts to develop a *Bund* within the *Bund* and if [this policy] continues there can be no other result than the separation of Austria from German trade interests. Austria, with its separate customs system, will stand against the other German governments in trading matters and will appear as a foreign place to them.

[*Metternich recognises that the obstacles to a single customs union including all the Habsburg Empire are too great although he suggests a milder alternative, such as agreement on maximum tariff levels.*]

Metternich to Emperor Francis, 11 June 1831. Hardtwig and Hinze, [9], pp. 154–6.

DOCUMENT 20   PRUSSIA EXTENDS ITS INFLUENCE THROUGH CUSTOMS AGREEMENTS, NOVEMBER 1831

A British diplomat reflects.

... The establishment & extension of the Commercial System ..., has been for some years a favorite object with the Prussian Gov[t]. The Union [Central German Commercial Union of 1828] formed in opposition to it under the Auspices of Hanover, Saxony & Electoral Hesse, has just been broken up, by the Secession of the Elector who has signed a Treaty of Commerce [25 August 1831] with Prussia, & by that of the King of Saxony, who is about to do so likewise. ...

I shall only observe that the object of Prussia is to unite those German Powers whose States are contiguous, in the uniform Commercial System now established in Prussia, Hesse-Darmsted, Coethen, & which is about to be introduced into Saxony & Electoral Hesse, & the principle of which is adopted in Bavaria & Wurtemberg, & on the point of being brought into action in the Grand-Duchy of Baden.

The main feature of this System is to abolish all Transit & all other Duties between the Countries leagued together, & to shut out from such united Countries, by heavy Duties, the produce of foreign Soils & of foreign Industry. Thus excluding from the States engaged in this Commercial league the productions of the rest of Europe, as Buonaparte endeavoured to shut out from the Continent the Production of Great Britain & of her Colonies. [The continental system begun in 1806.]

Prince Metternich, speaking to me in the Summer of 1830 of this System, called it 'Le Systeme Continental au petit pied' & added 'ne voyez vous pas que La Prusse cherche a <u>Jacobiniser</u> toute L'Allemagne contre le Commerce de L'Angleterre?' [A minor version of the continental system. ... Do you not see that Prussia seeks to 'jacobinise' all of Germany against British commerce?]

Prussia has made pecuniary sacrifices in order to advance this System, from which she expects not only advantageous future financial returns, but also an augmentation of political Influence in Germany; & her geographical Position, although disadvantageous in many respects, enables her, by making her the frontier of many different States, to act upon their direct Interests & thus to acquire Influence over them.

This Commercial System would not in its present immature State survive, it is thought, a war in Germany, a Consideration powerfully in support of Pacific Counsels.

FO 64/175: George William Chad to Viscount Palmerston, Private, Berlin, 28 November 1831. Freitag, [6], in press.

DOCUMENT 21   PAUL PFIZER: ON THE AIMS AND TASKS OF GERMAN LIBERALISM, TÜBINGEN, 1832

[Pfizer was an early liberal and one of the first to suggest Prussia had a national mission.]

...Following Germany's first reawakening in the war of liberation it was first Austria one hoped and wished ... would place itself at the head of Germany and lead Germans to unity and freedom internally and independence externally. [*But Austria refused the imperial title as going against interests of her own state.*]

Since then German hopes turned to Prussia, based on her efforts against Napoleon..., a very well designed administration and a clever use of all state power. ... And Prussia was ready to take over the function of protector to secure the unity and independence of Germany. However, the dominant party in Prussia wished to know nothing of freedom. ... They are quite happy to follow in the wake of Austria and to institute hateful measures against Germany's freedom in the interests of Austria and to the disadvantage of Prussia.

[*Pfizer then asks if France can be the instrument of German freedom. Although national unity and liberty are cherished French principles, France cannot act on behalf of Germans. Pfizer then considers where such a force might be forthcoming in Germany and finds it in the liberal-constitutional movements in south-west Germany. The problem is that this is very weak in relation to Austria and Prussia. The key then lies in transforming Prussia and excluding Austria.*]

...In order to complete the rebuilding of Germany on the basis of equality ... the Prussian state needs to be broken into several states about the size of Bavaria or Saxony, and Austria needs to be excluded from the Confederation or its German territory conquered for the Confederation and likewise broken into three or four medium states.

[*Concludes that Prussia could be won for the German cause but never Austria.*]

Gall and Koch, [7], vol. 3, pp. 67–94.

DOCUMENT 22   METTERNICH'S RESPONSE TO THE HAMBACH FESTIVAL, JUNE 1832

[Report from a British diplomat.]

I was sent for this morning by Prince Metternich whom I found in a state of much agitation. – He said the proceedings at Hambach had torn the veil asunder, that the Question now was whether the Sovereigns of Germany should descend from their Thrones without a struggle, or whether their Authority should be asserted by force. ... I had before been apprized that Austria and Prussia had agreed to employ their contingents for the suppression of revolt in Germany, a decision from which they had heretofore held back. The practical application of this principle appears to be at hand, & it is impossible not to foresee that it may be the forerunner of the most serious events. – Prince Metternich begged me to remark to Your Lordship that the events which are passing in Germany cannot be safely judged by an English Standard, – That if such a meeting as that of Hambach had passed at Leeds or Birmingham, he should have thought it no more serious than they generally are in England, but that in Germany it is revolution. – What Nations can support [he added] is determined by their previous habits, if ever you should see such a meeting in Vienna or a charivari given under my windows, be assured that the Austrian Empire is at an end. ... He thinks that the Mass of the People and the higher ranks of the Bourgeoisie are still attached to Monarchical Government and Enemies to this agitation, but that the Press, the Professors, the Students and the Employés who are exorbitantly numerous are its active promoters.

FO 7/235: Frederick Lamb to Viscount Palmerston, No. 66, Vienna, 6 June 1832. Freitag, [6], in press.

DOCUMENT 23   AUSTRIA AND PRUSSIA AGREE ON REPRESSIVE MEASURES IN GERMANY, AUGUST 1833

[A circular note drawn up by Metternich and the Prussian minister Ancillon and circulated to other German governments, 24 August 1833.]

The dangers ... which threaten the individual German states as well as the Confederation as a whole are undeniable. ...

These evils must be dealt with ... With this in mind the cabinets of Prussia and Austria, true to federalist principles, have considered how to respond and now make known their ideas to the other German governments.

[*How the constitution of the Confederation, especially as completed in the Final Act of 1820, provides the instruments for combined action. This is best achieved through the governments of the various states.*]

Droß, [3], pp. 204–7.

DOCUMENT 24   ASSESSMENT OF FORWARD PRUSSIAN POLICY IN GERMANY, JUNE 1836

[This dispatch from a British diplomat summarises two reports, one from the late Count Bernstorff who had led the government until 1833, the other by an unknown author said to be currently part of the Prussian mission in Frankfurt. What follows considers this second report.]

Count Bernstorff commences his Memoir by acknowledging the danger of the encreasing discontent of the German People, and shews the necessity of combating this evil, which he states is to be done by pursuing a system conformable to the general good, so as to conciliate the enlightened and possessing, and give them an interest to rally round their Sovereign in time of domestick danger or foreign War. He advises that the German Princes should not show any mistrust of their own Subjects – that they should endeavour to encrease and rely on their moral power, which should be strengthened by the application of legal means, that the Press should be brought to contribute to the maintenance of right and order, by placing it under the direction of writers of talents and good opinions, that an uniform system of commerce should be adopted, and that a general fusion of institutions should take place throughout Germany.

The second Memoir ... discusses at length that which Count Bernstorff only hints at, which is the means of extending the Power of Prussia over Germany, in fact of obtaining the ascendancy formerly in the hands of Austria, which has been declining since the Treaty of Vienna, and now depends solely upon the influence of Tradition.

Prussia, in order to make herself the directing Power of Germany must guide and govern publick opinions, and manage the machinery of the Commercial Union; by attention to these two objects she may in time become the Arbiter of the Confederation, dispose of the force of Germany in War, and model her institutions in Peace. But at this moment Prussia is far from exercising such an ascendancy. The formation of the Commercial League has certainly added, though not in a great degree, to her Political

Power; her real power is to be gained by adopting, exercising, and extending the means suggested by Count Bernstorff; and these I should say the Prussian Government had essentially neglected. The consequence is, that the small Constitutional States so far from looking to Prussia as an Example and Support, endeavour to take the lead in their progress towards improvement, and regard the close Alliance of Prussia with Russia, as putting her in the light of an enemy they should be on their guard against, rather than a friend on whom they could rely in the hour of need. Besides, the Prussian Government, after having given such development to the energies of the people, appears to be frightened at it's [*sic*] own work, and to wish to restrain those energies from acting upon the Political State of the Country; instead of following the line chalked out by Count Bernstorff, and leading publick opinion by the Press, and other legitimate means. The Prussian Press is only allowed to be a Register of facts, and the most enlightened Nation in Europe is not permitted to read the English Morning Chronicle. This erroneous system, however, whilst it prevents Prussia from having that moral and political ascendancy in Germany to which her Geographical position, as well as her Military strength, and free institutions entitle her to aspire, does not prevent her from being a tranquil, contented and powerful Nation. Tranquil and contented from the perfect justice that directs the actions of the King and Government – powerful, from the admirable organization of her immense Army. No Nation is in a better state to repel aggression than Prussia, and none, I should say at the same time, was less disposed or less fit to act aggressively.

FO 64/205: William Russell to Viscount Palmerston, No. 70, Berlin, [no date] June 1836.

Freitag, [6], in press.

DOCUMENT 25   RESPONSES TO THE CRISIS WITH FRANCE, NOVEMBER 1840

(A) BRITISH VIEW AS REPORTED FROM VIENNA

The frontier States of the Confederation have for some time past been addressing themselves to this Court upon the threatening aspect of France. Their language has been that of resistance to French aggression and of complaint at the inaction of Austria. ...

It is Prussia which takes the lead, and to Her all Germany looks in case active measures should become necessary, but thus stimulated and supported Austria will not in case of need remain behind.

If I can trust Prince Metternich's assurances, coupled with those of all the German Ministers with whom I converse, the spirit of Germany has been thoroughly roused by the juggling and boasting of France; there is no feeling towards her in Germany but a disgust at her constant state of internal change and agitation, and a lively indignation at Her assertions that Germany admires and is ready to affiliate with her. Far from this, the feeling of Germany is entirely national and its object is independence and peace; but if these should be violated there is every appearance that the whole country would rise as in 1813 to vindicate them. ...

FO 7/291B: Lord Beauvale to Viscount Palmerston, No. 170, Vienna, 11 November 1840.

(B) BRITISH VIEW AS REPORTED FROM BERLIN

(i) ...Lord Granville supposes that the French Army would take the field with about 200,000 Men, it is thought here that by leaving the Garrisons to the care of Veterans, Recruits and National Guards, 200,000 Men might be placed on the German Frontier and 100,000 on the Frontier of Italy. The German Confederation would be able in the space of four or six Months to put into motion 500,000 Men, and better Troops are not to be seen. ...

In the Military schemes discussed and adopted, some jealousy has arisen between Austria and Prussia. In former days the defence of Southern Germany was confided to Austria. This Power has, either willingly or from negligence ... allowed her influence amongst the Southern States to diminish, and they have made known to Prussia that they cannot trust their safety to the supineness and slow military movements of Austria – that in case of French Invasion they hope to be aided by Prussia. The King flattered by this appeal to his power, promised to send the 4th Corps d'Armée (30,000 men) towards the upper Rhine. The old Prussian Officers no sooner got knowledge of this promise than they remonstrated against it, as being contrary to the old Prussian System, and offensive to Austria. General Grollmann will probably rectify this misunderstanding at Vienna. ...

FO 64/229: William Russell to Viscount Palmerston, No. 59, Berlin, 25 November 1840.

(ii) ...Monsieur Thiers has involuntarily rendered great service to Germany by renewing the Union of the Confederated States which has been on the wane since 1820.

As far as the Sovereigns and Governments are concerned, it is now perfect. Two sources however of weakness exist, one is the deplorable state of the Finances of Austria – the other arises, or rather might arise, from an encreasing desire on the part of the People to obtain Institutions more liberal, which would make them reluctant to contribute to the Expenses of a War, unless they saw that the result would bring some benefit to themselves. Prussia for instance contains an enlightened and industrious Population without a particle of Civil Liberty, without control over the

Finances, without even having the free use of their own Judicial Tribunals. It is then scarsely [*sic*] to be expected that they would bear the burthen of War, without making their compact with the King. ...

FO 64/229: William Russell to Viscount Palmerston, No. 64, Berlin, 23 December 1840.

Freitag, [6], in press.

DOCUMENT 26 POPULAR SONG FROM THE RHINE CRISIS OF 1840

Wherever rings the German tongue
And praises God the German song, There shall it be!
There, German, make your Germany!
There shall the German's country lie,
Where scorn meets Gallic frippery,
Where France reaps hatred from the land,
And German clasps a German hand!
There shall it be!
There is the whole of Germany!
There is the whole of Germany!
O God, regard it from on high;
Grant German courage to us all
That we may love it true and well.
There shall it be!
There is the whole of Germany!

Open University A321, [13].

DOCUMENT 27 AUSTRIAN FEAR OF RISING PRUSSIAN INFLUENCE IN GERMANY

[Report from a British diplomat.]

... I should be inclined to doubt whether Prince Metternich's visit[1] to the King of Prussia ... has proved altogether as satisfactory to His Highness as he had promised to himself.

As a demonstrative measure imposing especially upon France the conviction that all Germany was united and exulting in the display of a military force upon her frontiers which had the power & the resolution to defend them, the presence of the Austrian Minister was doubtless of importance, but the increased ascendancy of Prussia became only the more apparent from it, and the whole demeanour of the King must have shewn the Prince that His Majesty is by no means disinclined to assume for Himself that leading position among the German States which may be said heretofore to have appertained to the House of Austria. ...

In matters of trade no approximation to the Prussian System has been come to by Austria, nor is it probable that She will ever see any benefit to be derived from Her associating with the Zoll-verein.

The establishment and extension of this League has given advantages and a preponderance to Prussia which are beginning to be regretted by some of the minor states. In Baden, for instance, the advantages of the League are more than problematical, and I have been credibly informed that already many of the manufactories in that Country are on the decline, and it is considered that they have been sacrificed to those of Prussia. ...

FO 7/305: Robert Gordon to Earl of Aberdeen, No. 56, Confidential, Vienna, 12 October 1842. Freitag, [6], in press.

---

1   In mid-September 1842 Prince Metternich visited Frederick William IV, who was at the Burg Stolzenfels near Koblenz to celebrate the building of Cologne Cathedral and for the German Confederation's military manoeuvres in the Rhineland.

DOCUMENT 28   **RADOWITZ'S MEMORANDUM ON MEASURES TO BE TAKEN BY THE GERMAN CONFEDERATION, NOVEMBER 1847**

[Radowitz was an adviser to Frederick William IV who had been sent to Frankfurt to report on the situation.]

The most powerful force of the present, that of nationality, is the most dangerous weapon in the hands of the enemies of law and order. This fact must be appreciated ... if there is to be any insight into present events. Through all hearts flows this desire for a community to develop in Germany, powerful and respected abroad, elevated and in harmony within. ... This is the only thought that extends beyond parties, to which conflict of different tribes, churches and political doctrines are subordinated. It is therefore the only principle on which a strong state system and society [*Lebensordnung*] can be constructed. It is Prussia's task, with the closest connection with the rest of Germany to pick up the reins lying on the floor and as a true moral authority to create the impetus towards a rebirth of Germany. ... Measures to be taken were threefold; to strengthen militarily, to extend and develop the protection of law, and to satisfy material needs. To achieve this it was necessary to bind Austria more narrowly to the Confederation, and to overcome the swindle of sovereignty and egoism of individual governments. The best means to prepare for reform of the Confederation was to call a ministerial conference representing the seventeen votes of the inner council of the Confederation. Its task must be to fix the basic principles for national state reform. 'In case this was not possible Radowitz recommended special associations to deal with different national problems, on lines of the customs union, however with the final aim of making these associations finally' the property of the confederation into which they will be merged.

This extract was translated from E. Huber, *Deutsche Verfassungsgeschichte seit 1789* (Kohlhammer, Stuttgart, 1980), vol. 1, pp. 588–9. Sections of the memorandum were paraphrased by Huber and thus inverted commas are used. Reprinted in Open University A321, p. 60.

DOCUMENT 29 OFFENBURG PROGRAMME OF SOUTH-WEST GERMAN DEMOCRATS, 10 SEPTEMBER 1847

1. We demand that our governments disassociate themselves from the Karlsbad Decrees of 1819, the Frankfurt Decrees of 1831 and 1832, and the Vienna Decrees of 1834. These decrees damage our inalienable rights as men as well as the Act of Confederation and our state constitutions.
2. We demand freedom of the press: the inalienable right of men to communicate their ideas freely can no longer be withheld from us.
3. We demand freedom of conscience and education. The relationship of men to God is a private matter and no external power can presume to determine it by their values. Every religion has the claim to the same rights in the state. ...
4. We demand the military take an oath to the constitution. ...
5. We demand personal freedom. The police must cease to patronize and pester the citizen. The right of association, a fresh communal life, the right of the people to assemble and free speech, and the right of the individual to freedom of movement within Germany, should be undisturbed.
6. We demand representation of the people at the German Confederation. The German people want a fatherland and a voice in its affairs, justice and freedom internally, and a firm position *vis-à-vis* the outside world to guarantee our existence as a nation.
7. We demand a popular military system. Only the trained and armed citizen can protect the state. Give the people weapons and take from them the huge burden of a standing army.
8. We demand a just system of taxation. Each should bear the burden he can carry. In the place of existing taxes there should be a progressive income tax.
9. We demand that education be available to all. The resources to achieve this will be raised.
10. We demand that the imbalance between labour and capital be rectified. Society is responsible for creating and protecting labour.

11. We demand laws worthy of free citizens and their application by trial through jury. Citizens will be judged by citizens. The implementation of justice is an affair of the people.
12. We demand a popular state administration. The fresh life of the people requires free institutions. They cannot be governed and directed by scribblers. Self-government of the people will replace the over-government of bureaucrats.
13. We demand the abolition of all privileges. Respect for a free citizen is the only right and due of all.

Huber, [10], pp. 323–4.

DOCUMENT 30 HEPPENHEIMER PROGRAMME OF THE SOUTH-WEST GERMAN LIBERALS, 10 OCTOBER 1847

One can expect nothing useful in the way of leadership or representation from the Federal Assembly in the promotion of national needs. The Assembly has not solved those tasks, such as creating state constitutions, free trade and traffic, river shipping, free press etc., which are laid down in the Act of Confederation; the confederal military constitution has led neither to a popular militia nor an organized army of the Confederation. On the contrary, the press is censored, the Assembly meetings are hidden in darkness, with an occasional decision coming to light which obstructs any free development. The only bond of common German interests, the Customs Union, was not created by the Confederation but outside it through treaties between individual states; even discussions of a law of exchange and a postal service are carried on by representatives of individual governments, not by the assembly. This and other considerations are connected to the question – will national representation in the Federal Assembly improve matters and thus be a worthwhile aim for all friends of the fatherland? Those will answer in the affirmative who feel that a representation of all the states of the Confederation can only be established through the existing institution of the federal governments, and expect that the growing strength of public opinion will seek to bring about the development of a German policy, with the aid of all the spiritual and material resources of the nation. Against this it will be maintained that however sublime the idea, yet its realisation is not possible. The Confederation contains members, such as Denmark and the Netherlands, which, as external powers, will never ally themselves to a German policy and the strengthening of German power. Other members are not exclusively German powers or contain territory, such as East Prussia, which is German but does not belong to the Confederation. Furthermore, national representation requires national government, armed with all the powers of a sovereign state, powers which the *Bund* does not have. The aim of uniting Germany for a German policy and common leadership and concern for national interests will rather be achieved when public opinion has been won over.

Huber, [10], pp. 324–6

DOCUMENT 31 **TYPICAL EXAMPLE OF DEMANDS AT THE OUTSET OF REVOLUTION**

The most urgent wishes of the people which the second chamber brings to the attention of the government at this most desperately serious time are as follows:

1. The government immediately declares that the following provisional emergency laws are no longer recognised in Baden: the Carlsbad Decisions of 20 December 1819, the Frankfurt decisions of ... 1832, the decisions of the secret Vienna conference of 1834.
2. That all citizens of the state, including soldiers, swear an oath of loyalty to the constitution.
3. That all restrictions on political rights on grounds of religious confession be abolished. ...
4. That a law be drafted on ministerial responsibility. ...
6. That the government will act very soon to remove remaining feudal burdens. ...
7. That measures be taken for a more just distribution of state and communal taxes. ...
8. That legal privileges be removed.
9. That a democratic system of communal administration be introduced.
10. That the government press urgently upon the Confederal Assembly the establishment of a representative assembly of the German people.
11. The independence of judges. ...
12. That state ministers and envoys of the Grand Duchy at the Confederation only be appointed from men who have the confidence of the people.

Resolution of the Second Chamber of the Grand Duchy of Baden, 2 March 1848. Fenske, [5], pp. 48–9.

DOCUMENT 32 BLUM AND JORDAN EXPRESSING DIFFERENT VIEWS ON THE POSEN ISSUE

[From the debate in the German National Assembly on the Posen question, 25 July 1848.]

Robert Blum

I have only one question. If we are deciding here on matters of European politics, matters of the greatest importance not merely for our fatherland, but for the whole of Europe, then I would like to know according to what principles you are acting. Is it the territorial aspect of the problems which is determining your attitude as would appear to be so in the case of Schleswig-Holstein, the Slavs and Trieste? Why then do you not proceed on the same principle when it is a question of discussing another nation which incorporates a number of Germans, just as we have incorporated a number of Danes, Slavs, Italians and whatever else they may be called. Or is it the nationalistic point of view which guides you? Now in that case you should be just as fair to the other side, and when you cut Posen in half so as to reclaim the Germans living there, then it would also be better if you cut Schleswig in half, liberate the Slavs who form part of Austria and also separate the South Tyrol from Germany; indeed I shall go further. If you possess such lively patriotic feelings and will let yourself be governed by them alone, then you should free the German Baltic provinces from Russian rule, and liberate the 600,000 unfortunate Germans in Alsace, who, what is more, languish under the rule of a republic. *(Prolonged applause.)* Either one or the other principle is right, for to adapt your politics according to what happens to suit you at that moment, is in my opinion not politics at all.

Wilhelm Jordan

It is high time that we finally woke up from that dream-like abandonment, in which we enthuse for every other nationality under the sun, whilst we ourselves lie down under humiliating subjugation, with the whole world trampling all over us. It is time we awoke to a healthy national egoism (and I use the expression candidly) which would make the welfare and honour of the fatherland the most important issue in all problems. But this very egoism, without which a people can never become a nation, is described as extremely condemnable by those who sympathise with Poland. ... Our right is none other than the right of the stronger, the right of conquest. Yes we have done some conquering. ... In the West it is only us who have been conquered, in the East we have had the great misfortune of ourselves doing the conquering, and by so doing have provided whole hosts of German poets with the opportunity of writing moving jeremiads about the various nationalities who have had to succumb to the weight of the German race.

(Laughter from the right, hissing from the left.) If we wanted to be ruthlessly fair, then we must give up not merely Poland, but also half of Germany. ... Therefore I maintain that the German conquests in Poland were a physical necessity. The laws of history are different from laws in text books. History only recognises the laws of nature, and one of these says that a nationality does not possess the right of political autonomy merely because of its existence, but only when it has the strength to affirm itself as a state amongst the others. The latest act in our conquests, the much decried division of Poland, was not the murder of a nation, as some have called it, but was nothing more than the proclamation of a death that had already taken place, the funeral of a corpse already in the process of decomposing, whose existence could no longer be tolerated by the living. For indeed a nation, which consisted of an aristocracy, Jews and bondsmen was, following the degeneration caused by a long period of anarchy, no longer fit for a rational freedom and could no longer exist when such a freedom became an essential condition for life.

Open University A321, [13], pp. 77–8.

DOCUMENT 33 CREATION OF A PROVISIONAL GERMAN AUTHORITY

[Decision of the German National Assembly.]

1. Until the definite foundation of a government authority for Germany, a provisional central power for all common affairs of the German nation is to be established.
2. This is: (a) to exercise the executive power in all affairs which concern the general security and welfare of the German federal state;
   (b) to take supreme command of the complete armed force and particularly to appoint its Commander-in-Chief;
   (c) to exercise the international and commercial representation of Germany and for this purpose to appoint ministers and consuls.
3. The establishment of the constitution remains excluded from the sphere of the Central Power.
4. Concerning war and peace, and treaties with foreign powers, the Central Power decides in agreement with the National Assembly.
5. The Provisional Central Power is to be entrusted to the Vicar of the Empire, who will be elected by the National Assembly.
6. The Vicar of the Empire exercises his authority through ministers appointed by him and responsible to the National Assembly. All his dispositions require for their validity the countersignature of at least one responsible minister.

7. The Vicar of the Empire is not responsible [to the National Assembly].

8. The National Assembly is to make a special law about the responsibility of the ministers.

9. The ministers have the right to attend the deliberations of the National Assembly and to be heard by it.

10. The ministers are obliged to appear in the National Assembly at its request and to provide information.

11. The ministers have the right to vote in the National Assembly only if they have been elected as its members.

12. The position of the Vicar of the Empire is incompatible with that of a member of the National Assembly.

13. The existence of the Federal Assembly ceases with the beginning of the functioning of the Provisional Central Power.

14. In connection with executive measures, the Central Power has to come to an understanding, in so far as is possible, with the plenipotentiaries of state governments.

15. The activity of the Provisional Central Power ceases as soon as the constitution for Germany has been completed and put into operation. ...

Eyck, [4], pp. 93–4.

DOCUMENT 34   DECLARATION BY HEINRICH VON GAGERN, 18 DECEMBER 1848

[Gagern, President of the German National Assembly, opts for the *kleindeutsch* solution to the national question.]

The Austrian ministry's programme of 27 November declares:

1. that the various states within Austria are united in one political unit;
2. that the political relations between Austria and Germany can only be settled when the two political complexes have both reached a new stable structure, i.e., they have decided on their own internal organisation.

This view of Austria's attitude towards Germany did not merely meet with the approval of the Austrian parliament at Kremsier, but it also seems to be in accord with the wishes and opinions of the vast majority of the population of the German regions of Austria.

Thus an answer has been delivered by the Austrian side to the question, contained in paragraphs (1)–(3) of the resolution on the draft constitution, 'Concerning the Reich and the power of the Reich', which was asked of her by the National Assembly.

The Reich ministry believes that in its assessment of the position to be adopted by the Central Authority towards Austria, it must start out from the following propositions:

1. Concerning the kind of association between Austria and the German states, the duty of the Reich authorities should be restricted at this time and for the whole period of the provisional government to maintaining in general the existing federal relations between Austria and Germany. Austria's special position should however be acknowledged according to which she claims the right not to enter into the as yet unconstituted German federal state if the terms were to alter the existing political alliance between the German parts of Austria and the non-German parts of Austria within the Confederation.

2. Therefore, judging from the resolutions passed so far by the National Assembly, which have determined the nature of the federation, Austria should be regarded as not participating in the as yet unconstituted German federation.

3. Any special act of union designed to settle the federal relations between Austria and Germany by attempting, where possible, to satisfy all the spiritual, political and material wants of two kindred nations, wants which from time immemorial have united Germany and Austria and could still unite them on an even more intensified level, must be left for the future.

4. As Austria is inextricably bound to Germany, now represented by the provisional Central Authority, but is not a participant member of the federation, then agreements concerning already existing as well as all future obligations and rights within the Confederation should be begun and/or maintained through ambassadorial channels.

5. The constitution of the German federal state, the speedy conclusion of which is in the interests of both parties, cannot however be a subject of any negotiations with Austria.

At the same time as delivering these propositions to the National Assembly for examination, I am petitioning for the Reich ministry to be given, on behalf of the Central Authority, the authority to exchange ambassadors with the Imperial Austrian government, thus acting in accordance with the circumstances outlined above.

Huber, [10], 1, pp. 291–2.

DOCUMENT 35   REPLY BY THE AUSTRIAN PRIME MINISTER, PRINCE SCHWARZENBERG, 28 DECEMBER 1848

[This is Schwarzenberg's response to von Gagern's *kleindeutsch* position.]

Directive to this country's plenipotentiary von Mensslingen

In this statement[1] the view has been expressed that Austria is claiming that she does not wish to enter the as yet unconstituted German federation, i.e. that she is excluding herself from it.

However the policy statement issued by the Austrian cabinet in Kremsier on the 27th, ult. explicitly left a settlement of the German problem to some further agreement in the future, and in no way expressed the intentions which Herr von Gagern's declaration seems to attribute to us.

It follows therefore that we do not acknowledge his premises, and so we also find it impossible to declare ourselves in agreement with any of the resulting conclusions.

Austria today is still a German federal power. Nor does she intend to abandon this position which has arisen from the natural development of circumstances going back for 1000 years.

Should there prove to be a successful end, as we sincerely wish and readily expect, to bringing about a more thorough fusion between the differing interests of the various parts of Germany; should the work on the constitution, in which Austria herself is taking part, be brought to its objectives successfully, then Austria will be able to maintain her position in this new political structure. In any event it would be a substantial anticipation of the future shape of the existing German federation if the withdrawal of Austria from this 'as yet unconstituted' federation (as it is termed in the above named declaration) were already now assumed to be a foregone conclusion.

One consequence of this assumption – rejected by us as completely invalid – appears to be the authorisation which the Minister is seeking from the German National Assembly, namely to be allowed to establish ambassadorial relations with the Austrian Empire.

Just like all the other German federal states we have a plenipotentiary at the seat of the Central Authority. His agency will be sufficient, now as before, for maintaining working relations with the Ministry.

You, Sir, have accordingly been charged with impressing upon Herr von Gagern that, for the above listed reasons, he should desist from his desire to establish diplomatic relations with us.

What we are looking for is a favourable outcome to this problem. This can only be achieved – of this the Minister may be certain – by way of an agreement between the various German governments, amongst which the Imperial government occupies the first place.

Gladly would we be ready to extend him our hand in this difficult task. For his part we would expect a correct assessment of the situation (his outstanding diplomatic qualities lead us to feel justified in this expectation) and also that willing sense of cooperation which alone can lead to a satisfactory solution.

Huber, [10], pp. 292–3.

---

[1]Gagern's speech of 18 December.

DOCUMENT 36 **PRUSSIAN CIRCULAR TO ITS ENVOYS AT THE SEATS OF THE GERMAN GOVERNMENTS, 23 JANUARY 1849**

[Prussia pursues the *kleindeutsch* possibility.]

The royal government views with great satisfaction the confirmation from Austria that, like us, she considers the German federation as continuing to exist and wishes to remain within it, taking part in its energetic development, and that she is prepared to come to some understanding in this matter with the National Assembly and the other governments in Germany. Undoubtedly this understanding will have to be of such a nature that nothing should stand in the way of either (a) the Imperial state in its efforts to achieve a strong constitutional framework for all the countries within its complex, sufficient to meet its internal needs; or (b) those German efforts directed towards presenting the outside world with a united political body, as well as those efforts aimed at producing a merging of commercial and material interests and the greatest possible balance of internal legislation. It is to be expected of the Imperial Austrian government that in these matters as well she will proffer help to the best of her ability and that in the restructuring of the internal circumstances of that monarchy she will show the greatest possible consideration for her relations with Germany. If nevertheless she should believe that she will not be able to show complete sympathy with the development of Germany indicated above, if moreover she feels unable to permit the requisite limitations of her sovereign rights in favour of a strong central federal authority and if she is unable to permit the application of this material unification of interests to take place in her German provinces, then clearly two things can be concluded from this. On the one hand Austria would not wish to exercise rights not matched by corresponding obligations; on the other hand it could not be expected of the other German states that they should concede rights to an agency made up of the whole population of the federation, to a federal government guiding the affairs of the entire federation, in which Austria maintains her position, her rights connected with foreign and commercial policies in general, and her rights connected with internal legislation and management of public funds, in the execution of which the Austrian area of the federation would not be subject to the same extent to the resolutions of that Central Authority. But it would not yet be correct to infer from this that Germany alone should return to the fundamental principles of the confederation, and that the enthusiastically received plan for a centralised federal union must be completely abandoned. On the contrary, the preservation and development of the German confederation – including Austria as well as the German areas of the Netherlands and Denmark – as well as the maintenance of a position in Germany befitting the Imperial house of Austria will prove completely compatible with the coalition of the other German states in a closer union, in a federation within the confederation. Thus, just as within the confederation the Customs Union could represent not just a closer internal union concerned with trade, industrial activity and commerce, but could carry within it the seeds for the formation and continuing existence of a common commercial agency dealing with the outside world, without destroying the confederation itself nor the relations between those members of the confederation who belong to the Customs Union and those who do not, so too can a union be concluded between the majority of members of the federation: a union, which could exist within the federation, embracing much broader interests.

The royal government recognises its duty now as before in continuing to advance along the path taken in summoning the German National Assembly.

Prussia is not striving for any extension of her power nor any honour for herself; no matter how the German constitution may be formulated, she desires no share in the running of the federal authority other than that which her position within Germany and the importance of the power, both spiritual and material, which she can place at the disposal of the common fatherland, would by their very nature assign her. She will not accept any tendered position unless offered with the full consent of all the allied governments; however she regards herself as duty bound to declare herself ready to render such service to Germany as may be required of her in furthering the interests of the whole community, even when this can only be achieved by some sacrifice on her part. At the same time she will willingly concur with everything, which, without endangering any common goal, is suitable for maintaining the independent autonomy of the individual states. In consequence of this intention I can now make the following pronouncement: his majesty the King and his supreme government are of the opinion that the establishing of a new German imperial house is not necessary for achieving a real and far reaching unification of Germany; that on the contrary we must fear that to struggle exclusively for a unifying feature of precisely this kind (although a unifying feature in itself is very necessary) would place fundamental and almost insuperable barriers in the way of actually achieving that very goal of unification. It should prove possible to find another form, under which, without sacrificing a single fundamental requirement, the urgent and totally justified demands of the German nation for a genuine union and strong robust commercial development can meet with complete gratification.

Huber, [10], pp. 295–7.

DOCUMENT 37 DESPATCH FROM SCHWARZENBERG TO SCHMERLING AT THE REICH AUTHORITY, 4 FEBRUARY 1849

[Schwarzenberg makes clear Austrian opposition to any national state.]

The formation of a unified state seems to the cabinet to be impracticable for Austria, and undesirable for Germany. It is impracticable for us because the government must not neglect the rights and duties incumbent on her in relation to the non-German elements within the monarchy in favour of her position in the federation. Just as she is unable to untie the knot which has bound together the German and non-German provinces for centuries, so too is she just as unable to accede to the unilateral abolition of the German federation which forms an essential part of the European network of treaties. But a unified state such as envisaged appears to us to be undesirable for Germany as well. For it would not only offend, extremely often and extremely deeply, against numerous and variously constituted requirements, the closest moral and material interests, traditions gained from the past and demands to be made of the future, but it would stand as a barrier in the way of the development of political and personal freedom in Germany, which is passionately yearned for and jealously watched over.

There is no point in trying to reply that it is not a unified state which is being aimed at, or that we are dealing here with a federation. It is impossible for us to let such a statement and designation pass by undisputed. The majority of the National Assembly has declared itself in favour of the programme outlined by Minister von Gagern. Should this programme be realized then it would mean the foundation of the so-called closer federation, that is to say just that unified state described by us above, and it is irrelevant whether its focal point remains in Frankfurt or is removed to some other place in another part of Germany. From no matter what standpoint this scheme is examined, it displays on all sides immense, insuperable problems. For Germany, because, if we are not greatly mistaken, each individual member, contrary to its history and its present needs, will have removed from it any form of independent existence which will be transferred to some artificially created central focal point. For Austria, because, either it will completely exclude us from this new Germany or else it will dissolve the union between the German patrimonial dominions and the non-German parts, that is to say it would, *de facto*, call into being paragraphs 2 and 3 of the section of the constitution dealing with the Reich. One should recall how the latter were received throughout Austria, including the provinces, with a howl of indignation, and how many arguments and doubts were raised against those paragraphs in the *Paulskirche* itself by many Austrian speakers and especially by the present Prime Minister at the 103rd sitting. Thus either we have the exclusion of the German provinces of Austria – in other words a truncation of Germany – or we have the loosening of those bonds between various parts of Austria, so closely interwoven and intimately bound together, so that from then on only thin threads of personal union would hold them together; these are the two end results, to which Germany and Austria would be driven with compelling logic by the foundation of this so-called federation, which is anything but a federation. The duty of self-preservation, for a German no less than for an Austrian, induces us in the same way to reject such statements. We will say it once more – Austria and Germany will not have their development furthered in any way by these proposals but rather weakened and discredited, and both will be hurt deep down in their political being, perhaps incurably. For as we felt obliged to state in another place, it is 'not in the dismembering of the Austrian monarchy that Germany's future greatness lies, nor a strengthening of Germany in a weakening of the monarchy: the continuation of Austria as a political unit is needed by Germany as well as by Europe'.

Huber, [10], pp. 298–9.

DOCUMENT 38 EXTRACTS FROM THE IMPERIAL CONSTITUTION OF MARCH 1849

SECTION I: THE REICH

1. The German Reich consists of the area of the heretofore existing German Confederation. The stipulation of the position of the Duchy of Schleswig remains reserved [for future arrangement].

2. If a German territory has the same head of state as a non-German one, then the German territory must have its own constitution, government and administration separate from the non-German one. Only German citizens may be appointed to the government and administration of a German territory.

   The Reich constitution and Reich legislation have the same binding force in such a German territory as in the other German lands.

3. If a German territory has the same head of state as a non-German one,

then the head of state must either reside in his German lands, or a regency must be installed in a constitutional manner to which only Germans may be appointed.

4. Apart from already existing associations of German and non-German lands, no head of state of a non-German territory may at the same time take over the government of a German territory, nor may a prince governing in Germany, without resigning his German government, accept a foreign crown.

5. The individual German states retain their independence in so far as it is not limited by the Reich constitution; they have all the state sovereignty and rights in so far as these are not expressly assigned to the Reich Authority.

SECTION II: THE REICH AUTHORITY

1/6. The Reich Authority exercises the exclusive international representation of Germany and of the individual German states towards foreign countries. ...

2/10. The Reich Authority has the exclusive right of war and peace.

3/11. The Reich Authority has at its disposal the whole armed force of Germany.

7/33. The German Reich shall form one customs and trading area, surrounded by a common customs frontier, with the abolition of all internal border dues. The exclusion of individual places and areas from the customs area remains reserved to the Reich Authority. It remains further reserved to the Reich Authority to attach even territories ... not belonging to the Reich to the German customs area by means of special treaties.

[*Other articles place regulation of currency, weights and measures with the Reich Authority.*]

SECTION III: THE HEAD OF THE REICH

Article I

68. The dignity of Head of the Reich will be assigned to one of the reigning German princes.

69. This dignity is hereditary in the house of the prince to whom it is assigned. It devolves in the male line according to the right of primogeniture.

70. The Head of the Reich has the title: Emperor of the Germans.

Article II

73. The person of the Emperor is inviolable. The Emperor exercises the authority assigned to him through responsible ministers appointed to him.
74. All government actions of the Emperor require for their validity the countersignature of at least one of the Reich Ministers, who thus assumes responsibility.

Article III

75. The Emperor exercises the international representation of the German Reich and of the individual German states. He appoints the Reich Ministers [resident] and the consuls and conducts diplomatic relations.
76. The Emperor declares war and concludes peace.
77. The Emperor concludes alliances and treaties with foreign powers, with the collaboration of the Reichstag in so far as this is reserved to it in the constitution.
79. The Emperor summons and closes the Reichstag; he has the right of dissolving the popular chamber [*Volkshaus*].
80. The Emperor has the right of proposing bills. He exercises the legislative power in common with the Reichstag under the constitutional limitations. He proclaims Reich laws and issues the decrees necessary for their execution.
82. The Emperor is charged with the preservation of the peace of the Reich.
83. The Emperor has the right of disposal over the armed forces.

SECTION IV: THE REICHSTAG

Article I

85. The Reichstag consists of two houses, the House of States [*Staatshaus*] and the House of the People [*Volkshaus*].

Article II

86. The House of States will be formed from the representatives of the German states.
87. [*Sets out the numbers from each state based on population. This includes Austria.*]

Article V

99. Each house has the right of initiation, of legislation, of complaint, of address and of the investigation of facts, as well as of the impeachment of ministers.

100. A resolution of the Reichstag can only validly be made by agreement of both houses.
101. A resolution of the Reichstag which has not obtained the consent of the Reich Government may not be repeated in the same session. If the Reichstag in three immediately consecutive ordinary sessions makes the same resolution without change, it becomes law with the end of the third Reichstag, even if the Reich Government does not give its consent. ...
102. A resolution of the Reichstag is necessary in the following cases:

(1) if it is a matter of the issue, abolition, alteration or interpretation of Reich laws.

(2) when the Reich budget is fixed, when loans are contracted, when the Reich takes over expenditure for which provision has not been made in the budget, or levies contributions from the states [*Matrikularbeitragel* or taxes].

(6) if territories not belonging to the Reich are included in the German custom area or particular places or areas are excluded from it.

(7) if German territories are ceded, or non-German territories incorporated in the Reich or to be associated with it in some other manner.

SECTION V: THE BASIC RIGHTS OF THE GERMAN PEOPLE

130. The following basic rights are to be guaranteed to the German people. They are to serve as the norm for the constitutions of the individual German states, and no constitution or legislation of an individual German state may abolish or limit them.

Article I

131. The German people consists of the members of the states which form the German Reich.
132. Every German has German Reich citizenship. He exercises the rights arising from it in every German state.

[*There then follows a catalogue of civil rights.*]

SECTION VI: THE GUARANTEE OF THE CONSTITUTION

[*Sets out the conditions under which constitutional changes can be made.*]

Huber, [10], pp. 149–65.]

NB. A translation of the whole constitution can be found in [20].

DOCUMENT 39   AUSTRIAN PROPOSAL CONCERNING THE REICH GOVERNMENT, 8 MARCH 1849

1. The Reich government should be run by a Directory.
2. This Directory should consist of seven ruling princes or their representatives. [*Then one seat for each of Austria, Prussia and Bavaria and details of how the other four are to be rotated amongst the remaining states.*]
3. At the head of the Reich government should be the Reich governor.
4. Alternating year to year, the Emperor of Austria and the King of Prussia should be invested with the dignity of being Reich governor.

Huber, [10], p.301.

DOCUMENT 40   FINAL PRUSSIAN REJECTION OF THE IMPERIAL CONSTITUTION, 28 APRIL 1849

When the King received the message that he had been offered the imperial crown from the deputation of the National Assembly he received on 3 April, he expressed his sense of the significance of this moment for the whole future of Germany and that he had a high estimation of this decision of the representatives of the German people. … However, he also made it clear that he could not come to a decision on this until he knew that consent to this was freely given by the princes and free cities of Germany as this would be of crucial significance for them and the peoples they governed.

[*The document continues by stating that Prussia has therefore consulted other German states and reports on the results of this consultation. The other states recognise that the Imperial Constitution is significant and lays down the basis for the formation of a federal state but that it is necessary to modify the constitution in various ways in order to:*]

1. Limit the competence of the Reich Authority. …
2. Preserve the existence of the individual states as independent entities and to limit them no more than is necessary in order to achieve the essential properties of a federal state.

[*How the National Assembly has failed to make such modifications. Also how, although some states have expressed support for the King of Prussia accepting the imperial title, others, including the most important, oppose this. Also objections to some of the Basic Rights and to the suspensive veto power of the emperor.*] This principle [the suspensive vote] threatens the constitutional-monarchical principle to which most of the German people are committed and, in conjunction with an electoral franchise which does away with any restrictions, gives to the constitution a character which makes it appear simply as a method, gradually and in an apparently legal way, to remove the supreme authority and introduce a republic.

...The conditions are lacking which would enable the king to accept this offer and, taking account of the duties he has to Germany and his own land ... and following the advice of his ministers, he has decided to reject ... the imperial title offered to him.

[*Concludes by saying that Prussia will still seek to lead the way towards the formation of a federal state but following a different path from that of the National Assembly. On the same day, 28 April, the Prussian government invited the other German governments to a conference in Berlin to consider such a way forward, thus inaugurating the Union policy which was only given up at the end of 1850.*]

Huber, [10], pp. 412–15.

DOCUMENT 41   ERFURT CONSTITUTION, 28 MAY 1849

[The constitution was designed to achieve a *kleindeutsch* arrangement shorn of any democratic or revolutionary features.]

PART I: THE EMPIRE

§1. The German Empire consists of the territories of the former German Confederation recognised in the Imperial Constitution.[1] The determination of the relation of Austria to the German Empire remains to be settled by mutual agreement.

§§2–5. As §§of Frankfurt Imperial Constitution.

PART II: THE IMPERIAL AUTHORITY

[*Most of this duplicates the Imperial Constitution.*]

PART III: THE HEAD OF THE EMPIRE

§65. The government of the Empire will be conducted by an Imperial President at the head of a college of princes.

§66. The office of Imperial President is bound to the Prussian crown.

§67. *Sets out the college with one seat each for Prussia and Bavaria and then five seats for the other states on a regional basis, each of which is respectively dominated by Saxony, Württemberg and Baden, Hannover, and the two Hessian states.*

...

PART IV: THE REICHSTAG

[As with the Imperial Constitution, there were two houses: an upper house consisting of half of the state delegates and half of the nominations from state parliaments; a lower house elected by the German people. The veto right of the lower house, which was written into the Imperial Constitution, does not appear in the Erfurt Constitution.]

Huber, [10], pp. 551–9.

---

[1]That is, the constitution agreed by the German National Assembly in early 1849.

DOCUMENT 42   **AGREEMENT BETWEEN BAVARIA, SAXONY AND WÜRTTEMBERG ON THE MAIN PRINCIPLES FOR A REVISION OF THE CONFEDERAL CONSTITUTION, 27 FEBRUARY 1850**

[A preamble declares that the Bundestag and the German National Assembly decisions of 1848–49 have failed to get agreement on a constitution by all members of the Confederation so these states are seeking the basis for an agreement which will not divide Germany.]

Art. 1. As common confederal concerns are recognised:

1. The diplomatic representation of Germany to the outside world. ...
2. Decisions on war and peace. ,
3. Command of armed forces at land and sea.
4. Maintenance of peace, law and order.
5. Supervision over common trade and tariff matters.
6. Supervision of transport, shipping, post, railways, telegraph.
7. Promotion of an understanding on matters to do with currencies, weights and measures.
8. Provision of necessary finance through state contributions.
9. Protection of those rights agreed by all German states.
10. Legislation on common confederal concerns.
11. Judicial competence over common confederal concerns.

Art.2. The confederal institutions are: the confederal government, the national representation, the confederal court.

Art.3. The confederal government is formed from seven members as follows: Austria, Prussia, Bavaria, Saxony, Hannover, Württemberg, the two Hesses.

[The other states can attach themselves to one or other of these seven.]

Art.5. The confederal government decides by simple majority.

Art.8. The national representation consists of 300 elected members, 100 from Austria, 100 from Prussia and 100 from the other states.

Art.9. The national representatives will be elected by the representatives of the state assemblies.

Art.11. The national representation participates in law making and without its consent the confederal government cannot make law. The national representation has the right of legislative initiative.

Art.12. The consent of the national representation is required for the determination of confederal expenditures and the financial contributions from the states. ...

Huber, [10], pp. 568–70.

DOCUMENT 43   OLMÜTZ AGREEMENT BETWEEN AUSTRIA AND PRUSSIA, 29 NOVEMBER 1850

[Sometimes called the Olmütz 'humiliation' because the result of a retreat by Prussia.]

§1. The governments of Austria and Prussia declare their intention finally and definitively to resolve the Hessian and Holstein affairs by means of a common decision of all German states. ...

§3. Taking into consideration that it is in the general interest that in both Kurhesse and Holstein there be created a situation in conformity with the law and confederal obligations, and that Austria and her allies have provided guarantees to Prussia concerning the occupation of Kurhesse, the two governments of Austria and Prussia have agreed the following. ...

(a) Prussia will place no obstacles in the way of troops invited into the state by the Elector. ... The two governments and their allies will ask the Elector to keep a batallion of Hessian and a batallion of Prussian troops in Cassel to maintain law and order. ...

§4. The ministerial conference will take place immediately in Dresden. ...

[*A second part of the agreement regulates the way in which troops will be demobilised, first by Prussia and then by Austria and its allies.*]

Huber, [10], pp. 580–2.

DOCUMENT 44   BISMARCK'S SPEECH TO THE PRUSSIAN *LANDTAG* ON THE OLMÜTZ AGREEMENT, 3 DECEMBER 1850

Why do great states go to war? The only good reason is state egoism, not romantic ideas. It is not worthy for a great state to fight for something which is not in its own interest. Gentlemen, show me a cause worthy of war and I will join with you. It is easy for a statesman ... to sail with the popular wind ... and sound the trumpet of war ... but woe to anyone who cannot justify the war once it is over. ...

Prussian honour in my view does not require Prussia to play the role of Don Quixote for parliamentary celebrities whose local constitution is under threat. Prussian honour rather requires us to keep clear of any shameful links with democracy ... but rather requires agreement between Prussia and Austria on the basis of common interests. ...

No one threatens our material interests, our borders, our internal security. We do not seek conquests ... The key question ... the arrangements for Germany, will be dealt with in a few days in a conference. ...

I would only ask the government not to stand down troops until the conference has produced a positive result. ...

When people connect the cause of German unity to that of a parliamentary union I must warn them against confusing two distinct matters. ... It is a peculiar unity which creates a separate league against our fellow Germans in the south. ... Just think of what will happen if it comes to war between the two parts of Germany. The difference in power between them is not significant so that even less powerful states than Russia and France could play a decisive role. I do not understand why we should allow this. ...

It is a peculiar idea that Austria is not a German power just because it rules over Slavs and Ruthenians. ... I recognise in Austria the representative and heir to an ancient German power which has often and gloriously wielded the German sword. ...

Huber, [10], pp. 582–4.

DOCUMENT 45 AUSTRIAN IDEA OF A CENTRAL EUROPEAN CUSTOMS UNION, JUNE 1850

[The Minister of Trade reports his views to the Prime Minister.]

... Austria has, above all, one thing to prevent, namely that, at the Conferences of Cassel[1], the *Zollverein*, due to expire at the end of 1852, should be renewed before the Austro-German Customs Union is irrevocably settled on a sure foundation. Such a renewal would bind all the German states for twelve years longer to Prussia's will in all national economic affairs. If Prussia were to see her supremacy assured for so long a time, she would scarcely be persuaded to enter the Customs Union with Austria – even though it offered the most convincing economic advantages – and to share, to that degree, her supremacy with her. The matter would, however, stand quite differently, if the renewal of the *Zollverein* were put in question by several of its members, or if it were made dependent upon the previous achievement of a Customs Union with Austria; for rather than endanger the intellectual and economic supremacy that she has gained through the *Zollverein*, Prussia would prefer an attempt to share it with Austria. ...

At the Cassell tariff conference, however, Austria has to protect other interests than the negative ones so far mentioned. She has to strive that the Austro-German Customs Union shall be seriously and thoroughly discussed there; that principles, harmonizing with the Austrian proposals, shall be laid down for these discussions; and that a time and place shall be fixed for a general Austro-German tariff conference; or, if this cannot be the aim, she should see that one or two of the states of the *Zollverein* are empowered to enter into negotiations with her in the name of the whole body. ...

In order to support this proposition, all the advantages will have to be circumstantially described. The advantages that Germany might expect from such a Customs Union would be: the moral unity which the same tariff and commercial laws, the common administration of these affairs, and an unobstructed internal economy would stimulate; closer political links; a large market; complementary industries in the various states, strengthening and stimulating each other; greater power and still greater standing abroad; the multiplication of shipping routes and a most remunerative overseas trade; finally, the satisfaction of the just wishes and expectations of the nation, to whom would be assured all the advantages of German unity without the dangerous disadvantages to particularist interests. Perhaps one might also mention that Austria herself, notwithstanding the political differences still outstanding, unreservedly offers her hand to help forward this unity, because she does not wish to withhold these advantages from the nation any longer and because she hopes to succeed through this unity in settling agitation on other matters. ...

Bruck to Schwarzenberg, 6 June 1850 (Vienna, Haus- Hof- und Staatsarchiv, PA II, no. 75).

Böhme, [1], pp. 77–8.

---

[1]The general conference of the *Zollverein* states sat at Cassel from 7 July to 2 November 1850. It was interrupted by the political disorders in Hesse-Cassel and was resumed at Wiesbaden in January 1851.

DOCUMENT 46 PRUSSIAN HOSTILITY TO AUSTRIA'S CUSTOMS UNION PLAN

...Prussia was able to give up the Erfurt Union and return to the Federal Diet, because the Confederation of 1815 is simply an international league in which a state of Prussia's power and standing may hope to be able to assert its independence even against a majority of smaller states. Prussia, however, can never comply with the Austrian demands in commercial policy without denying the whole political position she has up to now held, and without consenting to her own 'mediatization' [i.e., absorption by a more powerful state]. Prussia must, therefore, make it her resolve in commercial policy to maintain the *Zollverein*'s power of free self-determination, which is independent of any Austrian veto. However painful she may find a separation from the Confederation of 1815 and the disturbance of the long-accustomed relationships in many parts of the country and branches of industry, even so in this question of political life or death, Prussia will be obliged, quite decisively, to prefer a north-German, but independent, *Zollverein* to a greater Customs Union dependent upon Austria. ...

Extract from the *Constitutionelle Zeitung*, 9 April 1852. Böhme, [1], p. 87.

DOCUMENT 47   BISMARCK CONSIDERS AUSTRO-PRUSSIAN RELATIONS, 1856

Vienna's policy has made Germany suddenly too small for us both. So long as an honourable arrangement over the influence of each in Germany is not reached and executed, we shall both plough the same narrow furrow, and, just so long, Austria will remain the only state to whom we continually lose and from whom we could continually gain. ... We have ... a great number of conflicting interests, which neither of us can give up, without renouncing the mission in which each believes for itself; they are, therefore, conflicts which cannot be peacefully unravelled by diplomatic correspondence. Even the most serious pressure from abroad, the most urgent danger to the existence of us both, could not in 1813 nor in 1849 forge this iron. German dualism has for a thousand years, off and on, settled our mutual relations by internal war, and since the time of Charles V, it has done so at regular intervals once a century. In this century, too, war alone will set the time-piece of history at its right hour.

I do not intend by this reasoning to reach the conclusion that we should immediately direct our policy to bringing about the *decision* between Austria and ourselves in as favourable circumstances as possible. I only wish to express my conviction that we shall be obliged, sooner or later, to fight Austria for our *existence* and that it does not lie in our power to evade the fight, because the course of events in Germany can have no other outcome. If this is correct, which, of course, remains more a question of faith than knowledge, then it is not possible for Prussia to take self-denial to the point where she puts her own existence at stake in order to protect the integrity of Austria – in what is in my opinion a hopeless struggle ... [*Bismarck is referring to the situation after the end of the Crimean War where Franco-Russian* rapprochement *endangered Austria's position both in the Balkans and Italy.*]

Supposing we should be victorious against a Franco-Russian alliance, what in the end should we have fought for? For the maintenance of Austria's superiority in Germany and the pitiable constitution of the Germanic Confederation. We cannot possibly exert our last ounce of strength for that nor even set our own existence at stake for it. Were we to seek, however, in cooperation with Austria to put through alterations to the Germanic Confederation in our favour, we should fare as we did in 1815. ... Every deceit would be practised, now as then, in order to prevent Prussia from reaching a higher standing in Germany and to keep her under the pressure of her geographical position and the unfavourable Federal Constitution. ...

Bismarck to Manteuffel, Frankfurt, April 1856. Böhme, [1], pp. 89–90.

DOCUMENT 48   AUSTRIAN FEARS OF A PRUSSIAN ALLIANCE WITH LIBERAL NATIONALISM, OCTOBER 1859

[The Austrian ambassador in Berlin reports to Vienna.]

... In the attitude which Prussia as a German Power ... has recently observed, the Liberal direction of the present Cabinet is as unmistakable as a red streak. The evident purpose to which its endeavour is directed consists in this: to set Prussia up as the shield of a blossoming Liberalism to which the future in Germany belongs; to defeat the influence of Austria in this way by a political theory; and to enlarge her own moral influence and, if the opportunity occurs, her material power – perhaps without any anxious regard for legal right. In this connection the saying that 'the Kingdom of Prussia's skin is too tight for it' rings as true as the genuine Prussian wish: 'If we only had a Frederick the Great!'...

Since the Italian campaign the newspapers and the temper of the people show a malicious spirit against Austria. It is as if by their fits of anger they wished to stifle their sense of the injustice that has been done to true German interests. ...

Koller to Rechberg, Berlin, 27 October 1859 (*Die Auswärtige Politik Preussens*, vol. I, No. 535, p. 814). Böhme, [1], p. 93.

DOCUMENT 49   FOR OR AGAINST AUSTRIA? POLICY DISPUTES IN BERLIN, MARCH 1860

[The Prince Regent describes policy discussions to the Prussian Foreign Minister.]

The Council in its sitting today under my chairmanship determined to set out clearly the present position of Europe and to survey Prussia's policy in relation to it, to see how it should be shaped in the future. All were agreed that France, with its unpredictable Emperor, was the Power that was the source of danger to Europe, Germany, and Prussia. ... The nearest ally to whom we have to look is obviously Germany. She is as much affected by France's hankering after the left bank of the Rhine as Prussia and, because of her obligations to the Confederation, as much bound to ward off a hostile attack upon the Prussian Rhine Province as Prussia is to ward off a similar attack upon the Rhenish Palatinate [part of Bavaria]. At first sight, it seems obvious that Prussia need make no special exertions in this direction, since federal help is reciprocal. Almost all Germany for the last forty years has, however, cherished a hostile spirit against Prussia, and for a year this has been decidedly on the increase. One must admit, therefore, the sad possibility that south Germany at any rate may seek to preserve its neutrality by means of separate negotiations with France, so that Prussia may be left to endure the struggle alone, and be defeated, whereupon the spectral fear that she is out to devour Germany would be laid for a long time to come. It is a matter, then, of finding ways and means to put an end to German animosity against Prussia. By virtue of Prussia's superiority in moral and physical power, this would be easy if Austria, as our antagonist with her own enmity to us, were not also the moving spirit of German opposition. She could be as ready as the rest of Germany to leave her federal obligations unfulfilled, in the event of an attack upon Rhenish Prussia. The necessity, therefore, arises that we should enter into an understanding with Austria such as would make such an extreme eventuality impossible.

Agreement on this prevailed in the Council. Two decidedly different views, however, prevailed about the means to this end. The Minister von Schleinitz developed the view that, since he, with the whole Council, recognized France as the source of danger, any intimate connection with her in order to improve Prussia's position in Germany must be repudiated. Nothing then remained but to give up our hitherto sharp opposition to Austria and Germany, especially in the Federal Diet ..., and then to bring about a defensive alliance with Austria. After this it would automatically follow that Germany would go closely hand in hand with her two Great Powers. ...

The remaining members of the Council declared themselves, for the reasons adduced above, against such an alliance and also against any alteration of Prussia's German policy. Some even urged that Prussia's German policy should be taken to its logical conclusion, that she should not jib at a breach between subjects and governments. (I declared myself most decidedly against this course, for I will never play a part in Germany such as that played by Victor Emmanuel in Italy. This extreme was therefore set aside.)

Since I, in general, acceded to this point of view, I give the following directive for our future policy: we shall continue to follow a course in the

Federal Diet, calculated to keep the Diet within its legal limits or to bring it back to them. We must sedulously endeavour to take our stand on the basis of law. ... If we do that, it is quite unnecessary to enter a special alliance with Austria for German purposes. Should Austria request an alliance for non-German purposes, it should not be discussed, until she actually faces an enemy that she is unable to withstand alone. ...

The Prince Regent William to Schleinitz, 26 March 1860. Böhme, [1], pp. 93–5.

DOCUMENT 50 BEUST'S MEMORANDUM ON FEDERAL REFORM, 15 OCTOBER 1861

[The Saxon Prime Minister outlines a reform programme.]

...[In federal reform] one must above all keep in mind the character of what is already established and accordingly must remember that the Germanic Confederation is a league of states. There have been many attempts to set up a German federal state [a United States of Germany] yet, from this stand-point, the question whether it is at all possible will always be answered in the negative. This is because of the simple consideration that to set up a federal state would be tantamount to dissolving the Confederation. It is sufficient to draw attention to the fact that the defenders of this idea have only been able to think of its realization in terms of a single leadership in the hands of one Great Power. Quite apart from doubt whether the states, jointly placed under this leadership, would submit to it, the withdrawal of the other Great Power from the the Confederation would certainly follow. Nor can anyone, who looks at things with open eyes, be in doubt that the wider league [with Austria] which is part of this plan, could be nothing but an alliance treaty whose duration and execution would, like that of every other political alliance, remain dependent on changing circumstances.

This simple consideration is the foundation of the standpoint, that every attempt at reform that does not take the league of states as its starting point is impracticable.

The proposal, therefore, of a Parliament arising from direct, universal and popular election is impracticable. Such a national representative assembly, which, according to its mandate, would know nothing of the individual federated states, cannot be an institution integrated into a league of states, without either dissolving the league or being dissolved by it. This is the lesson of the years 1848 and 1849. The first alternative was intended, the outcome was the second. There is no place for this idea, then, in a plan of federal reform. The idea of a single central government is also impracticable. ... For the same reasons, a supreme army command, permanently in one hand, and an exclusive diplomatic representation abroad would seem equally impracticable. These ideas, therefore, do not belong ... to the area of federal reform.

Is this to ascribe the character of an absolutely wretched, spiritless thing to the league of states? Is the league of states, to which Germany owes the finest flowering of her cultural life, of her economy, and her prosperity, completely incapable of satisfying the needs of the national sense of community and the development of national power? Surely not. It is only that one does not wish to attain at *one stroke* what must be the work of patient and persistent cooperation and will surely succeed that way. ...

DRAFT REFORM

(a) The Federal Assembly is composed of representatives of the German governments. ...

The Federal Assembly meets twice a year, on 1 May and 1 November, for a period of four weeks at the longest. The holding of the meetings takes place, alternately in a city of south and in a city of north Germany (Regensburg and Hamburg). In the first Austria presides and in the second Prussia. ...

(b) The Assembly of Representatives is formed from representatives of the Parliaments of the states; Austria sends 30 members, drawn from the several representative bodies of her German provinces; Prussia, 30 members, chosen from the two Houses of her *Landtag*; Bavaria, 10, chosen from the two Houses of her Parliament: Saxony, Hanover, Württemberg, each 6. ... Total, 128. ...

The Assembly of Representatives does not meet regularly. It may only be summoned by the Federal Assembly. ...

In the intervals between the meetings of the Federal Assembly, a Federal Executive Power comes into operation. This Executive Power the Confederation places in the hands of Their Majesties the Emperor of Austria, the King of Prussia, and a third Prince of the Confederation, who act as plenipotentiaries for all the remaining states. ...

The Executive Power is endowed with the full power of the Confederation for the event of the occurrence of extraordinary political crises. ...

Böhme, [1], pp. 96–7.

DOCUMENT 51   FRANKFURT REFORM ACT, 1 SEPTEMBER 1863

[A programme agreed at a congress of German rulers convened by Austria but not attended by the King of Prussia.]

Art.1. The purpose of the German Confederation is to preserve the security and power of Germany against the outside world, to preserve internal order, to promote the welfare of the German nation ..., to protect the constitutional independence of the individual German states. ...

Art. 2. Conduct of confederal matters shall be undertaken by a Directory drawn from the princes and free cities of Germany.

A *Bundesrat* will be formed from envoys of the governments.

An assembly of confederal deputies shall meet periodically.

An assembly of princes shall meet periodically.

A confederal court shall be established.

Art. 3. [*A Directory with 6 votes, one each to Austria, Prussia and Bavaria, another three on a shared/rotating basis.*

In later clauses the Directory is given extensive executive powers, is chaired by Austria, and decides on a simple majority.

The assembly of deputies is elected by state parliaments with 75 each from Austria and Prussia and 152 deputies from the other states. The assembly had certain rights of participation in law making.]

Huber, [11], pp. 142–53.

DOCUMENT 52   RESPONSE OF THE PRUSSIAN GOVERNMENT TO THE FRANKFURT REFORM ACT, 15 SEPTEMBER 1863

[*The document begins by pointing out that neither Austria nor Prussia could ever submit to the will of the other or of the remaining German states. Any constitution which assumed such submission cannot work.*]

Prussia as a German power is not only equal to Austria but within the Confederation it has a greater population. ... Prussia cannot accept any preferential position for Austria but insists on complete equality.

[*It goes on to suggest that the way forward in reform should be to have a properly elected German parliament, independent of the states.*] ... The interests and needs of the Prussian people (*Volk*) are essentially and indivisibly identical with those of the German people. ...

Huber, [11], pp. 154–7.

DOCUMENT 53   RESOLUTION OF *NATIONALVEREIN* ON THE FRANKFURT REFORM ACT, 16 OCTOBER 1863

...The proposals drawn up by Austria and discussed at the princes' congress are inadequate to the claims of the nation to unity and freedom. ... They allow the continuation of all the defects of our constitution ... they strengthen the political influence of Austria and the particularist position of the kingdoms at the cost of Prussia and the other states. ... Equally unsatisfactory are the Prussian counter proposals, if such a government can be taken seriously. The national party holds firm to the Imperial Constitution [i.e., the constitution drawn up in 1849 by the German National Assembly]. ...

Huber, [11], p. 160.

DOCUMENT 54   RESOLUTION OF *REFORM VEREIN* ON FRANKFURT REFORM ACTS, 28 OCTOBER 1863

1. The assembly recognises in the princes' congress a patriotic act.
2. The assembly recognises in the Reform Acts a suitable basis for the development of the German constitution to firm unity and greater freedom. ...
3. The assembly hopes that all governments and parliaments which need to work together for reform recognise what will happen if they reject these proposals or tie them to impossible conditions. ...

Huber, [11], p. 160.

DOCUMENT 55   REPORT OF RECHBERG TO FRANZ JOSEPH, MAY 1864

[The Austrian Foreign Minister reflects on Austria, Prussia and customs union matters.]

The negotiations, which Your Majesty's Government has conducted for fully two years, to prevent the Franco-Prussian commercial treaty from applying to the whole area of the *Zollverein* and to avert from Austria the disadvantageous consequences of permanent exclusion from all share in guiding Germany's commercial policy, have reached the point when I must respectfully beg the favour of a decision as to Austria's further commercial policy at home and abroad.

First, so far as relations abroad, that is with the governments of the *Zollverein* states, are concerned, Prussia, in spite of her political relations with Austria, which are friendly, has deliberately continued to proceed in such a way as to make it impossible for the Imperial Government ever to realize the Customs Union, which by the treaty of February 1853 was set as Austria's and Prussia's common aim. Prussia has already significant results to show along this path. ... Despite its lack of reciprocity, the French commercial treaty has silenced all opposition in Prussia itself and, by its approach to the free trade system of the western Powers, has clearly won favour for itself in the Kingdom of Saxony and the Thuringian states, in Brunswick and Oldenburg. Moreover, the temper of the Parliaments in the medium-sized and southern states, in Bavaria, Württemberg, both Hessen, Nassau, etc., has quite turned in favour of the treaty and the maintenance of the *Zollverein* despite it. It is only the governments in the last-named states and still more their princes personally who, for political reasons and in order to counteract the sole dominance of Prussia in economic matters, continue their opposition and seek support from Austria. Hanover and Hesse-Cassel still offer for this reason to persevere in opposition. ... It is the only resistance north of the Main. Prussia does not owe these great successes only to her progressive industrialists and to their consciousness that they can stand up to competition from abroad. She owes them too to the consistency and singleminded direction with which the Berlin Cabinet, whether Liberal or Conservative statesmen hold the rudder, steadily uses the implementation and extension of the *Zollverein* as the foundation and guideline for Prussian power in Germany and thoroughly exploits it against Austria. Finally, the correctness of the economic principles, which have guided Prussian commercial policy, has very substantially contributed to her successes. It has been a policy of breaking free from artificial assistance to protect particular branches of industry, and has favoured the free exchange of the products of the soil and of manufacturing industry in natural competition.

These principles ... have latterly made further progress in Austria too. ... Unfortunately, the present Austrian draft tariff appears, to most of the governments friendly to us, still insufficient in its lowering of duties and approach to the system of the Franco-Prussian commercial treaty. These governments desire a further considerable reduction of duties to make it possible for them and for us to prove to Prussia that no economic barrier lies in the way of a German-Austrian Customs Union and that, therefore, only unjustifiable political motives dictate her wishes at all costs to exclude Austria from participation in the *Zollverein* and from leadership of the economic interests of Germany.

Böhme, [1], pp. 124–6.

DOCUMENT 56   BISMARCK TO WERTHER (VIENNA), 6 AUGUST 1864

[Bismarck in favour of Austro-Prussian cooperation.]

...A true German and Conservative policy is only possible when Austria and Prussia are united and take the lead. From this high standpoint an intimate alliance of the two Powers has been our aim from the outset. We see in its pursuit an earnest of the durability and fruitfulness of firm combination. We consider combination, though it is true both Powers and even all Germany already owe important successes to it, from a wider standpoint than that of the moment and as the means to consolidate the successes we have won. We consider combination (such as the joint action in waging war which is our immediate political purpose) as the foundation of an enduring unity and as the basis of a firm and healthy evolution of German policy in the future, and we have seen Austria's welcoming response in the *same* light. We consider the uncontested leadership of Germany by her two Great Powers as a peremptory requirement both for Germany and for the two Powers themselves. This leadership alone can guarantee to the complicated body of the Confederation, in itself little suited to action, a firm and assured attitude towards foreign Powers, and secure to it that influence on European politics which the nation justly demands. If Prussia and Austria are not united, politically Germany does not exist. If they are united, leadership belongs to them of right and in undertaking it they do no more than fulfil their duty to themselves and to the rest of Germany. At the same time, if they do so, but only if they do, they gain an increase in their own strength and security. This natural relationship existed to a certain extent before 1848. Unfortunately, events have since caused it to be almost forgotten. Quarrelling between Austria and Prussia has left some of the smaller states unsure, and made others presumptuous. ...

If we hesitate or weaken on the path we have so far trodden, or even if we tread with too great circumspection, timidity or disunity will be thought to impair our resolution. Courage will be found for majority decisions, to which we *cannot* conform, and the collapse of Germany will be brought about by an absurd effort to cause the European policy of two monarchs, powerful and victorious in arms, to be taken along in the wake of a few unarmed small states whose whole significance consists in the misdirected courage of their Parliaments and newspapers. If, on the contrary, we come forward firmly and energetically, the other German states will hardly venture to bring about majority decisions. They will not fail to understand the fruitlessness, indeed the danger, of such decisions, as soon as the two Powers face them in clear and united resolution. They will conform as soon as they see the firm will of Austria and Prussia. ...

Böhme, [1], pp. 128–9.

DOCUMENT 57 GASTEIN CONVENTION BETWEEN AUSTRIA AND PRUSSIA, 14 AUGUST 1865

[Austria and Prussia divide Schleswig-Holstein.]

Article I. The exercise of the Rights acquired in common by the High Contracting Parties, in virtue of Article III of the Vienna Treaty of Peace of 30th October, 1864, shall, without prejudice to the continuance of those rights of both Powers to the whole of both Duchies pass to His Majesty the Emperor of Austria as regards the Duchy of Holstein, and to His Majesty the King of Prussia as regards the Duchy of Schleswig.

Article II. The High Contracting Parties will propose to the Diet the establishment of a German Fleet, and will fix upon the Harbour of Kiel as a Federal Harbour for the said Fleet.

Until the resolutions of the Diet with respect to this proposal have been carried into effect, the Ships of War of both Powers shall use this Harbour, and the Command and the Police Duties within it shall be exercised by

Prussia. Prussia is entitled both to establish the necessary Fortifications opposite Friedrichsort for the protection of the entrance, and also to fit up along the Holstein bank of the inlet the Naval Establishments that are requisite in a Military Port. These Fortifications and Establishments remain likewise under Prussian command, and the Prussian marines and troops required for their Garrison and Protection may be quartered in Kiel and the neighbourhood.

Article III. The High Contracting Parties will propose in Frankfort the elevation of Rendsburg into a German Federal Fortress.

Until the Diet shall have issued the regulations respecting Garrisoning the said Fortress, the Garrison shall consist of Imperial Austrian and Royal Prussian troops under a command annually alternating on the 1st July.

Article IV. While the division agreed upon in Article I of the present Convention continues, the Royal Prussian Government shall retain two Military Roads through Holstein; the one from Lubeck to Kiel, the other from Hamburg to Rendsburg.

All details as to the Military Stations, and as to the transport and subsistence of the Troops, shall be regulated as soon as possible in a Special Convention. Until this has been done, the Regulations in force as to the Prussian Military Roads through Hanover shall be observed.

Article V. [*Prussia retains the disposal of one telegraphic wire for communication with Kiel and Rendsburg.* She will in due course request the granting of the concession for a railway from Lubeck through Kiel to Schleswig.]

Article VI. [*The duchies shall in due course enter the* Zollverein.]

Article VII. Prussia is entitled to make the Canal that is to be cut between the North Sea and the Baltic, through the Territory of Holstein, according to the result of the professional investigations undertaken by the Prussian Government. ...

Article VIII. [*Stipulations of the Treaty of Vienna relative to the financial obligations of the Duchies will remain unaltered.*]

Article IX. His Majesty the Emperor of Austria cedes to His Majesty the King of Prussia the Rights acquired in the aforementioned Vienna Treaty of Peace with respect to the Duchy of Lauenburg; and in return the Royal Prussian Government binds itself to pay to the Austrian Government the sum of 2,500,000 Danish rix-dollars, payable at Berlin in Prussian silver, 4 weeks after confirmation of the present Convention by their Majesties the Emperor of Austria and the King of Prussia.

Article X. The carrying into effect of the foregoing division of the Co-Sovereignty, which has been agreed upon, shall begin as soon as possible after the approval of this Convention by their Majesties the Emperor of Austria and the King of Prussia, and shall be accomplished at the latest by the 15th September.

The joint Command-in-Chief, hitherto existing, shall be dissolved on the complete Evacuation of Holstein by the Prussian troops and of Schleswig by the Austrian troops, by the 15th September, at the latest. ...

(L.S.) G. BLOME

(L.S.) VON BISMARCK

Medlicott and Coveney, [12], pp. 46–8.

DOCUMENT 58   AUSTRIAN MANIFESTO OF WAR, EMPEROR FRANZ JOSEPH, 17 JUNE 1866

The most pernicious of wars, a war of Germans against Germans, has become inevitable, and I now summon before the tribunal of history – before the tribunal of an eternal and all-powerful God – those persons who have brought it about, and make them responsible for the misfortunes which may fall on individuals, families, districts, and countries.

I decide upon fighting, confident in the goodness of my cause and upheld by the feeling of the inherent power of a great Empire, and in which the prince and the people are united in one and the same idea, in one and the same hope, those of defending the rights of Austria.

At the sight of my valiant armies, so ready for the fight, which form the bulwark, the rampart against which the forces of the enemy will dash themselves to pieces, I feel my courage and my confidence redoubled, and I can but feel a good hope when I meet the gaze of my faithful peoples, united and determined, and their ready devotion for every sacrifice.

The pure flame of patriotic enthusiasm strives with the same intensity throughout my empire. At the first call, the soldiers on furlough immediately joined their standards; volunteers enroll themselves in special regiments; the whole population able to bear arms in the threatened provinces fly to arms, and with the noblest self-denial they all strive to lessen the evils of war, and to provide for the wants of the army.

But one feeling animates the inhabitants of my kingdoms and provinces: they feel the ties which unite them, the strength which comes from union.

At this serious, but at the same time such an edifying moment, I doubly regret that the understanding on the constitutional questions are not sufficiently advanced to admit of my assembling the Representatives of all my kingdoms around my throne; actually deprived of that prop, my duty as a Sovereign is only the clearer, and my resolution to secure for ever the constitutional rights of my empire can but be strengthened.

We shall not be alone in the struggle which is about to take place. The princes and peoples of Germany know that their liberty and independence are menaced by a power which listens but to the dictates of egotism and is under the influence of an ungovernable craving after aggrandizement; and they also know that in Austria they have an upholder of the freedom, power, and integrity of the whole of the German Fatherland. We and our German brethren have taken up arms in defence of the most precious rights of nations. We have been forced so to do, and we neither can nor will disarm until the internal development of my empire and of the German states which are allied with it has been secured, and also their power and influence in Europe.

My hopes are not based on unity of purpose or power alone. I confide in an Almighty and just God, whom my house from its very foundation has faithfully served, a God who never forsakes those who righteously put their trust in Him. To Him I pray for assistance and success, and I call on my peoples to join me in that prayer.

Hamerow, [8], pp. 64–6.

DOCUMENT 59   PRUSSIAN MANIFESTO OF WAR, KING WILLIAM, 18 JUNE 1866

At the moment of the departure of the Prussian army for a decisive struggle, I feel called upon to speak to my people, to the sons and grandsons of the brave fathers to whom, a century ago, my father, who rests in God, addressed these memorable words:

'The country is in danger!'

Only a few years since, of my free will, and ignoring all previous injuries, I gave the emperor of Austria a friendly hand, when there was an intention of delivering up a German country to foreign dominion.

From blood shed in common, I was in hopes that an alliance based upon mutual esteem and furthering the prosperity and power of Germany would issue from the Austrian and Prussian brotherhood in arms. I have been deceived. Austria will not forget that her princes formerly reigned over Germany; and will not consider Prussia as her natural ally, but as a hostile rival.

In her opinion, Prussia must be opposed in all its tendencies, … because that which is beneficial to Prussia is objectionable to Austria.

The old and fatal jealousy has been revived: Prussia must be weakened, destroyed, dishonored; treaties have no longer any value. Not only are the princes of the Germanic Confederation called upon, but they are drawn into a breach of the Confederation. Wherever we cast our eyes in Germany, we are surrounded by enemies whose war cry is the humiliation of Prussia. But the spirit of 1813 lives in the Prussian people.

Who shall wrest from us an inch of Prussian territory if we are firmly resolved to keep the conquests of our fathers – if the king and the people, united more firmly than ever by the dangers of the country, consider as their first and most sacred duty to give their possessions and their blood to preserve her honor?

In the foresight, full of solicitude of what has just happened, I was obliged for years past, as the first duty of my royal functions, to prepare the civil portion of the Prussian people for a great development of power.

Like myself, every Prussian will confidently cast his eyes upon the armed force which defends our frontiers.

With their king at their head, the Prussian nation will truly feel itself a people in arms.

Our opponents deceive themselves if they imagine Prussia to be paralysed by dissensions at home. Before the enemy these disappear, and all hitherto opposed to one another stand henceforth united in triumph or misfortune.

I have done everything to save Prussia from the expenses and sacrifices of a war; my people know it; God also knows it, He who searches our hearts.

Up to the last moment I have striven in conjunction with France, Great Britain, and Russia, to come to an amicable arrangement.

Austria refused, and other German states have openly sided with her.

Let it then be so!

It is not my fault if my people are forced to maintain a difficult struggle, and perhaps to bear hard trials; but no other choice was left.

We are compelled to fight for existence. We must go forth to battle for life or death against those who wish to humiliate the Prussia of the great Elector, of the great Frederick, of the Prussia such as she has come out of the War of Independence, from the position to which the spirit of her princes, the bravery, devotedness, and morality of her people have raised her.

Let us implore the Almighty, He who rules the destinies of peoples and battles, that He may bless our arms.

If God give us the victory, we shall be strong enough to reunite more firmly and more prosperously those loosened ties of Germany which they who fear the right and the power of the national spirit have torn asunder.

Hamerow, [8], pp. 66–8.

DOCUMENT 60   **PRELIMINARY PEACE OF NIKOLSBURG, 26 JULY 1866**

[Preliminary settlement between Austria and Prussia.]

Art. I. With the exception of the Lombardo-Venetian kingdom,[1] the territory of the Austrian monarchy remains intact. His Majesty the King of Prussia engages to withdraw his troops from the Austrian territories occupied by them as soon as the peace shall be concluded, under reservation of the arrangements to be made upon the definite conclusion of the peace for guaranteeing the payment of the war indemnity.

Art. II. His Majesty the Emperor of Austria recognises the dissolution of the Germanic Confederation as it has existed hitherto, and consents to a new organisation of Germany without the participation of the Empire of Austria. His Majesty likewise promises to recognise the closer union which will be founded by His Majesty the King of Prussia, to the north of the line of the Main, and he declares that he consents to the German states south of that line entering into a union, the national relations of which, with the North German Confederation, are to be the subject of an ulterior agreement between the two parties.

Art. III. His Majesty the Emperor of Austria transfers to His Majesty the King of Prussia all the rights which the Treaty of Vienna of 30th October, 1864, recognised as belonging to him over the Duchies of Schleswig and Holstein, with this reservation, that the people of the northern districts of Schleswig shall be again united to Denmark if they express a desire to be so by a vote freely given.

Art. IV. His Majesty the Emperor of Austria undertakes to pay His Majesty the King of Prussia the sum of 40,000,000 thalers to cover a part of the expenses which Prussia has been put to by the war. But from this sum may be deducted the amount of the indemnity for the costs of war which His Majesty the Emperor of Austria still has the right of exacting from the Duchies of Schleswig and Holstein, by virtue of Article XII of the Treaty of Peace of 30th October, 1864 before cited, say 15,000,000 thalers, with 5,000,000 in addition, as the equivalent of the cost of providing for the Prussian army, maintained by the Austrian countries occupied by that army until the time of the conclusion of the peace.

Art. V. In conformity with the wish expressed by His Majesty the Emperor of Austria, His Majesty the King of Prussia declares his willingness to let the territorial state of the kingdom of Saxony continue in its present extent, when the modifications are made which are to take place in Germany; reserving to himself, however, to regulate in detail, by a special peace with His Majesty the King of Saxony, the questions as to Saxony's part in the expenses of the war, as well as the future position of the kingdom of Saxony in the North German Confederation.

On the other hand, His Majesty the Emperor of Austria promises to recognise the new organisation which the King of Prussia will establish in the north of Germany, including the territorial modifications consequent thereon.

Art. VI. His Majesty the King of Prussia undertakes to prevail upon His Majesty the King of Italy, his ally, to give his approval to the preliminaries of peace and to the armistice based on those preliminaries, so soon as the Venetian kingdom shall have been put at the disposal of His Majesty the King of Italy by a declaration of His Majesty the Emperor of the French.

Art. VII. The ratifications of the present convention shall be exchanged at Nikolsburg in the space of two days at the latest.

Art. VIII. Immediately after the ratification of the present convention shall have been effected and exchanged, their Majesties the Emperor of Austria and the King of Prussia will appoint plenipotentiaries, who will meet at a place to be hereafter named, to conclude the peace upon the basis of the present preliminary treaty, and to agree upon the details of the conditions.

Art. IX. For that purpose the contracting states, after having decided upon these preliminaries, will conclude an armistice for the Austrian and Saxon armies on the one part, and for the Prussian army on the other part, of which the detailed conditions, from the military point of view, are to be immediately determined. That armistice shall date from the 2nd of August, the day to which the present suspension of arms shall be prolonged.

The armistice shall, at the same time, be concluded with Bavaria, and General the Baron von Manteuffel will be instructed to conclude with the kingdom of Württemberg and the grand duchies of Baden and Hesse-Darmstadt, as soon as those states shall propose it, an armistice beginning on the 2nd August, and founded on the state of military possession at the time.

Hamerow, [8], pp. 68–70.

---

[1] The Lombardo-Venetian kingdom was ceded by Austria to Italy by the Treaty of Prague of 23rd August, 1866.

DOCUMENT 61   KING WILLIAM ADDRESSES THE LEGISLATURE IN BERLIN AFTER THE VICTORY OVER AUSTRIA, 5 AUGUST 1866

[Proposal of an Indemnity Bill to bring the constitutional crisis to an end.]

On seeing the representatives of the country gathered around me, my feelings impel me before all else to give expression from this place to my own and my people's thanks for God's grace which has aided Prussia, at the cost of heavy but productive sacrifices, not only to avert the dangers of a hostile attack from our frontiers, but also by the rapid victories of our army, to add new laurels to the hereditary renown of the nation, and to pave the way for the national development of Germany.

Under the evident blessing of God all who could bear arms answered with enthusiasm the call to the combat for the independence of the Fatherland; and our heroic army, supported by few but faithful allies, proceeded from success to success, from victory to victory, in the east as well as in the west. Much precious blood has flowed; the Fatherland bewails many a brave one, who, rejoicing in victory, died the hero's death, till our banners waved in one line from the Carpathians to the Rhine.

By their united endeavours the government and the representatives of the people will have to bring to maturity the fruits that must proceed from the bloody seed, if it is not to have been sown in vain.

Dear Gentlemen of both Houses of the *Landtag*!

My Government can look with satisfaction on the financial condition of the state. Careful foresight and conscientious economy have placed it in a position to overcome the great financial difficulties which are the natural result of the present situation of affairs.

Although in late years considerable sacrifices have been imposed on the treasury through the war with Denmark, it has been possible to defray the expenses of the war up to the present time out of the revenues of the state and other available resources, without further burthen to the country than the legal supplies in kind demanded for warlike purposes. I the more confidently hope that the supplies necessary for the successful termination of the war, and for the payment of the supplies in kind, while still maintaining order and security in the finances, will be readily granted by you.

It has not been possible in late years to come to an agreement with the representatives of the country on the settlement of the estimates. The state disbursements which have been made during that period, therefore, have not the legal basis which, as I again acknowledge, can only be given to the estimates according to Article XCIX of the constitution, by a law which is to be agreed upon every year between my government and both Houses of the *Landtag*. If my government has nevertheless for several years carried on the financial department of the state without this legal basis, it has been after careful consideration, and with the conscientious conviction that the continuation of a regular administration, the fulfilment of the legal obligations towards the creditors and the functionaries of the state, the maintenance of the army and of the state institutions, were vital questions, and that therefore such a proceeding was one of those unavoidable necessities from which no government that studies the interests of the country can or ought to withdraw. I feel confident that late events will aid in so far attaining the indispensable understanding, that the indemnity which is to be solicited of the national representatives will be readily granted to my government for the administration conducted without the budget law, and that thus the conflict that has been going on may be the more surely terminated for ever, as it may be hoped that the political situation of the Fatherland will allow an extension of the frontiers of the state and the establishment of a united federal army under the command of Prussia, the charges of which will be equally borne by all the members of the Confederation. The proposals which are requisite in this respect for a convocation of the national representatives of the federal states will be immediately laid before the *Landtag*.

Gentlemen, you feel with me, the whole Fatherland feels, the great importance of the moment which brings me back to my home. May Providence bless Prussia's future as graciously as the time just past has been visibly blessed. God grant it.

Hamerow, [8], pp. 80–2.

GLOSSARY

Bundesrat One of the main institutions created by the **North German Confederation** (see below) and which continued after 1871 under the constitution of the German Second Empire. It was intended to be the institution which drafted national legislation.

Bundestag The main institution created by the *Deutsche Bund* (see below).

Deutsche Bund (German Confederation) Established at the Congress of Vienna in 1815 with further additions to its constitution in 1820, this consisted of some thirty-eight states, ranging from Austria and Prussia to some tiny territorial princedoms and four city-states. The Hungarian half of the Habsburg Empire and the Italian provinces of Lombardy and Venetia were outside the Confederation, as were, until 1848, the Prussian provinces of East and West Prussia and the Grand Duchy of Posen. Some member states were ruled through personal union by foreign princes such as the King of Denmark (Holstein) and of the Netherlands (Luxemburg).

An assembly of state delegations formed the *Bundestag* which met in permanent session in Frankurt am Main. Voting was roughly related to the size of member states. *Bundestag* business was divided between an inner committee and the plenary body. There were no executive or judicial institutions. The *Bundestag* did not function between March 1848 and early 1851. It effectively ceased to exist with the outbreak of the Austro-Prussian War in June 1866.

Deutsche Zollverein (German Customs Union) The general customs union agreement, which commenced on 1 January 1834, covered the states of Prussia, the two Hesses, Bavaria, Württemberg, Saxony and some small central German states. New members joined as follows: Baden and Nassau (1835); Frankfurt (1836), Brunswick (1841), Hannover (1851), Oldenburg (1852), Schleswig-Holstein (1866), the Mecklenburg states and Lübeck (1868); Alsace-Lorraine (1871); Hamburg and Bremen (1888). The *Zollverein* abolished internal tariff barriers and negotiated common tariffs with other states. Until 1867 its affairs were managed by a general conference which met annually. In 1867 it handed over control to the **North German Confederation** in association with the south German states outside the Confederation. In 1868 a parliament was set up consisting of delegates from the *Reichstag* of the North German Confederation and directly elected deputies from the south German states. In 1871 the powers of the *Zollverein* were taken over by the government of the Second Empire.

Großdeutsch This means 'great(er) German'. It refers to the policy of including Austrian Germany within a German national state. It was often an anti-Prussian rather than a pro-Austrian position.

This position is not to be confused with 'pan-German' or 'greater German' views which took shape after 1871. Pan-Germans in Austria advocated the attachment of Austrian Germany to the 1871 *Reich*. Pan-Germans in the Second Empire advocated more general expansion in central Europe.

Großpreußisch   This means 'great(er) Prussian'. It refers to the policy of Prussian territorial expansion. Bismarck consistently took this view, seeing it as a long-established Prussian policy. The major territorial transformation of 1867 can be described as *großpreußisch* in that it involved such expansion with the annexation by Prussia of Hannover, Schleswig-Holstein, Hesse, Nassau and Frankfurt.

The relationship between *großpreußisch* and **Kleindeutsch** positions is complex. For example, the exclusion of Austria from Germany and the formation of the **North German Confederation** in 1866–67 can be seen as *kleindeutsch* but the simultaneous annexation of Hannover, Schleswig-Holstein, Hesse, Nassau and Frankfurt by Prussia can be seen as *großpreußisch*.

Kleindeutsch   This means 'little German'. It refers to the policy of excluding Austrian Germany from a German national state. It is usually associated with a liberal nationalist position which often included demands for reforms of the Prussian state and left the door open for Austrian Germany to join the nation-state later.

Mitteleuropa   This means 'middle (or central) Europe'. In the pre-1871 German context it refers to the policy of union or some other very close link between the German lands and the rest of the Habsburg Empire. After 1871 the position overlaps with that of Pan-German advocacy of expansion into non-German territories, as put into practice briefly by the Second Empire during the First World War and by the Third Reich during the Second World War.

North German Confederation   This was created in 1867 and consisted of the newly enlarged Prussia and the other German states north of the river Main. Its principal institutions were a **Reichstag** elected by universal manhood suffrage and a **Bundesrat** made up of delegations from the member states along the same lines as the now defunct **Bundestag** (see above). The Presidency of the Confederation was held by the King of Prussia. The Chancellor (who was Bismarck) was appointed by the President and conducted confederal business through the **Bundesrat** as well as appearing before the **Reichstag** to explain policies.

Reichstag   This was a parliament elected on the basis of universal manhood suffrage, originally established as part of the **North German Confederation** in 1867 (see above) and then extended to the remaining south German states under the constitution of the German Second Empire.

Trias policy   This refers to reform proposals put forward by various combinations of the medium German states. Such proposals normally tried to enhance the authority of the **Deutsche Bund** while preventing either Austrian or Prussian dominance and retaining autonomy for the other German states.

Union policy   This refers to the Prussian policy initiated by Radowitz in early 1849 which aimed to bring other parts of non-Austrian Germany under Prussian influence, principally through agreements between medium states and Prussia but also with liberal support. It was abandoned at the end of 1850 when directly opposed by Austria. It was briefly revived during the 'New Era', especially in 1861–62. It was abandoned by Bismarck, who relied instead on direct dealings with Austria (whether through cooperation or war) and the cutting out of the medium states as the way to make progress on the national question.

Arndt, Ernst Moritz (1769–1860)   Historian and poet. After 1800 taught history and philosophy at Greifswald University. Lived in Sweden in 1803, 1806–9. Secretary to Baron Stein (1812–16) during which time he produced much nationalist, anti-French propaganda based on romantic and language ideas. Opposed to peace settlement of 1815, he was suspended from his post as Professor of History at Bonn University in 1820 on suspicion of 'demagogy'. Only restored to his post in 1840 after Frederick William IV acceded to the Prussian throne. Elected to the German National Assembly in 1848 where he supported the offer of the hereditary emperorship to Frederick William.

Benedek, Ludwig August Ritter von (1804–81)   Soldier. Born into Austrian Lutheran nobility. Entered Austrian army in 1822, joined General Staff in 1833 and played a leading role in repressing the Galician uprising of 1846. Active in counter-revolutionary measures in Italy and Hungary in 1848–49. Chief of Staff to Radetzky in Italy, 1850–57. Played a distinguished role in the 1859 war against Piedmont and France. Created Field Marshal. Appointed commander of the Northern Army in 1866. Following Königgrätz stripped of his offices and brought before a court martial. Franz Joseph halted the proceedings. Benedek never sought subsequently to explain or justify himself.

Graf von Bernstorff, Christian Günther (1769–1835)   Diplomat. Born in Denmark. Entered Danish foreign ministry in 1788; envoy to Berlin in 1791. Back in Denmark in 1797, he tried to steer foreign policy on a path of neutrality. The failure of this policy by 1807 was followed by his resignation from Danish service in 1810. He entered Prussian service in 1818, soon becoming Foreign Minister. Increasingly unhappy with subordinating Prussian policy to Austria and with Metternich's repressive response to all reform movements, he retired on health grounds in 1832.

Graf von Beust, Friedrich Ferdinand Freiherr (1809–86)   Statesman. Grew up in Dresden, studied law at Göttingen and Leipzig, entered Saxon diplomatic service in 1830. In 1849 appointed Foreign Minister, added Ministry of Interior in 1853 and in effect chief minister. Called in Prussian troops to repress revolution in 1849. Policy concerns after 1850: to maintain a balance between Prussia and Austria, to promote confederal reform to the benefit of the medium states, especially Saxony, and to combine authoritarian politics with economic liberalism at home. In June 1867 appointed Chancellor of Austria-Hungary where cautiously tried to undo some of the effects of 1866. Failure of this policy led to his resignation in October 1871. After terms as ambassador to Paris and London, he retired in 1882. His autobiography was published a year after his death.

Bismarck, Otto von (1815–98)   Born the son of a noble Prussian landowner he briefly entered state service after university study, soon deciding to run the family estate. In 1847 he was a delegate to the United Diet called by Frederick William IV. During the 1848–49 revolutions he made a name for himself as an outspoken reactionary. In 1850 as a deputy to the Erfurt Parliament he defended the Olmütz settlement. His reward for his royalism was appointment as Prussian envoy to the restored German *Bundestag* in Frankfurt. Here he constantly sought to challenge Austrian pre-eminence in Germany. He was removed from this sensitive post in 1859 and served as ambassador to Russia. After a brief period in 1862 as ambassador to France, he was appointed Minister-President of Prussia in September 1862. He governed unconstitutionally until 1866, forcing through army reforms. These paid dividends in the wars against Denmark and Austria. In 1867 he extended Prussian territory and established the North German Confederation, acquiring the new office of Chancellor to add to those of Prussian Minister-President and Foreign Minister. After the defeat of France in 1870–71 he became Imperial Chancellor. For twenty years he dominated the politics of the Second Empire with a mixture of autocracy, manipulation and populism. After the death of William I in 1888 he lost the crucial support of the emperor and was forced to resign in 1890. He remained politically active during his retirement, constantly criticising the new government.

Bonaparte, Napoleon (1769–1823)   Born in Corsica, he joined the French army in 1785. Led successful action against provincial resistance to the Jacobin regime in 1793. Out of favour following the fall of the Jacobins but recovered with suppression of royalist rising in Paris in 1795. First major military success against Austria as commander of the army of Italy (1795–97). Unsuccessful invasion of Egypt in 1798. Back in France in 1799 became First Consul in the new regime. Dictator by 1802, crowned Emperor in 1804. Initiated legal and administrative reform at home and a series of successful wars abroad marked by crushing battlefield victories, as against Russia and Austria (Austerlitz, 1805) and Prussia (Jena and Auerstadt 1806). Following Peace of Tilsit with Russia (1807) had established an empire extending from Spain to the Baltic, including satellite states in the Low Countries, the German and Italian lands, Polish and Balkan territories. 1808 saw the first effective challenge with the uprising in Spain but in 1809 a further war with Austria was conclusively won. The beginning of the end was the invasion of Russia in 1812. By early 1813 defeat and retreat had become a rout and his armies were pressed back by a general alliance including Britain, Austria, Prussia and Russia. He abdicated in 1814 and was exiled to Elba. In 1815, exploiting the unpopularity of the restored Bourbon regime, he escaped from Elba and took control in France. The Hundred Days was brought to an end with defeat at Waterloo (18 June 1815). Exiled to St. Helena where he died.

Ferdinand I (1793–1875)   Austrian Emperor (1835–48) in succession to his father Francis I. An epileptic, he was incapable of personal rule and largely left matters to members of the royal family and leading officials such as Metternich and Kolowrat, an arrangement that often induced governmental paralysis. When this incapacity became a major handicap during the year of revolution he was pressed into abdication in favour of his nephew Franz Joseph.

Francis I (1768–1835)   Succeeded his father Leopold as Holy Roman Emperor and ruler of Habsburg lands in 1792. Within a month he found his realm in a state of continual warfare with France (1792–97, 1799–1801, 1805, 1809, 1813–15), losing all but the last of these wars. Declared himself Austrian Emperor in 1804 and gave up the imperial title in 1806. In 1810 signalled accommodation with France by marrying his daughter Maria Louise to Napoleon. After 1815 a thorough-going conservative and defender of absolute monarchical powers. However, his own very frugal and unpretentious lifestyle ensured him some popularity. In his testament for his son he included the injunction: 'Rule and change nothing.'

Franz Joseph (1830–1916) Succeeded his uncle Ferdinand as Emperor in 1848, his own father having resigned his claim to the succession. Hardworking and dutiful, if unimaginative, he began his reign an energetic reactionary. His policy of restoring order and non-constitutional rule largely succeeded for a decade. Defeat in the 1859 war against France forced him into some constitutional concessions. The defeat of 1866 in turn compelled him to accept the role of a constitutional ruler in a dualist Austro-Hungarian system. He fatalistically accepted this role and the reduction of his country to the status of a second-rank power up to his death.

Frederick William III (1770–1840) Succeeded his father Frederick William II as King of Prussia in 1797. A cautious reformer before 1806, he also in that time sought territorial gains within the Holy Roman Empire through negotiations with France. This policy was shattered with the defeat of 1806–7 and the savage settlement imposed on Prussia. He could only return to Berlin in 1810 and, although allowing the reform party some achievements, strenuously sought to avoid giving offence to France. He played little active role in the mobilisation and war of 1813–15 or the peace negotiations. Increasingly supported a reactionary policy after 1815. One policy to which he did give energetic support was the union of the Lutheran and Reformed churches in Prussia.

Frederick William IV (1795–1861) Succeeded his father Frederick William III to the Prussian throne in 1840. His aesthetic enthusiasms as well as some of his political values led to him being dubbed 'the romantic upon the throne'. Active in the restoration of Cologne cathedral and overcoming Protestant/Catholic tensions. Resisted constitutional reform in 1847 after having convened a United Diet. Quickly gave way to the revolutionary movement in early 1848 but persuaded to move in a counter-revolutionary direction by the end of the year. In 1849–50 supported the 'Union policy' of Radowitz until compelled to abandon Radowitz at Olmütz. In the 1850s especially concerned with a conservative revision of the December 1848 constitution he had himself imposed and with maintaining neutrality during the Crimean War. Already mentally unstable, in 1858 an illness left him with brain damage and his brother William was declared Regent and effective ruler.

Gagern, Wilhelm Heinrich August (1799–1880) Politician. One of a family of active politicians in Hesse-Darmstadt. As a young soldier in the service of Nassau he fought and was wounded at Waterloo. Involved in student nationalist movements after 1815. After university study (including abroad where his father prudently sent him) he entered government service in Hesse-Darmstadt, combining this with serving as a liberal member of the lower house of the Hesse *Landtag* from 1832. Persecution led to temporary withdrawal into private life but he returned as a *Landtag* deputy in 1847. Active in liberal oppositional meetings and in the early steps to secure a national parliament in 1848, he was elected to the German National Assembly. He sought to reconcile Prussian and Austrian positions, notably with his scheme for an inner and an outer union and, on this basis, was placed in charge of the provisional government in December

1848. After the failure of the policy of offering the Emperorship to Frederick William IV and the dissolution of the parliament he once more withdrew into private life. Later he renewed his support for Prussian-Austrian parity but subsequently accepted the Prussian-led unification and enthusiastically supported an alliance between Austria and Germany.

Hardenberg, Prince Karl August von (1750–1822)   Statesman. A German imperial noble he entered Prussian service and began his reforming career as administrator of the Hohenzollern enclave of Ansbach-Bayreuth. State minister by the time of the 1806 war. He advised continuing resistance to France after initial military defeats. Following the peace with France in 1807 he was dismissed from office on Napoleon's insistence. In enforced retirement he set out his reform programme in the Riga Memorandum. He was recalled to power in 1810 in the new office of state chancellor. Here he sought to build on the reform movement which had started with Stein's ministry of 1807–8 – especially financial rationalisation, consultation with representative bodies, centralised administration, and guild and land tenure reform. However, much of this was undermined by the desperate postwar crisis in the rump state of Prussia and the continued burdens of occupation and war to 1815. In foreign policy Hardenberg sought to restore Prussia to the ranks of the major powers, in which he succeeded by 1815. However, lack of support from the king and the rise of conservative opposition undermined the reform impulse at home and left Hardenberg looking increasingly ineffective. When he died in 1822, the office of state chancellor lapsed.

Humboldt, Wilhelm von (1767–1835)   Statesman and scholar. Born into an aristocratic Prussian family, early education at home and study of law and classics, the latter dominating his values. After travel, including to revolutionary France, and brief state service in 1791, he lived the life of an independent scholar and traveller. Re-entered state service in 1802, serving in Rome. Returned to Prussia in 1808 and for ten years played a leading role first in educational reform and then diplomacy. A key achievement was the foundation of Berlin University in 1810. Subsequently served as ambassador to Austria and, with Hardenberg, represented Prussia at the Congress of Vienna. With the onset of reaction in 1819 he was dismissed from office. He returned to scholarship, using his phenomenal range of languages, ancient and modern, to make major advances in the fields of philology and linguistics.

Jahn, Friedrich Ludwig 'Turnvater' (1778–1852)   Teacher. After theological, historical and Germanic studies, never satisfactorily completed, and becoming a Free Mason, Jahn travelled a good deal, supporting himself as a private tutor. He settled in Berlin in 1809 as a school teacher. In 1810 he founded the *Deutsche Bund*, forerunner of the post–1815 student nationalist movements known as the *Burschenschaften*. Drawing mainly on officers and teachers, its aim was liberation from French rule and German unity. In 1810 Jahn established the first gymnastic club; its organised drills intended to inculcate 'Germanic' virtues – physical and moral. Jahn served in a volunteer unit fighting in the war of 1813–14. After 1815 he played an active role in the *Burschenschaften*. He was arrested in 1819, imprisoned for a year, and remained in protective custody until 1825. He was only fully rehabilitated when Frederick William IV acceded to the throne in 1840. He was elected to the German National Assembly in 1848 but played little active part in its affairs.

List, Friedrich (1769–1846)   Economist and politician. After working in his
father's tannery, he undertook secretarial jobs in various town governments in
Württemberg. He went late to university, studying law and administration. By
1816 he was active in the early constitutional politics of Württemberg; in 1818
teaching economics at Tübingen; in 1819 writing a petition in favour of a
German tariff system on behalf of some merchants and founding the German
Trade and Manufacturing Association. His publicist work led to an order for his
arrest and his flight abroad. He was arrested when he returned in 1824 but
released provided he emigrated to the USA. After a successful career as farmer,
businessman and publicist, he returned to Germany in the 1830s, acting as US
consul to various German states. To his propaganda and promotional activity for
a customs union List added the cause of nation-building through a railway
system. His major work, *The National System of Political Economy*, went
through several editions in the early 1840s. In the midst of activity but exhausted
and depressed, he committed suicide in November 1846.

Metternich, Prince Clemens von (1773–1859)   Born of German nobility in the
Rhineland he moved to Vienna in 1794 and joined the Austrian diplomatic
service. Following service in Dresden and Berlin he was posted to Paris (1806–9).
Here he observed a triumphant Napoleon at first hand. Following the Austrian
defeat in 1809 he became Austrian foreign minister, concerned to appease
Napoleon and prevent radical reform at home. He organised the marriage of the
daughter of Francis I to Napoleon in 1810. Reluctant to break off the alliance
with Napoleon in 1813 and tried to broker a peace which would retain
Napoleon's rule in France. Eventually he joined the anti-French alliance and
presided over the Congress of Vienna (1814–15) where his policies of
monarchical restoration and conservative alliances against threats of war and
revolution largely prevailed. His subsequent policy was largely a defence of the
settlement of 1815, using methods of diplomacy, surveillance and mild
repression. Although predominant in foreign policy he was compelled to share
domestic power with other figures, especially during the reign of the ineffectual
Ferdinand. In early 1848 he was a personal focus for much of the anger of the
popular movement and fled to England. However, with the counter-revolution he
returned to Austria and was, until his death, constantly consulted by figures such
as Rechberg on the conduct of foreign policy.

Moltke, Helmut (1800–91)   Soldier. Born in Holstein, the son of an officer, Moltke
joined the Danish cadet school at the age of eleven. Family contacts enabled him
to move in literary and intellectual circles. He joined the Danish army in 1819
but, because of limited prospects, transferred to the Prussian army in 1822. He
studied in Berlin, joining the map section of the General Staff in 1828 and
becoming a staff officer in 1832. Leave to travel in the Middle East saw him
advising the Ottoman Sultan in war against Mehemet Ali of Egypt. His published
accounts of these experiences established his literary reputation. Back in Berlin
from 1840 he held a series of staff posts, and also acted as adjutant to members
of the royal family and tutor to the later Emperor Frederick. This was when the
then Prince William got to know and respect him. He was appointed Chief of
Staff in 1858. William I turned to him as his principal military adviser and
effective commander-in-chief in the last phase of the Danish war of 1864 and
confirmed that position just prior to the wars of 1866 and 1870–71. Thus

Moltke's argument for effective command by the war planners and also his modern principles of war making could be put into effect. He remained Chief of Staff until 1888 when William II permitted him to retire.

Napoleon III (1808–73)   Nephew of Napoleon Bonaparte he became pretender to the Bonapartist imperial throne in 1832 when his cousin 'Napoleon II' died. Led unsuccessful risings in 1836 and 1840. In December 1848 he exploited monarchist splits, continuing Bonapartist sentiments and popular disaffection with the new republic to achieve a massive victory in the Presidential election. After uneasy cohabitation with the republic, he instituted a coup in December 1851. A plebiscite in 1852 ratified the restoration of empire. His first decade of rule saw military and foreign policy successes (Crimean War, 1859 war against Austria) and a combination of liberalising and populist measures at home. In failing health in the 1860s, setbacks in Mexico and in Europe (above all, the failure to profit from the Austro-Prussian War of 1866) led the regime into the reckless decision to go to war against Prussia in 1870. Military defeat led to his overthrow and the installation of the Third Republic. He died shortly afterwards in exile in England.

Radowitz, Joseph Maria Ernst Christian Wilhelm von (1797–1853)   Soldier and politician. Born in Hesse-Cassel, son of a noble Catholic family which originated in Hungary. Raised as a Protestant (his mother's religion) until the age of thirteen and thereafter as a Catholic. Military education in Paris and Westphalia. Wounded fighting on the French side at Bautzen in 1813. Teaching and service with the Hesse state but disputes with the prince led to his arrest and subsequent switch to Prussian military service in 1823, rising rapidly in rank. Resided in England as tutor to the crown prince of Hesse, married into Prussian aristocracy, played leading role in confederal military affairs and collaborated on the conservative periodical, the *Berliner Politische Wochenblatt*. Became a close acquaintance of Frederick William IV. As envoy on a range of missions to other German states, he developed general reform ideas in which Prussia should take the lead. Concerned that his continued presence might embarrass the king after the outbreak of revolution, he resigned from service in early 1848 and retired to Mecklenburg. Elected to the German National Assembly. Frederick William IV recalled him to service in early 1849 to develop an alternative national policy following the king's rejection of the offer of the imperial Emperorship. Radowitz led foreign policy, especially in German matters, until late 1850, although only appointed Foreign Minister in September 1850. When confrontation with Austria finally led the king to abandon Radowitz's policy in November 1850, Radowitz resigned as Foreign Minister. In his remaining years he was engaged in minor diplomatic and military tasks and writing.

Graf Rechberg, Johann Bernhard (1806–99)   Diplomat. Born in Regensburg (Bavaria). His father was Bavarian minister at the Congress of Vienna. After his studies, he entered Austrian diplomatic service in 1828, holding posts in Europe and Brazil. Briefly envoy to the *Bundestag* in Frankfurt in 1849. In the early 1850s he was entrusted with negotiations over Austria's relationship to the *Zollverein*. Back in Frankfurt in 1855 where he frequently clashed with Bismarck. With the dismissal of Buol-Schauenstein at the start of the 1859 war, Rechberg became Foreign Minister in the midst of a crisis, having to negotiate a settlement after military defeat and working in a constitutional government for which, as a disciple of Metternich, he had no sympathy. In the Metternichian tradition he pursued a defensive and conservative policy, including dualism with Prussia in the war with Denmark. When this policy began to break down after the end of the war, and also at loggerheads with Schmerling, he was forced to resign in August 1864.

Schmerling, Anton Ritter von (1805–93)   Statesman. Born to a noble family, studied law in Vienna. Entered state service but also in 1846 became noble member of the Austrian *Landtag* and then worked for the *Landtag* on issues of legal reform. Played a leading role in the moderate constitutional movement in Vienna in early 1848. Briefly served as Austrian envoy to the *Bundestag* in Frankfurt. Elected to the German National Assembly. The first cabinet appointed by Archduke Johannes in July 1848 included him as Minister of Interior and soon after Minister-President. In this capacity he invited troops into Frankfurt to put down the September disturbances. As an Austrian he utterly opposed Gagern's programme of an inner and an outer union, resigning the Presidency when this programme received majority support. On returning to Vienna appointed Minister of Justice in the new constitutional order in July 1849. As the regime moved back to neo-absolutism he resigned in 1851 and for ten years worked as a judge. In the changed political situation of 1860 he became head of government and pursued a centralist but constitutionalist policy against Hungarian and Slav opposition. Resigned along with his whole cabinet in 1865 when he no longer had the Emperor's support. He resumed his career as a judge and played a prominent role in the Austrian Upper House after 1867.

Schwarzenberg, Prince Felix zu (1800–52) Soldier and statesman. Born into high Bohemian nobility. His uncle was a leading military commander in the Napoleonic period and he entered military service in 1818. In 1824 he transferred to diplomatic service and between then and 1839 served as attaché and on missions in many European capitals as well as Brazil. From 1839 to 1848 held ambassadorial posts in Parma and Turin and then Naples. Revolution forced him to leave Naples. He resumed military office under Radetzky and was active in the reimposition of Austrian control in northern Italy in 1848, during which time he was wounded. His experience of counter-revolution extended to Vienna in October/November where he worked closely with his brother-in-law Windischgrätz. Effectively first minister in October, he was publicly confirmed in that office in November. In early December he was closely involved in the abdication of Francis I and his replacement by Franz Joseph. His policy was resolute counter-revolution in defence of a unitary Habsburg state – a policy already implemented in Italy, developed in response to the pro-Prussian line of the German National Assembly and pursued against the Hungarian rebels. However, unlike Windischgrätz, who wanted absolutism and a federalist system based on historic provinces, he preferred to maintain a constitutional form for some time accompanied by a centralised administrative system. His policy prevailed with the transfer of the Austrian *Reichstag* from Vienna to Kremsier, then its dissolution and the imposition of a constitution in March 1849 which was immediately suspended. He was hostile to Radowitz's Union policy, supporting the opposition of the medium German states while pressing for Austrian entry into the *Zollverein*. He forced Prussia to give up the Union policy in late 1850 and at the Dresden conference of the following year agreed on the restoration of the *Bund*. In 1851 he brought about the abolition of the Austro-Hungarian customs barrier and a general shift to lower tariffs. At the end of 1851, following Louis-Napoleon's *coup d'état*, the constitution of March 1849 was set aside, signalling a formal return to absolutist rule. It was his last significant act; ill health compounded by an intense work regime induced his early death in April 1852.

Stein, Baron Heinrich Friedrich Karl von (1757–1831) Statesman. Born in Nassau, an imperial knight who entered Prussian state service, early making a reputation as a mining administrator. A Prussian minister by the time of defeat of 1806, he was dismissed by the king for 'insolence' in the way he advised the adoption of decisive policies. In enforced retirement he elaborated a reform programme (the Nassau Memorandum). Recalled to office in October 1807 he presided over the first wave of reforms, especially the formation of cabinet government, peasant emancipation and urban self-government. His contacts with groups plotting uprisings to coincide with renewed war between Austria and France led to his dismissal in October 1808 on Napoleon's insistence. He moved to Austria until the end of the 1809 war and then to Russia where he advised the Tsar on German policy. Placed in charge of occupied territory in 1814 he argued for a much more radical and national policy than Austria or Prussia were prepared to adopt. After 1815 he returned to his Nassau estates, holding the largely ceremonial office of marshal to the Westphalian diet. His last major achievement was initiating the great historical source collection, the *Monumenta Germaniae Historica*.

William I (1797–1888) The younger brother of the future Frederick William IV, he was especially devoted to military affairs during his long years as prince. He disagreed on many issues with his brother after 1840 and at times constituted almost a political opposition within the royal family. An unpopular figure in 1848, he was forced to flee to England following the March insurrection. A stalwart defender of royal and Prussian power, he bitterly opposed the climb-down at Olmütz at the end of 1850, at which time he also became acutely aware of Prussia's military weaknesses. During the 1850s, however, he came to accept the need for constitutional rule. On becoming Regent in 1858, he appointed a moderate liberal cabinet, arousing expectations of a 'new era' in Prussian politics. However, his resolute pursuit of military reform, both as Regent and after assuming the crown in 1861, led to constitutional crisis and the appointment of Bismarck as Minister-President in September 1862. Although at times resistant to Bismarck's policies (e.g., the refusal to participate in the Princes' Congress in May 1863), he invariably deferred to his first minister. Likewise, having come to know and trust Moltke through the latter's court offices and as Chief of Staff in the 1864 war, William was prepared to entrust him with effective military command. This delegation of political and military leadership to Bismarck and Moltke respectively was arguably his greatest achievement. After 1871 he refused all attempts by Moltke to resign as Chief of Staff and continued to defer to Bismarck until his death.

BIBLIOGRAPHY

I. DOCUMENTS

Sources for documents

1   Böhme, H. (ed.), *The Foundation of the German Empire: Select Documents*, translated by Agatha Ramm (Oxford, 1971)
2   Demel, W. and Puschner, U. (eds), *Deutsche Geschichte in Quellen und Darstellung: Bd. 6: Von der Französischen Revolution bis zum Wiener Kongreß 1789–1815* (Stuttgart, 1995)
3   Droß, E. (ed.), *Quellen zur Ära Metternich* (Darmstadt, 1999)
4   Eyck, F. (ed.), *The Revolutions of 1848–49* (Edinburgh, 1972)
5   Fenske, H. (ed.), *Quellen zur deutschen Revolution 1848–49* (Darmstadt, 1996)
6   Freitag, S., Mößlang, M. and Wende, P. (eds), *British Envoys to Germany, 1816–1866: Vol. 2: 1830–1847* (London, 2002)
7   Gall, L. and Koch, R. (eds), *Der europäische Liberalismus im 19. Jahrhundert*, 4 vols (Frankfurt/M, 1981)
8   Hamerow, T. (ed.), *The Age of Bismarck: Documents and Interpretations* (New York, 1973)
9   Hardtwig, W. and Hinze, H. (eds), *Deutsche Geschichte in Quellen und Darstellung: Bd. 7: Von Deutschen Bund zum Kaiserreich 1815–1871* (Stuttgart, 1997)
10   Huber, E.R. (ed.), *Dokumente zur deutschen Verfassungsgeschichte. Vol. 1: 1803–1850* (3rd. edn, Stuttgart, 1978)
11   Huber, E.R. (ed.), *Dokumente zur deutschen Verfassungsgeschichte. Vol. 2: 1851–1900* (3rd. edn, Stuttgart, 1986)
12   Medlicott, W.N and Coveney, D.K. (eds), *Bismarck and Europe: Documents of Modern History* (London, 1971)
13   *Open University Course A321: The Revolutions of 1848. Unit 3: Document Collection* (Milton Keynes, 1976)
14   Spies, H.-B. (ed.), *Die Erhebung gegen Napoleon 1806–1814/15* (Darmstadt, 1981)
15   Walker, M. (ed.), *Metternich's Europe: Select Documents* (London, 1968)

Other English language document collections or texts

16   Bismarck, O., *Bismarck: The Man and the Statesman* (London and New York, 1899). A translation of *Gedanken und Erinnerungen* which is in a modern German edition (Berlin, 1990) with an introduction by Lothar Gall.
17   Bonin, G., *Bismarck and the Hohenzollern Candidature for the Spanish Throne: The Documents in the German Diplomatic Archives* (London, 1957)

18   Fichte, J.G., *Addresses to the German Nation*, translated by R.F. Jones and G.H. Turnbull (Westport, CT; reprint, 1979)

19   Hargreaves, D. (ed.), *Documents and Debates: Bismarck and German Unification* (London, 1991)

20   Hucko, E. (ed.), *The Democratic Tradition: Four German Constitutions* (Leamington Spa, 1987). Translations of the constitutions of 1849, 1871, 1919 and 1949

21   Mason, J.W., *The Dissolution of the Austro-Hungarian Empire 1867–1918* (2nd edn, London, 1997)

22   Meyer, H.C. (ed.), *Mitteleuropa in German Thought and Action, 1815–1945* (The Hague, 1955)

23   Schulze, H., *The Course of German Nationalism: From Frederick the Great to Bismarck, 1763–1867* (Cambridge, 1991). A selection of translated documents are contained at the end of this book

24   Snyder, L. (ed.), *Documents of German History* (New Brunswick, NJ, 1958)

25   Walter, J., *The Diary of a Napoleonic Foot Soldier: Jakob Walter*, edited and with an introduction by Mark Raeff (Gloucester, 1997)

26   Williamson, D.G., *Bismarck and Germany 1862–1890* (2nd edn, London, 1998)

II. ENGLISH-LANGUAGE LITERATURE

General works on European history and nationalism

27   Breuilly, J., *Nationalism and the State* (2nd. edn, Manchester, 1993)

28   Broers, M., *Europe under Napoleon 1799–1815* (London, 1996)

29   Ellis, G., *Napoleon* (London, 1996)

30   Gellner, E., *Nations and Nationalism* (London, 1983)

31   Hobsbawm, E., *The Age of Revolution* (New York, 1962); *The Age of Capital* (London, 1975); *The Age of Empire* (London, 1987)

32   Hobsbawm, E., *Nations and Nationalism since 1780: Programme, Myth, Reality* (2nd edn, Cambridge, 1992)

33   Kedourie, E., *Nationalism* (3rd edn, London, 1966)

34   Kennedy, P., *The Rise and Fall of the Great Powers: Economic Change and Military Conflict from 1500 to 2000* (London, 1988)

35   Langer, W., *Political and Social Upheaval 1832–1852* (New York, 1969)

36   Mann, M., *The Sources of Social Power. Vol. II: The Rise of Classes and Nation-states, 1760–1914* (Cambridge, 1993)

37   Millward, A. and Saul, K.B., *The Economic Development of Continental Europe 1780–1870* (London, 1973)

38   Millward, A. and Saul, K.B., *The Development of the Economies of Continental Europe 1850–1914* (London, 1977)

39   Mosse, G.L., *The Nationalisation of the Masses* (New York, 1975)

40   Özkirimli, U., *Theories of Nationalism: A Critical Introduction* (London, 2000)

41   Schroeder, P.W., *The Transformation of European Politics 1763–1848* (Oxford, 1994)

42   Smith, A.D., *Nationalism and Modernism* (London and New York, 1998)

43 Sperber, J., *The European Revolutions, 1848–1851* (Cambridge and New York, 1994)
44 Taylor, A.J.P., *The Struggle for Mastery in Europe 1848–1918* (Oxford, 1954)
45 Woolf, S., *Napoleon's Integration of Europe* (London, 1991)

General works on German, Austrian and Prussian history

46 Alter, P., *The German Question and Europe: A History* (London, 2000)
47 Blackbourn, D. and Eley, G., *The Peculiarities of German History: Bourgeois Society and Politics in Nineteenth-century Germany* (Oxford, 1984)
48 Blackbourn, D., *The Fontana History of Germany 1780–1918: The Long 19th Century* (London, 1997)
49 Breuilly, J. (ed.), *The State of Germany: The National Idea in the Making, Unmaking and Remaking of a Modern Nation State* (London, 1992)
50 Breuilly, J., *The Formation of the First German Nation-State 1800–1871* (London, 1996; reprinted, 2001)
51 Breuilly, J. (ed.), *Nineteenth-century Germany: Politics, Culture and Society 1780–1918* (London, 2001)
52 Brose, E.D., *German History 1789–1871* (London, 1997)
53 Dwyer, P.D. (ed.), *Modern Prussian History 1830–1947* (Harlow, 2001)
54 Gagliardo, J.G., *Reich and Nation: The Holy Roman Empire as Idea and Reality, 1763–1806* (Bloomington, IN, 1980)
55 Hughes, M., *Nationalism and Society in Germany 1800–1945* (London, 1988)
56 Kann, R., *The Multi-national Empire: Nationalism and National Reform in the Habsburg Monarchy, 1848–1918*, 2 vols (New York, 1950)
57 Katzenstein, P., *Disjointed Partners: Austria and Germany since 1815* (Berkeley, CA, 1976)
57a Nipperdey, T., *Germany from Napoleon to Bismarck, 1800–1866*, translated by Daniel Nolan (Princeton, NJ, 1996)
58 Okey, R., *The Habsburg Monarchy, 1780–1918* (London, 2000)
59 Sheehan, J., *German History 1770–1866* (Oxford, 1989)
60 Treitschke, H. von, *Deutsche Geschichte im 19. Jahrhundert*, 5 vols (Leipzig, 1879–94; Königstein, 1981). There is a seven-volume translation into English (London, 1915–19). This is unfinished and only reaches the eve of the 1848 revolutions.
61 Wehler, H.-U., *The German Empire 1871–1918* (Leamington Spa, 1985)
62 Wilson, P.H., *The Holy Roman Empire, 1495–1806* (London, 1999)

Diplomatic and military history

63 Austensen, R., 'Austria and the "struggle for supremacy in Germany", 1848–1864', *Journal of Modern History* 52 (1980), pp. 192–225
64 Austensen, R., 'The making of Austrian Prussian policy 1848–52', *Historical Journal* 27 (1984), pp. 861–76
65 Bourne, K., *The Foreign Policy of Victorian Britain, 1832–1902* (Oxford, 1970)

66   Bridge, F.R., *From Sadowa to Sarajevo: The Foreign Policy of Austria-Hungary, 1866–1914* (London, 1972)

67   Bridge, F.R., *The Habsburg Monarchy among the Great Powers 1815–1918* (Oxford, 1990)

68   Bucholz, A., *Moltke and the German Wars, 1864–1871* (London, 2001)

69   Carr, W., *The Origins of the Wars of German Unification* (London, 1991)

70   Clark, C.W., *Franz Joseph and Bismarck: The Diplomacy of Austria before the War of 1866* (Cambridge, 1934)

71   Chandler, D.G., *The Campaigns of Napoleon* (London, 1966)

72   Coppa, F.J., *The Origins of the Wars of Italian Independence* (London, 1992)

73   Craig, G., *The Politics of the Prussian Army 1640–1945* (New York, 1964)

74   Craig, G., *The Battle of Königgrätz* (London, 1965)

75   Elrod, B., 'Bernhard von Rechberg and the Metternichian tradition: the dilemmas of conservative statecraft', *Journal of Modern History* 56 (September 1984), pp. 430–55

76   Förster, S. and Nagler, J. (eds), *On the Road to Total War: The American Civil War and the German Wars of Unification 1861–1871* (Cambridge, 1997)

77   Friedjung, H., *The Struggle for Supremacy in Germany 1859–1866* (London, 1935; reissued, New York, 1966) with an introduction by A.J.P. Taylor. Abridged version of the German original.

78   Goldfrank, D.M., *The Origins of the Crimean War* (London, 1994)

79   Hallberg, C.W., *Franz Joseph and Napoleon III 1852–1864: A Study of Austro-French Relations* (New York, 1973)

80   Halperin, H.S., 'The origins of the Franco-Prussian war revisited: Bismarck and the Hohenzollern candidature for the Spanish throne', *Journal of Modern History* 45 (1973), pp. 83–91.

81   Howard, M., *The Franco-Prussian War: The German Invasion of France, 1870–1871* (London, 1961)

82   Kraehe, E., *Metternich's German Policy. Vol. I: The Contest with Napoleon, 1799–1814* (Princeton, NJ, 1963)

83   Kraehe, E, *Metternich's German Policy. Vol. II: The Congress of Vienna 1814–1815* (Princeton, NJ, 1983)

84   Mosse, W.E., *The European Great Powers and the German Question 1848–1871* (Cambridge, 1958)

85   Pottinger, E.A., *Napoleon III and the German Crisis 1865–1866* (Cambridge, MA, 1966)

86   Schroeder, P.W., 'Europe and the German Confederation in the 1860s', in Rumpler (ed.), [159], pp. 281–91

87   Showalter, D., *Railroads and Rifles: Soldiers, Technology and the Unification of Germany* (Hamden, CT, 1986)

88   Sybel, H. von, *The Founding of the German Empire by William I*, 7 vols (1890; reprint, New York, 1968)

89   Steefel, L.D., *The Schleswig Holstein Question* (Cambridge, MA, 1932)

90   Steefel, L.D., *Bismarck, the Hohenzollern Candidacy and the Origins of the German War of 1870* (Cambridge, MA, 1962)

91   Wawro, G., *The Austro-Prussian War: Austria's War with Prussia and Italy in 1866* (Cambridge, 1996)

92   Wengenroth, U., 'Industry and warfare in Prussia', in Förster and Nagler (eds), [76], pp. 249–62

Political, economic, social, cultural and intellectual history

93 Anderson, E.N., *The Social and Political Conflicts in Prussia 1858–1864* (Lincoln, NB, 1954)

94 Berger, S., *The Search for Normality: National Identity and Historical Consciousness in Germany since 1800* (Oxford, 1997)

95 Billinger, R.D., *Metternich and the German Question: States Rights and Federal Duties, 1820–1834* (Newark, NJ, 1991)

96 Borchardt, K., *The Industrial Revolution in Germany 1700–1914*, Vol. 4/Section 4 of *The Fontana Economic History of Europe* (London, 1972)

97 Breuilly, J., 'The revolutions of 1848', in David Parker (ed.), *Revolutions and the Revolutionary Tradition in the West 1560–1991* (London and New York, 2001), pp. 109–31

98 Carr, W., *Schleswig-Holstein, 1815–1848: A Study in National Conflict* (London, 1963)

99 Connelly, O., *Napoleon's Satellite Kingdoms* (New York, 1965)

100 Davis, J.R., *Britain and the German Zollverein, 1848–1866* (London, 1997)

101 Düding, D., 'The nineteenth-century German nationalist movement as a movement of societies', in H.Schulze (ed.), *Nation-building in Central Europe* (Leamington Spa, 1987), pp. 19–49.

102 Eyck, F., *The Frankfurt Parliament 1848–49* (London, 1968)

103 Ferguson, N., *The House of Rothschild: The World's Banker 1849–1998* (London, 2000)

104 Good, D.F., *The Economic Rise of the Habsburg Empire, 1750–1914* (Berkeley, CA, 1984)

105 Hamerow, T., *Restoration, Revolution, Reaction: Economics and Politics in Germany, 1815–1871* (Princeton, NJ, 1958)

106 Hamerow, T., *The Social Foundations of German Unification 1858–1871. Vol. 1: Ideas and Institutions* (Princeton, NJ, 1969); *Vol. 2: Struggles and Accomplishments* (Princeton, NJ, 1972)

107 Henderson, W.O., *The Zollverein* (2nd edn, London, 1968)

108 Hope, N., *The Alternative to German Unification: The Anti-Prussian Party in Frankfurt, Nassau and the two Hessen 1859–1867* (Wiesbaden, 1973)

109 Huertas, T., *Economic Growth and Economic Policy in a Multinational Setting: The Habsburg Monarchy, 1841–1865* (New York, 1977)

110 Iggers, G., *The German Conception of History* (Middletown, CT, 1969)

111 Kiesewetter, H., 'Economic preconditions for Germany's nation building in the nineteenth century', in H. Schulze (ed.), *Nation-building in Central Europe* (Leamington Spa, 1987), pp. 81–106

112 Komlos, J., *The Habsburg Monarchy as a Customs Union: Economic Development in Austria-Hungary in the Nineteenth Century* (Princeton, NJ, 1983)

113 Kraehe, E., 'Austria and the problem of reform in the German Confederation, 1851–1863', *American Historical Review* 56 (1950/51), pp. 276–94

114 Langewiesche, D., *Liberalism in Germany* (London, 2000)

115 Langsam, W., *The Napoleonic Wars and German Nationalism in Austria* (New York, 1930)

116 Marsh, P.T., *Bargaining on Europe: Britain and the First Common Market, 1860–1892* (New Haven, CT, 1999)

117 Murphy, D.T., 'Prussian aims for the *Zollverein, 1828–1833', The Historian*
     53 (1991), pp. 283–302
118 Namier, L.B., *1848: The Revolution of the Intellectuals* (London, 1944)
119 Pollard, S., *Peaceful Conquest: The Industrialization of Europe 1760–1970*
     (Oxford, 1981)
120 Schmitt, H., 'Count Beust and Germany, 1866–70: reconquest, realignment,
     or resignation', *Central European History* 1 (1968), pp. 20–34
121 Schmitt, H., 'From sovereign states to Prussian provinces: Hanover and
     Hesse-Nassau 1866–71', *Journal of Modern History* 57/1 (1985), pp. 24–56
122 Sheehan, J., *German Liberalism in the Nineteenth Century* (Chicago, 1978)
123 Showalter, D., *Railroads and Rifles: Soldiers, Technology and the Unification
     of Germany* (Hamden, CT, 1986)
124 Siemann, W., *The German Revolutions of 1848–1849* (London, 1998)
125 Simms, B., *The Struggle for Mastery in Germany, 1779–1850* (London, 1998)
126 Sperber, J., *Rhineland Radicals: The Democratic Movement and the
     Revolutions of 1848–49* (Princeton, NJ, 1991)
127 Voth, H.-J., 'The Prussian *Zollverein* and the bid for economic superiority', in
     Dwyer (ed.), [53], pp. 109–25
128 Windell, G., *The Catholics and German Unity 1861–1871* (Minneapolis,
     MN, 1954)

Biographical studies

129 Baack, L.J., *Christian Bernstorff and Prussia: Diplomacy and Reform
     Conservatism 1818–1832* (New Brunswick, NJ, 1980)
130 Barclay, D., *Frederick William IV and the Prussian Monarchy 1840–1861*
     (Oxford, 1995)
131 Bled, J.P., *Franz Joseph* (Oxford, 1994)
132 Eyck, E., *Bismarck and the German Empire* (London, 1950)
133 Feuchtwanger, E., *Bismarck* (London, 2002)
134 Gall, L., *Bismarck: The White Revolutionary*, 2 vols (London, 1986)
135 Henderson, W.O., *Friedrich List: Economist and Visionary, 1789–1846*
     (London, 1983)
136 Palmer, A., *Metternich: Councillor of Europe* (London, 1972)
137 Pflanze, O., *Bismarck and the Development of Germany. Vol. I: The Period
     of Unification 1815–1871* (2nd edn, Princeton, NJ, 1990)
138 Sweet, P., *Wilhelm von Humboldt: A Biography. Vol. 2: 1808–1835*
     (Columbus, OH, 1980)
139 Zucker, S., *Ludwig Bamberger: German Liberal Politician and Social Critic,
     1823–1899* (Pittsburgh, PA, 1975)

III. SELECT GERMAN LANGUAGE STUDIES

140 Aretin, K.O. von, *Das Alte Reich, 1648–1806* (Stuttgart, 1993–97)
141 Bartels, H. and Engelberg, E. (eds), *Die großpreußisch-militarische
     Reichsgründung 1871: Voraussetzungen und Folgen* (Berlin, 1971)
142 Berding, H., 'Die Entstehung des Deutschen Zollvereins als Problem
     historischer Forschung', in idem. (ed.), *Vom Ancien régime zum modernen*

Parteienstaat. Festschrift für Theodor Schieder (Munich and Vienna, 1978), pp. 225–37

143 Böhme, H., *Deutschlands Weg zur Grossmacht. Studien zum Verhältnis von Wirtschaft und Staat während der Reichsgründungszeit 1848–1881* (3rd edn, Cologne, 1974)

144 Brandt, H.-H., *Deutsche Geschichte 1850–1870: Entscheidung über die Nation* (Stuttgart, 1999)

145 Dann, O., *Nation und Nationalismus in Deutschland 1770–1990* (Munich, 1990)

146 Doering-Manteuffel, A., 'Der Ordnungszwang des Staatensystems: Zu den Mitteleuropa-Konzepten in der österreichsch-preußischen Rivalität 1849–1851', in A.M. Birke and G. Heydemann (eds), *Die Herausforderung des Europäischen Staatensystems* (Göttingen, 1989), pp. 119–40

147 Doering-Manteuffel, A., *Die deutsche Frage und das europäische Staatensystem 1815–1871* (Munich, 1993)

148 Düding, D., *Organisierter gesellschaftlicher Nationalismus in Deutschland (1808–1847). Bedeutung und Funktion der Türner- und Sängervereine für die deutsche Nationalbewegung* (Munich, 1984)

149 Dumke, R., 'Der deutsche Zollverein als Modell ökonomischer Integration', in H.Berding (ed.), *Wirtschaftliche und politische Integration in Europa im 19. und 20. Jahrhundert* (Göttingen, 1984), pp. 72–101

150 Dumke, R., 'Anglo-deutscher Handel und Frühindustrialisierung in Deutschland 1822–1860', *Geschichte und Gesellschaft* V (1979), pp. 175–200

151 Gruner, W., *Die deutsche Frage. Ein Problem der europäischen Geschichte seit 1800* (Munich, 1985)

152 Hahn, H.-W., *Geschichte des Deutschen Zollvereins* (Göttingen, 1984)

153 Hahn, H.-W., 'Mitteleuropäische oder kleindeutsche Wirtschaftsordnung in der Epoche des Deutschen Bundes', in Rumpler (ed.), [159], pp. 186–214

154 Kolb, E., *Der Kriegsausbruch 1870. Politische Entscheidungsprozesse und Verantwortlichkeiten in der Julikrise 1870* (Göttingen, 1970)

155 Lutz, H., *Zwischen Habsburg und Preussen. Deutschland 1815–1866* (Berlin, 1985)

156 Matis, H. and Bochinger, K., 'Oesterreichs Industrielle Entwicklung', in A. Wandruszka and P. Urbanitsch (eds), *Die Habsburger Monarchie 1848–1918. Vol. 1: Die wirtschaftliche Entwicklung*, edited by Alois Brusati (Vienna, 1973), pp. 105–232

157 Mommsen, W.J., *Das Ringen um den nationalen Staat: Die Gründung und der innere Ausbau des Deutschen Reiches unter Otto von Bismarck 1850 bis 1890* (Berlin, 1993)

158 Rumpler, H., *Die deutsche Politik des Freiherrn von Beust 1848–1850: Zur Problematik mittelstaatlicher Reformpolitik im Zeitalter der Paulskirche* (Vienna, 1972)

159 Rumpler, H. (ed.), *Deutsche Bund und deutsche Frage 1815–1866* (Munich, 1990)

160 Schnabel, F., *Deutsche Geschichte im 19. Jahrhundert*, 4 vols (Freiburg, 1929–37; Munich, 1987)

161 Siemann, W., *Vom Staatenbund zum Nationalstaat: Deutschland 1806–1871* (Munich, 1995)

162   Srbik, H. von, *Deutsche Einheit. Idee und Wirklichkeit von Heiligen Reich bis Königgrätz*, 4 vols (Munich, 1935–42)

163   Wehler, H.-U., *Deutsche Gesellschaftsgeschichte*, Vols 1–3 (Munich, 1987, 1995)

IV. OTHER USEFUL REFERENCES

Statistics

164   Bairoch, P., 'Europe's gross national product 1800–1975', *Journal of European Economic History* 5 (1976), pp. 273–340

165   Bairoch, P., 'International industrialisation levels from 1750 to 1980', *Journal of European Economic History* 1 (1982), pp. 269–333

166   Fischer, W., et al. (eds), *Sozialgeschichtliches Arbeitsbuch. Vol. I: Materialien zur Statistik des deutschen Bundes 1815–1870* (Munich, 1982)

167   Flora, P. (ed.), *State, Economy and Society in Western Europe 1815–1975: A Data Handbook*, Vol. 1 (London, 1983)

168   Mitchell, B.R., 'Statistical Appendix', in C. Cipolla (ed.), *The Fontana Economic History of Europe: The Emergence of Industrial Societies*, Vol. 2 (London, 1973), pp. 738–820

169   Mitchell, B.R., *European Historical Statistics 1750–1970* (Abridged edition, London, 1978)

Handbooks

170   Belchem, J. and Price, R. (eds), *A Dictionary of Nineteenth-Century World History* (Oxford, 1994)

171   Cook, C. and Stevenson, J., *The Longman Handbook of Modern European History 1763–1985* (London, 1987)

172   Emsley, C., *The Longman Companion to Napoleonic Europe* (London, 1993)

173   Pearson, R., *The Longman Companion to European Nationalism 1789–1920* (London, 1994)

Non-print media: bibliography, documents and maps

There is a rapidly growing and changing set of resources for historians on the Internet. One can easily access the catalogues of major libraries throughout the world and search them by author, title or keyword. There are also specialised databases, for example of books in print or of literature published in various disciplines. All I will do here is give some examples, for documents and bibliographies respectively.

The Avalon Project at the Yale Law School: Documents in Law, Diplomacy and History (http://www.yale.edu/lawweb/avalon/avalon.htm) contains copies of many historical documents.

For bibliographies one resource is *Online Bibliographies for Historians: A Directory* (*http://www.geocities.com/historyguide/ebib/ebib-index-06b.html*).

Another bibliographical aid is *Historical Abstracts (1775–1945)*, edited by E. Boehm (Santa Barbara, California, 1955ff.), which has recently shifted to publishing in CD rather than print format. Its great advantage is that it does not just give bare bibliographical details but also provides short synopses of the work cited, both books and periodical articles.

Anyone wanting to consult good historical maps for Germany should look at the website of the Institute of European History at the University of Mainz entitled 'IEG-Maps'. The website address is: http://www.ieg-maps.uni-mainz.de

INDEX

STUART BRITAIN

Social Change and Continuity: England 1550–1750 (Second edition)
Barry Coward   0 582 29442 8

James I (Second edition)
S J Houston   0 582 20911 0

The English Civil War 1640–1649
Martyn Bennett   0 582 35392 0

Charles I, 1625–1640
Brian Quintrell   0 582 00354 7

The English Republic 1649–1660 (Second edition)
Toby Barnard   0 582 08003 7

Radical Puritans in England 1550–1660
R J Acheson   0 582 35515 X

The Restoration and the England of Charles II (Second edition)
John Miller   0 582 29223 9

The Glorious Revolution (Second edition)
John Miller   0 582 29222 0

EARLY MODERN EUROPE

The Renaissance (Second edition)
Alison Brown   0 582 30781 3

The Emperor Charles V
Martyn Rady   0 582 35475 7

French Renaissance Monarchy: Francis I and Henry II (Second edition)
Robert Knecht   0 582 28707 3

The Protestant Reformation in Europe
Andrew Johnston   0 582 07020 1

The French Wars of Religion 1559–1598 (Second edition)
Robert Knecht   0 582 28533 X

Phillip II
Geoffrey Woodward   0 582 07232 8

The Thirty Years' War
Peter Limm   0 582 35373 4

Louis XIV
Peter Campbell   0 582 01770 X

Spain in the Seventeenth Century
Graham Darby   0 582 07234 4

Peter the Great
William Marshall   0 582 00355 5

EUROPE 1789–1918

Britain and the French Revolution
Clive Emsley   0 582 36961 4

Revolution and Terror in France 1789–1795 (Second edition)
D G Wright   0 582 00379 2

Napoleon and Europe
D G Wright   0 582 35457 9

The Abolition of Serfdom in Russia, 1762–1907
David Moon   0 582 29486 X

Nineteenth-Century Russia: Opposition to Autocracy
Derek Offord   0 582 35767 5

The Constitutional Monarchy in France 1814–48
Pamela Pilbeam   0 582 31210 8

The 1848 Revolutions (Second edition)
Peter Jones   0 582 06106 7

The Italian Risorgimento
M Clark   0 582 00353 9

Bismarck & Germany 1862–1890 (Second edition)
D G Williamson   0 582 29321 9

Imperial Germany 1890–1918
Ian Porter, Ian Armour and Roger Lockyer   0 582 03496 5

The Dissolution of the Austro-Hungarian Empire 1867–1918 (Second edition)
John W Mason   0 582 29466 5

Second Empire and Commune: France 1848–1871 (Second edition)
William H C Smith   0 582 28705 7

France 1870–1914 (Second edition)
Robert Gildea   0 582 29221 2

The Scramble for Africa (Second edition)
M E Chamberlain   0 582 36881 2

Late Imperial Russia 1890–1917
John F Hutchinson   0 582 32721 0

The First World War
Stuart Robson   0 582 31556 5

Austria, Prussia and Germany, 1806–1871
John Breuilly   0 582 43739 3

EUROPE SINCE 1918

The Russian Revolution (Second edition)
Anthony Wood   0 582 35559 1

Lenin's Revolution: Russia, 1917–1921
David Marples   0 582 31917 X

Stalin and Stalinism (Second edition)
Martin McCauley — 0 582 27658 6

The Weimar Republic (Second edition)
John Hiden — 0 582 28706 5

The Inter-War Crisis 1919–1939
Richard Overy — 0 582 35379 3

Fascism and the Right in Europe, 1919–1945
Martin Blinkhorn — 0 582 07021 X

Spain's Civil War (Second edition)
Harry Browne — 0 582 28988 2

The Third Reich (Third edition)
D G Williamson — 0 582 36883 9

The Origins of the Second World War (Second edition)
R J Overy — 0 582 29085 6

The Second World War in Europe
Paul MacKenzie — 0 582 32692 3

The French at War, 1934–1944
Nicholas Atkin — 0 582 36899 5

Anti-Semitism before the Holocaust
Albert S Lindemann — 0 582 36964 9

The Holocaust: The Third Reich and the Jews
David Engel — 0 582 32720 2

Germany from Defeat to Partition, 1945–1963
D G Williamson — 0 582 29218 2

Britain and Europe since 1945
Alex May — 0 582 30778 3

Eastern Europe 1945–1969: From Stalinism to Stagnation
Ben Fowkes — 0 582 32693 1

Eastern Europe since 1970
Bülent Gökay — 0 582 32858 6

The Khrushchev Era, 1953–1964
Martin McCauley — 0 582 27776 0

The French at War, 1934–1944
Nicholas Atkin — 0 582 36899 5

NINETEENTH-CENTURY BRITAIN

Britain before the Reform Acts: Politics and Society 1815–1832
Eric J Evans — 0 582 00265 6

Parliamentary Reform in Britain c. 1770–1918
Eric J Evans — 0 582 29467 3

Democracy and Reform 1815–1885
D G Wright   0 582 31400 3

Poverty and Poor Law Reform in Nineteenth-Century Britain, 1834–1914:
From Chadwick to Booth
David Englander   0 582 31554 9

The Birth of Industrial Britain: Economic Change, 1750–1850
Kenneth Morgan   0 582 29833 4

Chartism (Third edition)
Edward Royle   0 582 29080 5

Peel and the Conservative Party 1830–1850
Paul Adelman   0 582 35557 5

Gladstone, Disraeli and later Victorian Politics (Third edition)
Paul Adelman   0 582 29322 7

Britain and Ireland: From Home Rule to Independence
Jeremy Smith   0 582 30193 9

TWENTIETH-CENTURY BRITAIN

The Rise of the Labour Party 1880–1945 (Third edition)
Paul Adelman   0 582 29210 7

The Conservative Party and British Politics 1902–1951
Stuart Ball   0 582 08002 9

The Decline of the Liberal Party 1910–1931 (Second edition)
Paul Adelman   0 582 27733 7

The British Women's Suffrage Campaign 1866–1928
Harold L Smith   0 582 29811 3

War & Society in Britain 1899–1948
Rex Pope   0 582 03531 7

The British Economy since 1914: A Study in Decline?
Rex Pope   0 582 30194 7

Unemployment in Britain between the Wars
Stephen Constantine   0 582 35232 0

The Attlee Governments 1945–1951
Kevin Jefferys   0 582 06105 9

The Conservative Governments 1951–1964
Andrew Boxer   0 582 20913 7

Britain under Thatcher
Anthony Seldon and Daniel Collings   0 582 31714 2

Britain and Empire, 1880–1945
Dane Kennedy   0 582 41493 8

INTERNATIONAL HISTORY

The Eastern Question 1774–1923 (Second edition)
A L Macfie   0 582 29195 X

India 1885–1947: The Unmaking of an Empire
Ian Copland   0 582 38173 8

The Origins of the First World War (Second edition)
Gordon Martel   0 582 28697 2

The United States and the First World War
Jennifer D Keene   0 582 35620 2

Anti-Semitism before the Holocaust
Albert S Lindemann   0 582 36964 9

The Origins of the Cold War, 1941–1949 (Second edition)
Martin McCauley   0 582 27659 4

Russia, America and the Cold War, 1949–1991
Martin McCauley   0 582 27936 4

The Arab–Israeli Conflict
Kirsten E Schulze   0 582 31646 4

The United Nations since 1945: Peacekeeping and the Cold War
Norrie MacQueen   0 582 35673 3

Decolonisation: The British Experience since 1945
Nicholas J White   0 582 29087 2

The Origins of the Vietnam War
Fredrik Logevall   0 582 31918 8

The Vietnam War
Mitchell Hall   0 582 32859 4

WORLD HISTORY

China in Transformation 1900–1949
Colin Mackerras   0 582 31209 4

Japan faces the World, 1925–1952
Mary L Hanneman   0 582 36898 7

Japan in Transformation, 1952–2000
Jeff Kingston   0 582 41875 5

China Since 1949
Linda Benson   0 582 35722 5

US HISTORY

American Abolitionists
Stanley Harrold   0 582 35738 1

The American Civil War, 1861–1865
Reid Mitchell   0 582 31973 0

America in the Progressive Era, 1890–1914
Lewis L Gould   0 582 35671 7

The United States and the First World War
Jennifer D Keene   0 582 35620 2

The Truman Years, 1945–1953
Mark S Byrnes   0 582 32904 3

The Korean War
Steven Hugh Lee   0 582 31988 9

The Origins of the Vietnam War
Fredrik Logevall   0 582 31918 8

The Vietnam War
Mitchell Hall   0 582 32859 4